Robert Dessaix

For many years the presenter of Radio National's 'Books and Writing' program, Robert Dessaix is widely known as a broadcaster, author, translator and literary critic.

After a Sydney childhood, he went to study at Moscow University, and then taught Russian language and literature at the Australian National University and the University of New South Wales for almost twenty years. The editor of *Australian Gay and Lesbian Writing: An anthology*, Robert Dessaix is also the author of short stories, essays and translations of Russian writers Chekhov, Dostoyevsky and Turgenev, and several books including the autobiographical *A Mother's Disgrace,* the acclaimed *Night Letters*, and *Secrets* (with Amanda Lohrey and Drusilla Modjeska).

Robert Dessaix lives in Melbourne.

Speaking
their minds

Intellectuals and the Public Culture in Australia

Edited by

Robert Dessaix

ABC
BOOKS

Robert Dessaix would like to thank all
those who took part in this series for their
generous and enthusiastic contributions
to the debate about the public intellectual
culture; Kate Bochner, Executive Producer
of Arts Talk (Radio) ABC Victoria and
producer of 'Rethinking Australia', for
her invaluable research and imaginative
shaping of the series; Mary Rennie for
her discerning and rigorous editing of
this book; and Susan Morris-Yates of
ABC Books for her exacting criticisms,
discriminating advice and unreserved
commitment to the project.

Published by ABC Books for the
AUSTRALIAN BROADCASTING CORPORATION
GPO Box 9994 Sydney NSW 2001

Copyright © Robert Dessaix 1998

First published May 1998

National Library of Australia
Cataloguing-in-Publication entry

    Speaking their minds: intellectuals and
    the public culture in Australia

    ISBN 0 7333 0653 5.

    1. Intellectuals – Australia – interviews.
    2. Australia – Intellectual life.
    I. Dessaix, Robert, 1944– .
    II. Australian Broadcasting Corporation.

305.5520994

*Designed and typeset by Brash Design Pty Ltd
in 9.5/14.5 Usherwood Book
Cover designed by RENO Design Group
Colour seporations by
Finsbury, Adelaide
Printed and bound in Australia by
Australian Print Group, Maryborough, Victoria*
5 4 3 2 1

Contents

Preface

THE FOLLOWING CONVERSATIONS with thinkers and commentators from various areas in the public intellectual culture were recorded between December 1996 and June 1997, and originally broadcast on Radio National between April and June 1997, under the title 'Rethinking Australia: Intellectuals and the public culture'. In the interests of clarity and readability, this transcribed version of the series includes changes in structure and wording as well as interview material not broadcast in the original series.

The original purpose of these conversations was to investigate the nature of Australia's public intellectual culture at the end of the century: what kind of Australians become 'public intellectuals' and how, what we expect of them, how the public culture of ideas functions, its strengths and weaknesses, its obsessions and also its silences. With this purpose in mind, and a desire to interview intellectuals from a variety of arenas (history, sociology, science, journalism and the arts, among others), I began asking friends and acquaintances, academics and ABC colleagues, journalists and writers which Australians they would include in a list of our most prominent public intellectuals. I would like to emphasise that I did not ask which Australian intellectuals they admired and would like to hear interviewed, but which they would call prominent public intellectuals.

Some names, such as Donald Horne's, Robert Manne's and Phillip Adams', appeared in almost all the lists, while others, such as Helen Garner's and David Williamson's, aroused enthusiasm and hostility in equal measure. (Revealingly, few of the people whose opinion I canvassed found it easy to name intellectuals of whom they disapproved, whether for personal or ideological reasons.)

Out of the scores of suggested participants, the final choice was made, as it has to be for a radio or television series, on the basis of diversity, availability and, of necessity, a sensitivity to the demands of 'good radio'. At no point was it the aim of this series to propose a list of Australia's most prominent intellectuals or to correct imbalances in the public intellectual culture. Nor was it my intention to present in detail particular individuals' programs for social or cultural change — this information is already widely available.

For this reason, and for reasons that emerge from the interviews themselves, I believe that the concentration on highly educated individuals, with a reputation in their fields of knowledge established over many years and, as a rule, oppositional political views, needs no apology. These appear to be the characteristics we look for in what we call public intellectuals. For other kinds of thinkers in the public domain Australians use other terms.

Except in the introductory chapter, which contains more of my own reflections than the original radio script or the other chapters, my opening remarks and questions are in italics.

Robert Dessaix
Melbourne, January 1998

What is a Public Intellectual?

Don Anderson

David Marr

Morag Fraser

Kerryn Goldsworthy

Nicholas Jose

Hilary McPhee

Judith Brett

McKenzie Wark

To the man-in-the-street who, I'm sorry to say,

Is a keen observer of life,

The word 'intellectual' *suggests straight away*

A man who's untrue to his wife.

W. H. Auden[1]

---

1 From 'Shorts', *Collected Shorter Poems 1927–57* (Faber & Faber, 1966).

IN JUST FOUR PITHY LINES Auden put his finger on several aspects of the deep-seated unease about the word 'intellectual' in English-speaking cultures. The faceless (and that's important) man-in-the-street, the representative of the suburban masses Auden's class both feared and held in contempt, was mistrustful of intellectuals for three very good reasons: he suspected, firstly, that intellectuals saw him as existing only to consume and be analysed; secondly, he had a hunch that intellectuals were so busy refining their exquisite sensibilities that 'real life' and its dreary practicalities (such as work and wives) were beyond their ken; and, thirdly, he got a whiff, quite rightly, of something sexually unsettling about intellectuals.

This unease has a long tradition: for the best part of a century, as John Carey has documented in *The Intellectuals and the Masses*[2], English intellectuals have generally regarded the non-intellectual classes as obtuse, unimaginative and dangerous, while these same masses have nurtured a suspicion that intellectuals are all basically effete layabouts who spend far too much time rabbiting on in a private patois about things of no practical importance. In fact, the cultural theorist Raymond Williams has claimed that words such as 'intellectual', 'intellectualism' and 'intelligentsia' were all used for the most part pejoratively in English until as late as the 1950s[3].

Yet is the situation so different half a century later? Even now, from the intellectuals' point of view, do the masses exist for much more than 'to consume and be analysed', particularly in their habits of consumption? Although there has been a wave of faintly self-congratulating academic interest in mass culture (soap operas, suburban architecture, shopping, the semiotics of food and so on), it is at least arguable that this interest, consciously expressed, as a rule, in terms and in forums totally inaccessible to anyone outside the intellectual elite, is scarcely different from the traditional intellectual habit of 'converting [the masses] into scientific specimens', in Carey's phrase[4]. The effect is as much to eliminate the humanity of the man-in-the-street, and, of course, nowadays his wife, as to enhance it — indeed,

---

2 (Faber & Faber, 1992).

3 In *Keywords: A vocabulary of culture and society* (Fontana, 1988).

4 *The Intellectuals and the Masses*, p. 25.

4

many academic theorists today would deny that the abstraction 'humanity' has any objective meaning at all. In other words, the 'unsociability' of intellectuals (to use a popular term from French discussions of what an intellectual is) is as much a problem as it ever was, despite the need to be 'sociable' if they want to be public. Their traditional dislike of what is going on in society is still often in conflict with their desire to communicate with a public which, for the most part, has accommodated itself to what is going on. Stanley Fish puts it slightly differently, arguing that, just because intellectuals talk about what the public does, it doesn't mean the public will want to promote or agree with what intellectuals say when they hear it. '[It] is quite possible, and even likely, that were they to be told about gender per-formativity and the social construction of merit, they would reject these notions even if in their own lives they were acting them out.'[5]

The man-in-the-street's gut feeling that there is something sexually on the nose about intellectuals is also still valid, at least up to a point: while the culture still apportions the serious discussion of ideas and the decision-making that follows to men, it apportions the sensitive use of language and a highly developed imaginative life to women. Consequently, whether a public intellectual is male or female, there is something about the very role which is sexually ambiguous. Indeed, the intellectual classes are often dismissed as 'the chattering classes' who allegedly 'sit around' 'not doing anything', terms which feminise and therefore trivialise what they do. Almost all those public intellec-tuals who are female are forced to assume cameo roles: they're wheeled out for a quick grab on abortion, lesbianism or women in the Church and then pushed off abruptly back into the wings before they can start chattering on about wider, weightier issues.

To some extent this general distrust of the intellectual appears to be a phenomenon in English-speaking societies in particular. To the French, for example, who probably invented the term during the Dreyfus affair, there's nothing suspicious about intellectuals at all as a category. Certainly they have disgraced themselves over the past

---

5 *Professional Correctness: Literary studies and political change* (Clarendon Press, 1995), p. 123. Stanley Fish is Professor of English and also Professor of Law at Duke University, a prominent critic, and author of *There's No Such Thing as Free Speech, and It's a Good Thing Too* (OUP, 1995).

few decades, jettisoning universal values while at the same time embracing the universal values of Marxism, not to mention one or two even odder philosophies, but as a category of Frenchman (more rarely Frenchwoman) they have complete legitimacy. According to the editors of the *Dictionnaire des intellectuels Français*[6] an intellectual is anyone who 'offers society as a whole an analysis, a direction, a moral standpoint which their earlier work qualifies them to elaborate'[7]. The Dictionary was conceived as a celebration of the thousands of French intellectuals who have 'added to the great family of thought, literature and art', and to be listed in it is presumably regarded as an honour. Any Australian whose name was included in a 'Dictionary of Australian Intellectuals' would very likely sue for libel. In Russia, too, while ideologues are mistrusted and action is sometimes valued over words, writers, film-makers, theatre directors and other members of the intelligentsia are respected for their contribution to 'the great family of thought'. Few Russians would preface their discussion of ideas, as so many of the Australians interviewed here did, with a denial that they consider themselves to be intellectuals.

It is all too easy to blame a supposed anti-intellectualism for the Australian unease. Yet, despite the fact that Australia's settler history favoured action over thought and imagination, and although relatively few of our post-War migrants have been drawn from the intelligentsia, there is no evidence at all of any greater ingrained hostility to the culture of ideas in Australia than anywhere else. On the contrary: in terms of the number and type of books bought, read and published in Australia, the quality of the programming on such publicly funded networks as Radio National and SBS television, the readership of our intellectual magazines, the extraordinary and growing popularity of Australia's numerous 'literary festivals', unmatched anywhere else in the world, and the high level of patronage of cultural events demanding serious intellectual engagement, particularly in the visual arts and performance, the signs of enthusiasm for ideas on the part of the

---

6 Edited by Jacques Juillard and Michel Winock (Seuil, 1996). An enlightening overview of the state of French intellectual culture in the last quarter of the century may be found in John Flower's 'New Clerics for Old' (*Meanjin*, 1/1993).

7 Compare Jean-Paul Sartre's notion of the intellectual as someone moving beyond his or her sphere of competence to make broad pronouncements on social, political and moral issues.

Australian public, if not Australian governments, are strong. As the essayist, columnist and academic Don Anderson[8] has remarked, musing on the myth of 'Paul Hogan's sun-bronzed, surfing, throw another shrimp on the barbie Australia':

> I think there's a lively intellectual scene here: if you walk along Bondi Beach at the height of summer, for example, you actually see a lot of people reading... even the newspapers, particularly the Australian, are quite happy to give space to intellectual debate, although often for the wrong reasons. (It's what I call the Paddy McGuinness syndrome: looking for a fight. Being able to write or talk seriously about intellectual matters in public without picking a fight is still something to be aspired to.)

Perhaps conducting the debate in terms of male rivalry rituals lessens the unease about intellectuals and their (sexually ambiguous) chatter.

There is also a widespread suspicion that Australians are contemptuous of their leading intellectuals because they are intolerant of tall poppies. But is there any evidence whatsoever that the Australian man-in-the-street abhors tall poppies? On the contrary, there's plenty of evidence that he idolises them in every field of endeavour — sport, business, the arts, entertainment, fashion, crime, medicine, finance. The media serve him up dozens of tall poppies for his veneration every day. What he does take deep umbrage at, however, is the spectacle of a tall poppy professing to being a tall poppy, frankly admitting to being better than anyone else at what he does. Hence the daily ritual, in television and radio interviews, of people who have excelled in some field explaining that they were just doing their job, just giving it their best, just being lucky. No one must ever appear to regard himself or herself as naturally tall.

In some practical sense, however, intellectuals *must* be understood to be speaking from a position of far greater than average knowledge

---

8 Don Anderson is Associate Professor of English at Sydney University. He has published three collections of his own articles and essays (*Hot Copy: Reading and writing now* [Penguin, 1986], *Real Opinions: Polemical and popular writings* [McPhee Gribble, 1992] and *Text and Sex* [Vintage, 1995]) and edited several collections of contemporary writing, including *Transgressions: Australian writing now* (Penguin, 1986) and *Contemporary Classics 65–95: The best Australian short fiction 1965–95* (Vintage, 1996).

and understanding of their field. Why else single them out for their insights? The public has every right to be less interested in my views on town planning than in those of the Professor of Town Planning at RMIT. What Australians are presumably deeply mistrustful of in the intellectual arena is the self-declared intellectual, the self-professed tall poppy, rather than the activities of tall poppies themselves. This is why, I think, camouflaged from head to toe as novelists, columnists, editors and academics 'just doing their job', none of the intellectuals interviewed for this series wanted to be caught out parading as a self-declared or self-styled intellectual. As Don Anderson hinted in his observation about Bondi Beach, it's not the consumption of ideas that makes us feel awkward, but any sense that the producers of ideas, the professional traffickers in ideas, regard themselves as belonging to a special caste, marked off from the rest of society.

David Marr, biographer of Sir Garfield Barwick and Patrick White[9], a former presenter of 'Arts Today' on Radio National and now a staff writer on the Sydney Morning Herald, singles out this self-declared quality to intellectualism, as well as its remoteness from practical, everyday concerns, as something that arouses our suspicions:

> Australia has learnt to its advantage to be sceptical of people who set themselves up as authorities. To claim to be an intellectual is to bring in a foreign notion — we want people who are intelligent to be doing more than just sitting around being intelligent. Perhaps that's anti-intellectualism, but perhaps it's more a requirement that the intellect needs to be applied before we respect it.
>
> What I think we're really sceptical of are people such as those bogus newspaper commentators who no longer have any real connection with the world we live in. Out pours this angry flummery based on whatever they've been reading lately from some publishing house in Chicago, and I think most of us find them pretty laughable. I don't think that's an anti-intellectual stance, but a stance which is contemptuous of that easy chucking around of ideas which all too often passes for intellectual debate in this country.

9 *Barwick* (Allen & Unwin, 1980) and *Patrick White: A life* (Random House, 1991). Marr is also the author of *The Ivanov Trail* (Nelson, 1984) and editor of *Patrick White: Letters* (Random House, 1994).

Morag Fraser, editor of *Eureka Street* magazine, also alludes to this kind of mistrust of the intellectual in her comments on what the term 'public intellectual' means to her:

> I think this mistrust has an ethnic root, an Irish in particular, or maybe Scottish, knocking of any pretension. I don't know that it's anti-intellectual as much as anti-pretentious, although it can sometimes take an anti-intellectual form. Then it becomes virulent and dangerous. So for me, and, I think, for many Australians, ['intellectual' is] an uneasy term — there's an Australian resistance to labels that differentiate people too markedly from everyone else.

The writer Kerryn Goldsworthy[10], noting that '"elite" is now used in public discourse as a term of abuse', agrees that 'ordinary Australians' (in Pauline Hanson's terms) might sneer at intellectuals because the term 'suggests pretentiousness', but probes further:

> A traditional Australian value is honesty, and the minute you suggest someone is being pretentious, you're partly suggesting they're being dishonest in their activities. So it's not just a matter of egalitarianism, but of someone putting one over you, pretending to be someone they're not.

The novelist Nicholas Jose[11] has more reservations about the quality of Australian intellectual life than Fraser, Marr or Anderson, but his reasons are different:

> I don't think you could honestly say that there's a great lust to undertake serious thought on difficult topics out there. Plenty of people are serious about their own lives, as well as the big questions, and are

---

10 Author of the short-story collection *North of the Moonlight Sonata* (McPhee Gribble, 1989) and *Helen Garner* (OUP, 1996). Until December 1997, Goldsworthy lectured in English at Melbourne University.

11 Jose's best-known novels, several with Chinese themes, are *Paper Nautilus* (Penguin, 1987), *The Avenue of Eternal Peace* (Penguin, 1989), *The Rose Crossing* (Hamish Hamilton, 1994) and *The Custodians* (Macmillan, 1997). He is also author of *Chinese Whispers: Cultural essays* (Wakefield Press, 1995).

keen to think about these things in ways they can handle, but if you try to push it too far you get isolated. What's interesting about Australia, I think, is that it's a highly visual culture. Architects, urban designers, environmentalists and visual artists grapple with how we live — and could and should live — but not in verbal ways. Australian culture is quite receptive to big and difficult ideas when they come in that form. The notion of wilderness, for instance, is hugely complex, but people understand it without having to have it explained to them in great tomes. This resistance to too much verbalising is sometimes mistaken, I think, for philistinism.

✧

While many Australians involved in intellectual pursuits seem to agree that, despite a resistance to the idea of 'the intellectual', there is no marked resistance in Australia to the culture of ideas, agreement about what constitutes a public intellectual — how the phrase is actually used — is more difficult to achieve.

The difficulty comes not with the basic definition, but with the detail. Stanley Fish, the prominent American public intellectual, has defined the public intellectual in terms few will argue vehemently against: 'A public intellectual is someone who takes as his or her subject matters of public concern, and *has the public's attention*.'[12] Where opinions differ is on questions of what matters of public concern public intellectuals should engage with, what 'the public' might mean, how and where its attention is secured, whether or not a public intellectual should lead or simply interpret to the public, and how independent an intellectual should be to earn the public's attention.

Matters of Public Concern

When asked what sorts of issues a public intellectual might be expected to write or speak about, virtually every participant in this series replied 'social issues'. Although archbishops and geneticists, for

---

12 *Professional Correctness*, p. 118.

example, apply their intellects to areas of knowledge of wide public interest, the media tend to provide them with a public for their views only when those views have social ramifications: not, in the archbishop's case (except at Christmas) reflections on the nature of altruism, but on gambling or homelessness; not, in the geneticist's case, on the complexities of gene-shearing, but on disease control or social engineering. It is here, incidentally, that the difference between 'thinker' and 'public intellectual' may lie: the thinker may be unaware of the social ramifications of his or her thought, whereas the public intellectual will emphasise them.

Hilary McPhee, former chair of the Australia Council, sums up this view of the public intellectual's area of concern in two words: public policy.

> The main issues for a public intellectual are related to public policy — education, race, class and so on. And by 'class' I mean issues of fairness, whether our society is fair or not. However, the intellectual debate must range more widely than those particular issues. One of the dangers of the current situation where the media are the sole outlet for debate is that debate is invariably tied to current issues, and this is limiting. Even when newspapers, say, recruit an academic to write a regular column on Australian history or the state of education, we know that what the writer will be asked to comment on will be in line with the newspaper's interest in that particular issue. It will have to be newsworthy, it will be difficult to introduce more wide-ranging, original discussion.

The need to be 'newsworthy' is clearly one of the traps created by the expectation that public intellectuals will link their ideas to issues — to the next election, say, rather than to a discussion of whether or not Australia is a democracy. Yet their need to be 'of their time' is also one of their strengths.

Judith Brett[13], who both teaches history at La Trobe University and writes a regular opinion column in the *Age*, while believing that public

---

13 Judith Brett is the author of *Robert Menzies' Forgotten People* (Macmillan, 1992) and editor of *Political Lives* (Allen & Unwin, 1997).

intellectuals should address themselves to social questions[14], defines
'social' broadly enough to have a chance of escaping this trap:

> By 'social' I mean questions relevant to people living at the same time
> as the writer, anything to do with the meaning of being alive in this
> place at this time, not just the issues of unemployment or poverty.

The question of what that place is, however, is not quite as straightforward as it seems: is it just Australia, is it the whole region, or can
it sometimes be the world?

> I think that the public intellectual when writing has to have a clear
> sense of an imagined audience, and it's easiest to imagine the audience
> you're living amongst. It is possible to be an international public intel-
> lectual, like, say, Susan Sontag, but that kind of public intellectual is
> essentially United States-based, with the United States standing in for
> the whole world. For an Australian the dilemma is greater: there's a
> choice you have to make between writing about the issues of existence
> in the late twentieth century in general or as they manifest themselves
> in Australian experience. If you choose the latter, you won't get an
> international audience. And you have to accept that. The other side of
> the coin is that, if you write for an international audience, your writing
> is likely to be dessicated, uninteresting and hardly known in Australia.
> A lot of academics take that option because a more exciting career path
> opens up and they're offered visiting positions at the University of
> California. With increasing globalisation, and with Australia's engagement
> with Asia, there's a chance now for regional intellectuals to emerge.
> But that would require Australian intellectuals to give up the thrall of
> the northern hemisphere metropolis.

The common linking of public intellectuals with issues of social
justice is a reflection, from Morag Fraser's point of view, of the moral
status we accord them in our society:

---

14 In 'The Bureaucratization of Writing: Why so few academics are public intellectuals' she has
written that a public intellectual's work 'is engaged with substantive social questions; and... the
person actively attempts to communicate with a public' *(Meanjin,* 4/1991) p. 513.

'Public intellectual' is a good instrumental term because it pushes people towards a sense of social responsibility. It makes people who think consider that there's also a public responsibility to discourse in public. Public intellectuals are people who spend a great deal of their time thinking hard about issues and make those thoughts accessible in a way that is, broadly speaking, for the public good. I use that word deliberately — I don't mean just for more public blather or more public chat.

Of course, notions of 'the public good' will often conflict with individual rights, access to pornography being an obvious example of an area of contention. However, mediating conflicts of precisely this kind is seen by many commentators as the heartland of the public intellectual's territory. The notion of 'the public good' is one that the novelist Nicholas Jose also finds himself examining in considering what the role of the intellectual is in Australia at the end of the twentieth century:

The interesting thing is that intellectuals in Australia are bound together by some sort of commitment to or responsibility for Australia. They don't identify Australia with the State — on the contrary, Australia is something which exists in potential, not something we can point out. So there's endless discussion of national identity and ideas about which way the society might go. In the racism crisis intellectuals jump to defend a non-racist idea of Australia. Now, I don't think that would happen in Britain, I don't think British intellectuals particularly care about the state of Britain or the future of Britain in the same way. Iris Murdoch, for example, cares about 'the good', but I don't think she cares too much about Britain.

Perhaps that's partly because we're less confident in Australia than the English or French are that we live at some centre of universal significance.

The ability to range widely, circling out from a core area of knowledge and concern, seems to be a commonly mentioned characteristic of the public intellectual as opposed to the well-known expert on a given subject. For Morag Fraser, as for Hilary McPhee and the editors of the *Dictionnaire des intellectuels Français,* it is a key characteristic:

> The first responsibility is for articulating an area of expertise as clearly and honestly as possible. The next step, which is rarely taken, is to move into some sort of broader philosophical or social analysis. The particular area of learning, in other words, is broadened out. Someone who knows their hard science very well, for example, will work out how their learning over many years can be applied to a whole social structure — what sort of responsibilities attach to the kind of work they do.
>
> The best of them, I think, are those who broaden out into another sense of social responsibility to take in another analytical level. So, when Edward Said talks about relations between Arabs and the rest of the world, it's a speciality, but it also has such broad political application that it's fascinating to listen to. In his case you don't feel you're listening to blather on top of some ideology. In Noam Chomsky's case, for all his extraordinary knowledge, you can sometimes feel that the specialisation is slipping away and what you're hearing is an ideological agenda. But not always.

Don Anderson also likes intellectuals to speak outside their area of expertise, but takes what they say with a pinch of salt.

> I don't think that literary intellectuals — or let's say literary practitioners such as poets, novelists or dramatists — ought to have more attention paid to them when they speak about larger issues of state than anybody else with an informed vote. I mean, on certain important issues sometimes advertisements are taken out in newspapers signed by the usual suspects — poets and playwrights and so on — and the implication is that their vote is more important on some issue, even though it's not connected with their area of expertise, than other people's. Well, I don't think it is, although, as I think about it, perhaps as people who think and read more and pursue matters further, their vote is worth about one and a quarter ordinary votes — but not two.

On the question of expertise and how free an intellectual should feel to range beyond its confines, Judith Brett has very liberal opinions indeed:

In a way I don't feel I write out of expertise so much as out of a sort of sustained moral introspection, trying to pick up in myself moral intuitions about what is happening in the broader political sphere. I then try to reflect on what that is a response to, to put it into a broader historical context. So, in a sense, one writes out of moral and social experience rather than expertise — or I feel I do.

Independence

In post-War Britain Cyril Connolly made a living writing a weekly review for the *Sunday Times*. He had a whole week to research, ruminate on and write his review essay without having to give any thought to selling himself to institutions, corporations or governments. This was as close to true independence as it is possible to imagine. There is hardly a single intellectual of any consequence with a public profile now who is in this position in Australia.

Quite a few of the luminaries in the international intellectual firmament have, of course, discussed the question of independence. Some, like Edward Said, consider that independence is a *sine qua non* of any public intellectual: the 'principal intellectual duty', he writes in *Representations of the Intellectual: The 1993 Reith Lectures,* is independence from allegiances to institutions and worldly powers[15]. In these lectures Said speaks at some length about the necessity for the public intellectual not only to be free of what he calls 'the State and worldly powers', but to wage war against the guardians of sacred visions or texts, confronting orthodoxies and dogma — in effect, to live as an exile. Said's intellectual must be free in order to set others free. In practice in Australia, since this kind of freedom is scarcely an economic possibility for most intellectuals, we set our sights a little lower.

In some traditions, of course, as Nicholas Jose with his strong Chinese connections is well placed to point out, independence plays no part at all in the intellectual's duty to society:

---

15 (Vintage, 1994), p. xiv. Professor of English and Comparative Literature at Columbia University, Edward Said is also the author of other books on a wide range of topics, including *Orientalism* (1978, republished with a new afterword by Penguin, 1995), *Culture and Imperialism* (Vintage, 1994) and *The Politics of Disposession: The struggle for Palestinian self-determination 1964-1994* (Vintage, 1995).

Traditionally the intellectual's role in China was to serve the Emperor and the State while remaining an honest courtier. When the things the intellectual said became inconvenient to the Emperor, there was usually a showdown of some kind and the intellectual had to go into exile taking a kind of Zen option. There he would lament the corruption, ignorance and folly at court, commenting on it much more mordantly than was possible when he was there, casting back darts designed to shatter the crystal. Sometimes, of course, he would be overwhelmed by despair and jump into the river.

So the intellectual's role was a double one: to be an honest courtier while acting as a mouthpiece — a propaganda role in the contemporary situation — interpreting what was happening in the country in a stylised way. Sometimes intellectuals would try subtly to influence the powers-that-be, but their role was basically to interpret for the powers-that-be to the public.

It's interesting to compare this situation with what happens in Australia. Since it's a small country, most intellectuals inevitably get co-opted to work for the system in one way or another — as spokespersons for institutions, in advisory roles to government, the Australia Council, Foreign Affairs and so on, losing the independence that is so absolutely vital to an intellectual. Then they become disaffected, either slinking away with their tail between their legs or finding themselves some funny little vantage point to keep saying their piece from, but with a sense of their own powerlessness.

Hilary McPhee believes that the intellectual life has its roots in creative thinking, out of 'thinking for yourself', while 'ranging widely and freely over a body of material':

Intellectuals are the ones in a society who can stand back and take a maverick and independent view, a view growing out of what is often quite a peculiar perspective telling and showing us things we'd never have thought of otherwise. Yet it's hard to think of more than half a dozen examples a year of an article, a radio broadcast or a book that does that. Still, that's what we should be aiming for.

David Marr is keenly aware of the paucity of intellectuals in Australia in a position to speak with the sort of independence everyone assures us is crucial:

> One of the tragedies of intellectual life in the English-speaking world is that absolute tenure does not seem to produce absolute courage. Judges, for example, are unbudgeable, yet, when prominent Australians were approached by *Outrage* magazine to speak, as homosexuals, about their professional lives, not a single judge would admit to being homosexual. And while I don't discount the courage of many thinkers in Australian universities, our universities, with their large number of tenured positions, have not in fact produced many courageous public commentators. We're actually more used to the courage of retired academics. Odd, isn't it? Many of our important intellectual commentators are people who have left the academy behind. Having retired from a tenured position, they then speak, often with great clarity and moral force.
>
> In journalism the situation is complicated. I can't tell the extent to which my independence is compromised by the fact that I work and write for the *Sydney Morning Herald*. Obviously it's compromised in matters of style — I have to adopt a new way of writing in order to say in just a couple of thousand words what I would prefer to say in ten thousand. But I hope that doesn't alter what I can say.
>
> Yet the freelance world is impoverished in Australia, and that, I think, is the principal problem for public intellectual life and its independence. In Britain, Italy, France and America, freelance intellectuals can live well, building careers as commentators, writers, book reviewers, speech-makers and so on. They're paid well and survive. In this country it's impossible to build a career as a freelance intellectual — it just can't be done. There's no market for the skills — so few media proprietors are anxious to publish the work of articulate commentators. So, what ought to be a vibrant, independent, intellectual community of the kind you have in London or New York can't exist here because there's simply not a willingness on the part of media proprietors to pay.

How 'independent' can a thinker be, regardless of his or her courage in the face of pressure from an employer, colleagues or powerful institutions, if he or she is openly committed to an established ideology — has an 'ideological agenda', in Morag Fraser's phrase, or is 'a guardian of a sacred text', in Said's? Is there not indeed some sort of contradiction, for example, in the notion of a Marxist or Catholic public intellectual? Traditionally, of course, there is no contradiction at all: in fact, commitment to a specific world view was the mark of the European intellectual until quite recently[16]. The usual response that 'no one is ideology-free' hardly resolves the problem, however: while few of us may be free of the influence of a variety of (often contradictory) ideologies, by no means are all thinkers committed to a single coherent ideology. Nor is an ideology quite the same thing as a philosophical position. Don Anderson, however, is inclined to agree that to describe yourself as ideology-free is a 'bourgeois humanist' position:

> I have no problem with the notion of somebody with a recognised ideological commitment being regarded as a public intellectual. I hope I'm not doing John Frow[17], for example, a disservice by describing him as a committed Marxist, but I think in his debate with Andrew Riemer over Pierre Ryckmans' 1996 Boyer Lectures — it was the usual editorial trick: he was pitted against him — he had the perfect right to be regarded as a committed Marxist intellectual engaging in public debate about matters of public concern.

In Australia, where in the absence of freelance possibilities so many of them are university-based, intellectuals often appear to regard it as their bounden duty to guard and propagate sacred visions and texts, usually with a European or North American provenance. The public reaction to their rituals of obeisance ranges from indifference to

---

16 For a discussion of commitment in the influential French context, see Elizabeth Rechniewski, 'Forms of Commitment in Contemporary France' (*Meanjin*, 1/1993).

17 John Frow, Professor of English at the University of Queensland, is the author of *Marxism and Literary History* (Harvard University Press, 1996) and *Cultural Studies and Cultural Value* (OUP, 1995), and edited with Meaghan Morris the widely read *Australian Cultural Studies: A reader* (Allen & Unwin, 1993).

scorn. It is hardly surprising that in any discussion of independence, some disenchantment with the Australian university system eventually comes to the surface.

The Academy

The Australian intelligentsia — the thinking middle class — seems to have reached a critical point in its scepticism about the role tertiary educational institutions are playing in the public intellectual culture. This scepticism appears to be bound up with doubts engendered by the transformation of universities into corporations, and therefore career bases, together with old suspicions about the humanities serving as ideological bridgeheads for a wacky elite.

In a university system which actually rewards narrow specialis-ation and the use of impenetrable language, which considers an ability to address a broad public as not only worthless but dangerous and which in many areas of the humanities enforces ideological conformity — in such a university system the emergence of a truly public intel-lectual is severely hampered. As Hazel Rowley has pointed out[18], DEETYA (the federal Department of Employment, Education, Training and Youth Affairs) would reward Salman Rushdie one quarter of a point for *Midnight's Children*, were he a lecturer in an English Depart-ment, but a fellow lecturer half a point for a brief critique of *Midnight's Children* in a refereed journal in Nebraska read by virtually nobody. The production of experts in narrow fields, the use of specialised languages fostered by a competitive, highly territorial intellectual culture, and a focus on careers within a bureaucratised system are unlikely to nurture the kind of maverick, free-ranging thinkers with wide public appeal Australians expect their public intellectuals to be[19].

---

18 In 'Universities are losing on points', the *Australian*, 18 December 1996, p. 13.
19 Although Kerryn Goldsworthy commented in her interview on the opposite tendency in some cultural studies departments: the tendency to range so widely that no expertise is needed at all. 'Now that the humanities have become more and more interdisciplinary, there are colleagues of mine theorising about the body (a hot topic at the moment) who know nothing about anatomy. I don't know if it worries you, but it worries me.'

In fact, intellectuals (and academics) of note such as Russell Jacoby[20], Stanley Fish and Edward Said have all suggested that it may now be impossible, given the rules tertiary institutions work by in countries like Australia, Canada and the United States, to be both a public intellectual and an academic at the same time.

To make matters worse, in the humanities, as opposed to the so-called hard sciences, there are particular problems: the contemporary unwillingness to claim authority for any single system of thought or values, and the tendency to offer explanations and analyses rather than to propose radical social transformations, have left many intellectuals in the humanities socially detached, virtually without a function, except as an occasional guest on Radio National. Their role is important and useful, but it falls far short of the role the public intellectual has traditionally played. Joanne Finkelstein, whose analyses of popular culture are witty, perceptive and disturbing, has plaintively asked why it is 'that the intellectual remains so remote and unknown' when he or she is 'detailing' the conditions 'the ordinary individual ... is living out', articulating so brilliantly 'the shifts and changes in cultural values and practices which many individuals ... incorporate into their daily existence'[21].

Stanley Fish's answer to questions such as these is simple: 'To think that by exposing the leaks in a system you fatally wound it, is to engage in a strange kind of deconstructive Platonism ... in which the surface features of life are declared illusory in relation to a deeply underlying truth or non-truth ... Bringing new grist to your mill does not in itself alter the basic manner of its operation.'[22] Yet altering the basic manner of society's operation, or at least having a strong opinion about how this might be done, seems to be part of the public intellectual's oppositional role, the active side to his or her 'unsociability'.

Those in the social sciences, according to some commentators, find themselves in a similar quandary. Writing in the *Times Literary*

---

20 Author of the highly controversial *The Last Intellectuals: American culture in the age of academe* (Basic Books, 1987).
21 'Intellectuals — an endangered species?' (*24 Hours*, July 1993), p. 59.
22 *Professional Correctness*, pp 74, 101.

Supplement, Michael Hechter, Professor of Sociology at the University of Arizona, argues that in the new tertiary environment, where the social definition of universities revolves around material usefulness and economic productivity, awkward questions can arise about what the contribution of the social sciences to society actually is. 'No one expects social scientists to find a cure for AIDS, but can social scientists help us make sense of an increasingly bewildering social world? Well, not exactly — they have too many internal disputes for that. Can they successfully predict the demise of entire social systems, like Communism? Not exactly. Are they good at making accurate long-term economic forecasts? Not exactly. Do they offer solutions to social problems like spiralling rates of crime, divorce and poverty? Not exactly. Can they resolve communal conflict in places like Bosnia, Northern Ireland or the West Bank? Not exactly. These reponses are worrying.'[23] They can, of course, help us to think lucidly about all these things, but universities are no longer the places where that is regarded as a valid occupation. Nor is thinking lucidly enough to make a social scientist a public intellectual.

This situation at times arouses significant resentment amongst those academics who feel eminently suited to the role of public intellectual while suspecting that, in some real sense, define and redefine the terms as they might, they have failed to become truly public. The resentment arises, I think, from quite a bitter awareness that, in Gramsci's terms[24], they have failed to become 'traditional intellectuals' and have ended up merely 'organic'. Some of them react by denying that there is any such thing as 'the public', claiming that there are many publics, each with its own validity. (All the same, few of them

---

23 24 January 1997, p. 11.
24 Antonio Gramsci (1891–1937), the Italian intellectual and politician, was one of the founders of the Italian Communist Party in 1924, arrested and imprisoned by the Fascists in 1926 and released just before his death. Gramsci distinguished between 'traditional intellectuals' such as priests and teachers (and we might add writers and philosophers to the list — people whose occupation is to disseminate ideas) and 'organic intellectuals' such as bureaucrats, lawyers and, in today's world, probably advertising executives. Organic intellectuals serve the interests of organisations, marshalling opinion, winning clients — merchandising ideas. Gramsci's writings are available in English in *Selections from the Prison Notebooks of Antonio Gramsci,* edited and translated by Q. Hoare and G. Nowell Smith (1971), *A Gramsci Reader: Selected writings 1916–1935,* edited by David Forgacs (Lawrence & Wishart, 1988) and progressively in a new translation of the *Quaderni del carcere (Prison Notebooks)* (Colombia University Press, vol. 1, 1992).

would opt for a weekly column for the *Open Road* or the *Bendigo Advertiser* over the *Australian* or a regular spot on the ABC.) Some react by launching vituperative attacks against those intellectuals, or even thinkers, who do have a public for their utterances, impugning their credentials and right to the public's attention. Others, of course, including a number represented in this series, take a more positive line: they seek ways to capture the public's attention.

Hilary McPhee thinks that a public intellectual can work from within the academy, but that it doesn't often happen:

> I think it's perfectly possible — there are some good examples of public intellectuals working within the universities — but, interestingly, there aren't many examples. That's because of the state of the academy. Our more interesting minds tend to operate outside the academy, finding they can operate there with much more freedom. It's a tragedy for the academy.
>
> I think that quite a long time ago ground was given up to managerialism. At the same time, some fifteen or twenty years ago, we also saw managerialism beginning to take over the publishing houses. Accountants and financial managers began to make the ultimate decisions about what would happen. In publishing houses you now have the situation where the marketing people, the promoters, actually have bigger budgets than the editors — the editors must come cap in hand to the promoters. If you have an ugly author who's written a brilliant book, you'll have a hard time convincing a publishing meeting that his book is more important than one written by somebody with a sports car, a suntan and a zippy style.
>
> Yet public intellectuals within the academy who had a strong sense of what was going wrong and could have spoken out didn't. Perhaps they didn't have the forums, being in the academy, and there were very limited outlets in the press. The press has tended to (and still does) limit debate to one-off columns rather than running with sequential discussion.

According to many commentators, there is something about the very nature of tertiary institutions in Australia, however, which militates against the development of an intellectual culture. As Don Anderson points out, the present Coalition government is not solely to blame for this state of affairs.

> This government inherited a situation in which universities are profoundly undervalued and devalued. They are not merely being bled of funds, but are being turned into something that universities were never meant to be: corporations, where corporate behaviour is valued; bodies which have to sell themselves, not to students, but to what are referred to as customers[25].

Judith Brett, who, as well as teaching history at La Trobe, is a former editor of *Meanjin* singles out the failure of academics to enter public discussion in terms which hold the public's attention as one of the main reasons for the widespread disenchantment with the academy's contribution to the intellectual culture:

> The reason it's difficult for academics in the humanities and social sciences to enter public debate is that increasingly their careers are governed by publications directed essentially towards academic audiences. It has seemed to me, both as a writer and as an editor, that the projected audience is one of the major determinants of a writer's style, and the practising academic is essentially trained to write for an examiner — to write for a higher authority. The PhD thesis, for example, a major piece of writing that may take five years to complete, is essentially writing for an examiner. And then they may go on to write articles for refereed journals — again, a form of examination.
>
> Now, it seems to me that academics have to make some sort of psychological break with the way in which they've been trained to write, to say at some point, 'Here I stand, this is how I'm going to write, too bad if Professor X thinks it's boring or daggy or passé or too simple'. It's a complex psychological transformation that's required, projecting quite a different audience in relationship to their writing.
>
> Writing for an academic audience affects their vocabulary, and even their grammar and syntax. It produces that characteristic of bad

---

25 Anderson expands on this theme in 'Death of the University' (*24 Hours*, August 1997).

academic prose — the endless qualification, the endless aside to let somebody know you've read the latest and do realise this generalisation is a slight overgeneralisation and so on. This slows the prose down, destroying any sense of the rhythms of a spoken voice, and makes for tedious reading. The constant use of the passive voice, for example, and abstract nouns as the subject of the sentence, is a rhetorical device to distance the author from what he or she is saying. Again, it's defensive writing, an attempt to be impersonal and let the argument stand on its own feet. Now, although there's something to be said for that, they're not imagining an audience who needs to be convinced, they're not writing persuasive prose. Unless the writer puts himself or herself into the writing, saying, for example, 'The reason I'm interested in this question is because of such-and-such an experience', the reader will find it difficult to relate to what's being said. Passionate argument is also often absent from academic articles, yet passion is very engaging for the reader. Passion means going out on a limb, taking a risk by arguing a case strongly, using polemical devices.[26]

Passion and lucidity, Judith Brett's two touchstones, are rarely ever mentioned in the discussion of what is considered valuable in the public intellectual.

McKenzie Wark[27], however, who teaches Communications at Macquarie University and also writes regularly for the *Australian,* takes a more forgiving stance than Judith Brett, suggesting that the work of many academics becomes 'public' in a different, yet important way:

There's a lot of excellent work coming out of the academy, badged as 'cultural studies', although it's actually a lot of different things. However, because of the requirement that writing meet certain criteria as research, enabling academics to build a career for themselves and a life around that career, the writing sometimes has an 'ingrown toenail'

---

26 Brett has written in 'The Bureaucratization of Writing' that 'experience outside an academic career' is vital to the development of the public intellectual, 'a deep commitment to extra-academic goals and values — to political or religious beliefs, for example, to give meaning to a writer's vocation beyond the service of a career' (p. 520).

27 McKenzie Wark is the author of *Virtual Geography: Living with global media events* (Indiana University Press, 1994) and *The Virtual Republic: Australia's culture wars of the 1990s* (Allen & Unwin, 1997).

style to it. This is blamed on the people who produce it, which I think is desperately unfair, given that they have to react to a whole series of institutional constraints which make their writing difficult to thread into public discourse. Where it actually more often ends up is in policy — State and Federal Government policy. The multiculturalism project, for example, is the product of the humanities academy, as are aspects of media policy and film industry policy.

The Forums

Once upon a time, the principal forum apart from newspapers and journals in which intellectuals influenced each other, and, since they were already influential, influenced society, was the café. In eighteenth-century Milan, for example, it was in the city's coffee houses that the Milanese Enlightenment might be said to have taken place — *Il Caffè* was even the name of one of the intellectual journals of the time. One of the denizens of those cafés was Count Cesare Beccaria whose ideas on penal reform[28] influenced Maria Theresa of Austria, Catherine the Great, Voltaire and even Thomas Jefferson. In Padua in the following century there was Pedrocchi's café. There were distant echoes of this culture in the Deux Magots in Paris and perhaps even in the bar at Stewart's Hotel in Elgin Street, Melbourne. Yet today, although some intellectuals like to be seen at certain cafés or bars — McKenzie Wark made it clear, for instance, in the recent ABC documentary 'Bohemian Rhapsody', that, for all his isolation as a writer, he spent a lot of time in Potts Point bars — they are hardly the intellectual cauldrons they once were. Although a good place to network and publicise which crowd you belong to, cafés are no longer needed as actual forums in which to disseminate ideas.

The Internet is turning into a forum, or web of forums, of a kind, but its very democracy and internationalism, at least in the late 1990s, makes it unsuitable as a site in which to become a public intellectual. The Larry Kramer home page, for example, is hit hundreds of times a day because hundreds of thousands of people have already been to

---

28 Elaborated in *Essay on Crimes and Punishment* (1764).

see his plays in theatres and read about him in newspapers. 'The audience', so crucial to the formation of a public intellectual, is too diffuse and fragmented on the Internet to create the kind of identity we associate with the public intellectual. As the Internet becomes more widely used and its function alters, this situation may, of course, also change.

In the end, it is still essentially in the newspapers and journals and on radio and television that public intellectuals perform and influence their audiences. Significantly, it is these channels, not the Internet, that critics like Mark Davis complain are clogged by people older than themselves (the supposed 'keepers of authorised culture', whatever that might mean). And, in fact, it is not newspapers and journals, radio and television *in general* they see as unjustly clogged, but the ABC and the major dailies — this is where you must still perform if you are to be recognised as a public intellectual in Australia. Governments of both persuasions certainly recognise the danger represented by the ABC: everything possible is being done to shatter the 'culture of the ABC' through funding cuts, redundancies and outsourcing.

At this point in our history, however, the skilled use of language, on paper or in performance, is still vital in the dissemination of ideas and in the creation of the public intellectual. As both a journalist and an academic, McKenzie Wark is in an excellent position to comment on two of the major problems in the development of a public intellectual culture in Australia's press and electronic media: the lack of forums in which to secure the public's attention and, in particular, the failure of the journalistic and academic worlds to accommodate themselves to each other to everyone's benefit.

Journalists and academics operate in little worlds unto themselves, creating their own aesthetic or ethic and talking amongst themselves. The difficulty lies in networking these little worlds together, getting journalists and academics talking to each other. The spaces where those things can happen, between the newspapers on the one hand and the literary quarterlies on the other, with circulations of, say, 100,000 and 3000 respectively, are narrowing to nothing. There's the ABC, or what's left of it, but, apart from that, there's really nothing.

There's a huge black hole right in the middle of Australian intellectual culture and no one has done anything about it. It would require institutional reform for that problem to be solved, but that's not happened.

For example, I think there's a space which a combination of subsidies and market forces could revive. It would require a substantial commitment from bodies such as the Australia Council and the Australia Foundation to make it work, and this in turn would involve taking money away from other things. It would require saying, 'All right, certain things now have to stand on their own two feet. After a decade or two, certain things have reached a threshold of success. Let's look around and see what's missing from our creative and intellectual world.' It's obvious, for instance, that we need a space for non-fiction writing that isn't book reviews. Book reviews seem to be the only thing you can make a living writing and it's tedious, mindless work. And the range of concerns in that area is astonishingly limited at the moment.

When you look at who's writing columns in Australian newspapers today, you find the same names as in the newspapers of twenty years ago. There's been a failure to provide a window for new ideas to enter public discourse. To that extent I think Australian newspaper columnists have failed their public. That's one of the reasons Australian newspapers are a declining institution: they're not the place where new ideas are being brokered into the public domain.

Is that in fact happening anywhere except in small corners of the public domain? SBS is the only television network consistently providing the Australian public with intellectual programming, and much of that is bought in from overseas. Radio National, an acknowledged 'place where new ideas are ... brokered into the public domain', has one of the smallest audiences in each capital city.

Books, of course, despite predictions of their early demise, remain one of the most powerful sources of new ideas. While McKenzie Wark might rightly bemoan the fixation of editors on book reviews as the place to discuss ideas, the fact remains that they do this, no doubt, in part because books are still considered one of the most important arenas for newsworthy and challenging ideas to emerge and points of debate to be contested. In recent months, for example, books such as Mark Davis' *Gangland*[29], *Bodyjamming* edited by Jenna Mead[30] and Christine Wallace's *Greer: Untamed shrew*[31] all spring to mind as the sources of vast webs of public debate about matters of widespread public interest and concern.

Intriguingly, more and more Australians are commenting on the phenomenon of so-called literary festivals as a new and valuable arena for debate about ideas. Unlike literary festivals overseas, with exception of the Hay-on-Wye and Cheltenham festivals in England and the Vancouver Writers' Festival in Canada, Australian festivals are remarkable for their presentation of prepared papers, debates and discussions about ideas, are attended by tens of thousands of people and take place in capital cities and regional centres across Australia, from Busselton to Brisbane. Even the increasingly popular 'readings' organised by festivals, bookshops and writers' centres throughout the country as often as not turn into discussion sessions between members of the audience and the writers.

But Hilary McPhee is doubtful that even this burgeoning of public discussion is reaching a wider, integrated public:

> There's a debate at a literary festival, there's a debate at a conference or some other forum, but it's not heard by the wider public. It reaches the same group of people who move around from forum to forum, reading the literary magazines and attending the festivals. Yet a public intellectual, as far as I'm concerned, has to be very public. He or she is not there just to speak to the same few thousand people on a regular basis for a small amount of money, but should have access to the mass media and be taken seriously. We need gurus like this.

✧

Is there a core of shared opinions about the role of the public intellectual emerging from these comments by journalists and academics? I think there is. The simplest way of describing it might be by refining

---

29 *Gangland: Cultural elites and the new generation* (Allen & Unwin, 1997).
30 *Bodyjamming: Sexual harassment, feminism and public life* (Vintage, 1997).
31 (Macmillan, 1997).

Fish's basic definition for Australian conditions: a public intellectual is an independent thinker and performer who, working from some core area of expertise, takes as his or her subject issues related to the public good (and particularly issues of social justice) and, by the grace of the media and an outstanding ability to communicate with many publics (even society as a whole), has the attention of a considerable segment of educated Australia. And denies it.

In the Western context, the definition might be further defined to suggest a straddling of faultlines of some kind in the public intellectual, the living out of a conflict between loyalty to some cause, such as Said's loyalty to the Palestinian cause, and an old-fashioned, impassioned belief in wider human values. However intellectually untenable 'wider human values' may be according to some philosophies, they make intellectuals attractive to certain publics.

There is also, I think, general agreement about the main problems militating against the development of a richer public intellectual culture than we have: an impoverished freelance world, the corporatisation of our tertiary institutions, the shrinking of serious national forums for intellectual debate and the tendency to bar women from a public intellectual role.

In the following interviews with prominent Australian intellectuals this definition and these problems are examined more closely in the light of personal experience.

Robert
Manne

'There's an extraordinary interest in ideas and a
large audience for ideas in this country...

any suggestion that this is an anti-intellectual

society seems to me wrong.

What is dispiriting is the lack of stamina in argument

which makes intellectual life exciting and the

absence of a critical audience...

there are plenty of intellectual forums, a hungry public...

but not a sufficient number of people watching everything...

all sorts of interesting things are said, but soon,

too often, a silence descends and

the silence stays.'

ROBERT MANNE *is a regular commentator on public issues, both in newspapers such as the* Age *and the* Sydney Morning Herald *and on ABC radio. From November 1989 (the very day the Berlin Wall came down) until November 1997 he was editor of* Quadrant *magazine. Robert Manne stands out from the crowd because he's what some doubt a true intellectual can be: a conservative thinker. He's not (as he points out) a Right-wing thinker — he's no free marketeer or supporter of authoritarian government — but he's no revolutionary, either.*

The impression Manne gives in his books and essays, whether his detailed account of the Darville/Demidenko affair[1] or a journalistic article on what's wrong with economic rationalism, is of a rational mind gently sifting the evidence, coming to logical conclusions in its own good time — Robert Manne appears unwilling to be rushed, even on crucial issues. He's also a deeply, perhaps even passionately, moral thinker, which is refreshing — because he's open about it, and open about not being able to define the precise moral shape of his ideal world. He's also open about having been wrong.

Like a number of high-profile public thinkers in the nineties, and reflecting a change of emphasis from the seventies, Robert Manne is concerned with rights. He's interested in the area where individual rights intersect with communal rights — your freedom with mine.

Robert Manne is also Associate Professor of Politics at La Trobe University in Melbourne. In fact, from the moment he first went to Melbourne University as an undergraduate in the mid-sixties, he's had at least one foot firmly inside the academy. His association with the academy over three decades gives particular force to his ideas about what constitutes a public intellectual.

I'VE ALWAYS THOUGHT that intellectuals occupy a special place in society. Perhaps the best way of understanding them is to think of what they're close to but not. For example, an intellectual is not a scholar. That is, an intellectual may be a scholar as part of his or her work, but is much more committed to the world, to the moral, political and economic direction of the world, than a scholar. An

---

1 *The Culture of Forgetting: Helen Demidenko and the Holocaust* (Text Publishing, 1996).

intellectual is engaged (to use that old term), whereas a scholar can do, and should do, fine work without that kind of engagement. So I think of an intellectual as someone who lives in the world of ideas, and who thinks the world of ideas matters to the direction that his or her own society or other societies take — and who, to be honest, wishes to influence that direction.

I mean that not just in the sense of changing policy. As I get older I think it's more and more important that the questions that worry us should be talked about in a certain tone, with a certain complexity, and also with generosity of spirit. The way we talk about things matters just as much as what we say. I'm also less interested as I get older in 'what should happen' — and more and more confused about it — while more and more committed to a society in which intellectuals can discuss what matters in a way that doesn't demean it. In some ways now that is almost the most important role that an intellectual can play, I think.

'Generosity of spirit' doesn't exclude the possibility of a coherent philosophy, by the way, but on the whole I think coherent philosophies are more likely to come from the scholars, the people working away, as it were, at the Grand Theory of Everything — or at least the Grand Theory of politics or economics. Here I think intellectuals are a bit more ragged in their thought than scholars, since by definition intellectuals have to respond to day-to-day events.

I actually suspect we live in an age when the great intellectual constructs are not going to be built — I don't think there can be great system-builders any more, a Hegel, for instance. (The great system-builders we do have turn out to be pretty flat.) Knowledge is too complicated now, and the aspiration to build a Grand Theory ('a Grand Narrative', as they say nowadays) has just about been discredited. We live in a world in which the achievements will be on a smaller scale, I think. It's difficult to imagine anyone being on top of enough, as it were, to do plausibly the kind of thing Hegel did or tried to do.

I think the great metaphor for intellectual life, and possibly societal life, is conversation, not theory. I think we change because we talk and listen to each other. The listening part is terribly important to intellectual life — not being completely sure one's right, being willing to change when an argument is convincing, and so on. When I spoke of generosity of spirit, I meant a desire to join in the conversation with vigour and a capacity to listen, with a willingness to change and a willingness to say if necessary 'No, that's shabby'. I don't think that approach to ideas is consistent with really great system-building or scholarly work of the system-building kind. Insofar as I choose, I choose for myself the role of just joining in the conversation.

Conversation is certainly an excellent metaphor for public intellectual life. It's particularly useful, perhaps, when considering why minority voices often fail to engage the public's attention, voices from specific ethnic communities, for example, or, until recently, Aboriginal voices: a case could be put, I think, that too often such voices are not raised as part of a wider, many-voiced conversation.

The question of where these conversations can best take place, though, is a complex one. There seems to be a hunger for the public exchange of ideas (and you have suggested that the extraordinary growth in literary festivals in Australia over the past few years may in part be the expression of this hunger for public forums for discussion) but the hunger does not seem to be matched by the availability of effective spaces to exchange them in. One problem, you suggest, is that while there are many active forums of ideas in Australia (magazines, seminars, newspapers, Radio National) they don't much intersect: young contemporary art enthusiasts talk to other young contemporary art enthusiasts, for example, and Left-wing radicals talk to other Left-wing radicals, but few mixed conversations are taking place. One place where that might have been thought to be happening is the university, but you suggest, I think, that universities aren't quite what they were in that regard in the 1960s.

I think there's a great tension between institutions and intellectuals. It's very hard for people who work in business, let's say, or the public service, or even perhaps the ABC, to speak their minds. I quite self-consciously chose a university to work in, taking it to be the one institution where, because of a kind of historical oddity, freedom of thought was preserved. Now I've discovered I was totally wrong in that — universities aren't at all as they were meant to be. Indeed, freedom of thought isn't even a topic for discussion at university any more. Universities have become quite ordinary institutions — trade-unionised, self-interested, with no clear conception of their role — the pursuit of truth, say, as was the case in the past.

Let me give you an example: I chose to work in a university partly because there was something called tenure. I took there to be a trade-off: if one went into the law, one could be very wealthy, whereas if one went into universities, one could have freedom of thought, you could more or less say whatever you wanted, without fear of the consequences. Tenure still exists in America, but in Australia we just gave it away. People have even forgotten what it once meant to have it — they just see it as a trade union issue to be traded for something else. That creates a sense of insecurity. In other words, I thought there was an institution where freedom of thought was really secure, but it's not true any more. If I were in my mid-twenties now, I suspect I wouldn't choose the university as a place to work. In most institutions now you're under all sorts of pressures not to speak your mind — there are probably none now where anyone except the writers of books are really free, and even that depends on being published.

To what extent do you think intellectuals in Australia form some kind of clerisy or elite?

I constantly use the term 'intelligentsia', a term with Eastern European origins, because I think it usefully refers to a social category. I believe there is an intelligentsia in Australia and I believe it forms one of the elites in Australia at the moment — indeed, in any Western society. But the intelligentsia and intellectuals aren't the same thing: the intelligentsia is a much broader category of people who, let's say, listen to the ABC, read the quality newspapers and to some extent discuss ideas, while not necessarily being productive in the world of ideas, being much more the audience for ideas. The intellectual class is much smaller. I don't know that it's a clerisy — I think it's more divided than that. It's an outsider's view, I think, to consider that intellectuals constitute a clerisy.

✧

In The Shadow of 1917 *Robert Manne writes of George Orwell (whom he greatly admires) that:*

What he possesses in abundance is high order sanity; anti-metaphysical, temperamental scepticism; an ear for cant; an understanding of power and its corruptions; a suspicion of utopianism; a feeling for the meaning of pain and deprivation; an instinctive love for established ways of life.[2]

I some ways Robert Manne could be seen to have modelled himself on this picture of the intellectual.

The way I've described Orwell clearly reflects that side of Orwell that spoke to me. It's also true that he was the first writer who got to me in some very deep way, and that was because all sorts of things — about the evil in totalitarianism, about the vice of nationalism and the virtue of patriotism, about the relationship of language and liberty, about social equity — struck me as true and deeply appealing. These were obviously the things I wanted to develop in my own thought, the things that struck chords I then tried to develop in my own writing.

The 'love for established ways of life' might sometimes be called conservatism — a word that doesn't seem to have a very settled meaning any more, often just used as a term of abuse. What do you think would be a useful way to use the word 'conservative'?

I've often said that I'm a conservative, but not a right-winger — which makes people double-take sometimes. There's a difference. I think that to be a conservative is partly to value certain traditions in one's own society. It's partly, too, to be sceptical of wide-ranging schemes of reform, to want to wait, to test, to be doubtful that people can deliver what they hope they'll deliver. And, as 'love for established ways of life' suggests, it means to cherish existing ways of life, to

---

2 *The Shadow of 1917: Cold War conflict in Australia* (Text Publishing, 1994), p. 240. On the same page he writes: 'I regard George Orwell as one of the greatest political writers of our century'.

think that a way of life that already gives people sustenance is to be in general preferred to a scheme for a radically new way of doing things. So it's an anti-utopian suspicion of broad change and a cherishing of what already exists over grandiose hopes for something better.

Because of what's happened in economic terms, I would nowadays actually call much of the Left more conservative than much of the Right, especially the New Right. The New Right has what I've called 'that glint in their eye', they believe that with a few pretty simple economic recipes you can make societies vastly better. At a certain point, perhaps in the mid-to-late eighties, the penny dropped for me and I suddenly saw that some of the things I'd been suspicious of on the Left were now taking place on the New Right. I'd become a slightly different person.

The word 'conservatism' is commonly used to mean 'on the side of social power and capital'.

Well, it can be used in that way — but then it's used in dozens of different ways. All I can say is that when power is on the side of rapid transformation, conservatism is almost always *not* on the side of power — it's on the side of preservation. Many on the Left now are concerned about the destruction of community. Now, I don't think it's entirely bizarre to call that a conservative stance, yet it's certainly not on the side of power. Obviously, I would never describe myself as a conservative if it were generally assumed that to be a conservative meant to be on the side of power, because most of the things that I truly hate have to do with the corruptions of power.

In your journalism you show the deepest concern for what we might call the faultline between liberalism — by which I mean the notion that the freedom of the individual is always paramount — and conservatism — maintaining some kind of system of shared values, even if that means sacrificing individual interests. What sort of criteria do you apply in order to decide where you're going to stand on these sorts of issues? Are they connected with a sense of unbearable social harm?

There was a time when the claims of individuals against the community, tradition, government or conformity were strong. The sixties represented that kind of absolute break-out of radical individualism on all sorts of levels, both against conformity and against tradition — and at that time I was, in regard to the sixties revolutions, a feeble fellow-traveller. At this particular moment in the culture I think radical individualism, both in the economy and in private lives, is the problem. As you've sensed from my writing, I would now like the balance to be redressed.

As far as my criteria for making judgments are concerned, I don't have criteria in general — indeed, that's not the way I think about anything. I take it issue by issue, looking for something like 'the social good'. In each case I try to argue it through, to think of the kinds of considerations one should keep in mind, the consistency of the arguments people put for this or that point of view, and so on. But, to be honest, I very much rely on moral instinct — a dangerous approach, I know, but one I don't think I can avoid. For example: I decided at a certain point that certain elements in the popular culture were likely to be harmful, particularly to the young people consuming them at a great rate — extreme violence in the cinema, for example, and the pornography, especially violent pornography, available on videos. I decided that everyone was pussyfooting around on this question, not wanting to admit to favouring censorship — including the feminists, many of whose arguments I share, who often seemed to favour something that looked to me like censorship, although, fearing this word, they wouldn't put a case for it. So what I tried to do was show up the inconsistency. But if you asked according to what criteria I would censor this kind of material, I wouldn't have an answer. It seems to me an impossible question. It would be better to look at something with you and discuss it, and then either come to a common understanding or at least see why we couldn't come to one.

Another thing I've written about recently is euthanasia. One would have to be utterly heartless not to see that in certain conditions people might wish to be relieved of suffering. I'm interested in trying to think through the social logic of events. In the case of euthanasia, for example, what worries me is that if it becomes a legal right — the

Last Right, as I've called it — then some years down the track, when there's pressure on public hospitals and the aged can no longer be kept in conditions they're accustomed to, we'll be tempted by the thought that if people are very sick or in a coma it might be better for all of us, including them, to take their lives involuntarily.

The difficulty with that kind of approach, though, is that someone can simply say to you, 'Well, I come to different conclusions according to different criteria'. And what can you then say?

But this is the whole point of intellectual culture. This is why one is involved in writing newspaper articles and editing magazines. When someone says that to you, you say: 'Well, come on, now we've got an argument. Tell me why you've reached the conclusions you have. It's not sufficient to say you disagree, it's not sufficient for you to argue that this is what you believe.' We can then have, as I say, a conversation, even an honest conversation, where we give and take when we have to, conceding points when good points are made, considering the examples others offer and seeing if we can arrive at something like a reasonable conclusion. If in the end we can't, then we can't, but going through that process of deep and complex conversations still seems to me worthwhile. Indeed, it's now probably the only reason that I'm involved in public intellectual life.

These 'conversations' go on everywhere all the time, of course — they're the sum of things being said and talked about in society. There's no one place where they're going on — on the radio, on television, in the newspapers and journals, in the universities. No one can follow them in total. We must follow them as best we can. One of the most important things a public intellectual can do, it seems to me, is deepen and make serious, make flexible and even humorous when necessary, this conversation, to make it a good conversation rather than a crude, abrupt or unproductive conversation. I think it's a terrible indictment of intellectuals that they don't follow what others are saying, that they turn their backs on all sorts of lines of thought. Even if a particular line of thought seems uninteresting or antithetical to what you believe, it may be worth following.

Could not the criticism be made of you, though, that you avoid conversations about environmentalism? Reading what you've written on the subject, I get the impression that you dismiss environmentalist arguments.

I think that would be a false criticism, but it's fair to make it. In the first place, I usually take a long time to get into issues. Apparently Russian peasants used to take years and years to acclimatise themselves to new ways of doing things — well, I think I'm a bit like that. For a long time I like to listen to what's being said, not saying much myself and maintaining a certain scepticism. (As I get older, though, I'm less like that than I used to be, strangely enough — I suspect I've changed.) I've been listening to what's being said on environmental issues — I'm not at all closed to its meaning, although I don't read as much in that area as I should.

In the second place, it seems to me that some areas of discussion require specialised knowledge. Environmentalism is one of them. To evaluate scientific argument without being a scientist is difficult. On the whole I prefer to remain silent when I think that the matter under discussion requires scientific capacity. There are certain kinds of arguments that I can follow and articulate in my writing, but in this area I feel that others can do it better than I. Life's too short for me to get on top of the scientific arguments on the environment.

✧

Robert Manne has remarked that if the 'new political conversations' taking place since the fall of the Berlin Wall and the collapse of the Soviet Union are to flourish, the meaning of 1917 must be neither 'fudged nor forgotten'. After all, as he sees it, 'the Bolshevik seizure of power in Petrograd is probably the single most important political event in our century'.

There are obviously two main areas of meaning here. When the Bolsheviks seized power in Petrograd, no one thought they would hold on to it — they were the extreme end of the radical socialist movement in Russia. But after destroying the alternative socialist movements, including the democratic socialist organisations, the Mensheviks, the Jewish Bund and the Socialist Revolutionaries (the peasant socialists), they held on to power against all the odds, creating a vast machinery of terror in order to do so, because they genuinely believed that the world would be a better place for their seizure of power. The regime they built up over the next 20 or 30 years was one of the most monstrous State regimes that history has seen — certainly until the Nazis. Then, after the Second World War, because of Hitler's attack on the Soviet Union, they created satrap states throughout East Central Europe. In East Asia parties built upon the Soviet or the Stalin–Lenin model took power in China, North Korea, North Vietnam and then South Vietnam, Laos and Cambodia. So, what was really a small event in the midst of the chaos of the decaying Russian Empire — a small, obscure party seizing power — had led, by the 1970s, to about half of humanity living in the grip of the fantasies of Lenin and the power structures Stalin had created (adapted slightly by Mao and others). Communism moulded the lives of, and caused extraordinary suffering for, hundreds of millions of people.

The other set of meanings lies in what happened in Western intellectual life. It's a huge topic but, briefly, the Bolshevik experiment gave socialism a very bad name. After the Bolshevik revolution, the socialist movement split in a much deeper way than ever before: the split was now between democratic socialism and communism. Insofar as part of the Left in the West took the side of the Communist parties, it seems to me that it was deeply corrupted. As well as that, from the 1920s through to the seventies or eighties, the Bolshevik myth really did exert a huge influence on Western intellectuals. One of the main themes in my thinking is just how deep that corruption went. I'm still genuinely astonished that for almost 50 years the most generous, the finest, the most intelligent people in Western societies thought that the future of humanity rested with communist societies.

While intellectuals are presumed to value freedom of speech and freedom of expression — indeed, they can't live without it — it was patently obvious that intellectuals within the Soviet sphere were not free in any sense of the word. Yet, astonishingly, the penny didn't drop until very late in the piece for many people. Again, I take it that the tradition of the Left is to oppose imprisonment, torture, capital punishment and other kinds of judicial brutality. Now, it was patently obvious that for 50 years Soviet-style societies were characterised by precisely this kind of judicial brutality, yet Western intellectuals went along with it, if it was done in the name of socialism. Similarly, I take it that a belief in scientific rationality is central to intellectuals. They believe that freedom of scientific culture and scientific work is necessary. Yet it was obvious that science was corrupted almost beyond redemption within Soviet-style societies. Our intellectuals failed to notice. These are all matters for genuine astonishment, I think. They have given intellectuals in societies such as ours a bad name and at the same time ask questions about them which are still very much open. There is still some mystery about the radical misjudgment which occurred.

Some of the most daring examples you give in the essays in The Shadow of 1917 *concern what happened in Cambodia and the reaction of certain intellectuals, whom you name, to these events.*

The Cambodian example was one I lived through from beginning to end, but there are earlier examples which are just as potent — remember how many intellectuals found the Maoist experiment attractive — this apparently radical, egalitarian movement, which was in fact just a form of worship of an extraordinarily brutal leader. Eyes were closed to the fact that between 25 and 30 million people died in the Great Leap Forward. Yet to me the worship of Stalin was more shocking. For a long time — almost 25 years — to say forthrightly that Stalin was one of the most monstrous figures that history had seen was to put oneself into the camp of reaction. Is it not astonishing that this was the case? It's not as if we didn't know. One of the illusions my students and young people naturally have is that you couldn't know what was going on. It needs to be documented for the next generation that a good newspaper reader knew exactly what was going on. In the 1930s the English, American and Australian press presented extremely detailed evidence of what was going on. And in the case of Cambodia, I knew exactly what was going on, not because I knew the

Khmer language or went to the refugee camps, but simply because I read newspapers with an open mind. Most of the Left in Australia and America didn't.

Perhaps part of the explanation for the way intellectuals sided with brutal authoritarianism may lie in their centuries-old desire to solve the problem of the masses.

It's certainly true that intellectuals like to plan societies, imagining it's a relatively easy task to plan for a better world for the masses while feeling a certain contempt for many of the ideas and attitudes they find amongst the masses — in 'the suburbs', for example. The attitudes of intellectuals towards the masses can also be coloured by sentimentality and a failure to judge — a failure to see what is actually pretty nasty.

At the moment in Australia, ordinary people (I can't think of a better term) seem to be taking their revenge against the intellectuals' dominance of public culture and contempt for the values of ordinary people through the Pauline Hanson phenomenon. My position would be that it's more important to judge the issues than it is to sympathise with the feelings of ordinary people. I don't agree at all with the popular sympathy for Pauline Hanson's ideas about Asian migrants swamping the country, say, or about the supposed privileges of Aborigines. Daniel Goldhagen's book[3], which I recently read, doesn't paint a pretty picture of what ordinary Germans were capable of thinking and doing during the War, either. I'm a bit suspicious now of the romanticisation of the good masses as against the effete intellectual. Here my emphasis is different from Orwell's.

All the same, without romanticising them, doesn't the intellectual have some sort of responsibility at least to try to understand the masses' anxieties?

Well, yes, that's the other side of it. And also to see what's good in lower middle-class and working-class culture. But it's important not to

---

3 *Hitler's Willing Executioners: Ordinary Germans and the Holocaust* (Little, Brown & Co., 1996).

pretend — and this must be traumatic for the traditional Left — that one of the most potent forces for a certain kind of conservatism in most Western societies is now the working class and lower middle class. The strongest resistance to what Christopher Lasch calls the revolt of the elites[4] is popular opinion in the non-elite part of the population. The challenge for intellectuals is to sympathise with what is good about that resistance while not pretending it has no negative sides.

Another defining moment in this century was 1989 — the year of the first free Polish elections, of Tiananmen Square and, of course, the fall of the Berlin Wall. What impact do you think 1989 has had on Australian intellectual life and is it the impact you expected?

Up until 1989 or perhaps just a little earlier, to be an anti-communist was to be regarded as a rather suspicious figure. I took part in Australian intellectual life until the late 1980s under a sort of cloud, and this cloud had nothing to do with anything other than my view on communism. That changed — the perception of communism changed: in 1989 I wrote a piece for the Melbourne *Herald* saying 'we're all anti-communists now' — a joke on the old 'we're all socialists now' line from the 1880s. And I think that is what happened: now, for example, the Left is not at all sympathetic to China, and virtually no section of the Left is still connected with the communist movement. Cuba still has an aura, of course, but even that will go eventually. North Korea has no aura at all.

On the broader question, what didn't happen after 1989 was a coming to terms with what had happened intellectually before then. And, again, that surprises me. Many Leftists in America and England have come to terms with their pasts and have said in a pretty forthright way how wrong they were. The best essay I've read along these lines is by Eugene Genovese[5] who was a pro-Soviet Leftist to the end. In it he points out what it means to have been so wrong for so

---

4 See *The Revolt of the Elites: And the betrayal of democracy* (W. W. Norton, 1995).
5 'The Crimes of Communism: What did you know and when did you know it' (*Dissent*, Summer 1994).

long. And Doris Lessing[6] has talked about the same thing — the Soviet or communist habits of mind that persisted for so many years[7]. What's really interesting about Australia is that this just hasn't happened here, as far as I can see. The anti-communists have said in a muted kind of way 'we were right', which is totally uninteresting, but on the Left there's been no coming to terms with this deep, systematic misunderstanding of half the world.

I've almost given up hope that that will ever change. It also worries me that somehow the old generation doesn't want to face up to these things, while the new generation isn't interested in them — they've moved on to something else. Perhaps there'll never be any coming to terms with this aspect of our intellectual history.

Well, while communist ideology may have had its day, Marxism in various forms still is influential in some university departments, wouldn't you say? Is there anything wrong with that state of affairs, do you think?

I suppose at some remove it's still influential in academic departments, although the connection, say, between Marxism and certain kinds of deconstruction, post-structuralism and post-modernism and so on is complicated and subtle — and, to be honest, it's not something I've thought through in any detail. Some of the hostility to the economy of contemporary Western societies, as well as to Western social and cultural forms, is also, I'm sure, the sediment of Marxism — that suspicion of capitalism, that rancour, that persists as if Marxism were still alive. I'd have thought that sort of suspicion would now have to be re-thought — not that one should be uncritical of how contemporary economics function, but the old forms of anti-capitalism, premised on a socialist alternative, have somehow persisted without

---

6 After growing up in Southern Rhodesia (Zimbabwe), Lessing moved to England in 1949, publishing her first novel, *The Grass is Singing*, in 1950. Her subsequent novels, written from a radical political perspective, also drew on her experience of a racially prejudiced, rigid society. Her most celebrated work was *The Golden Notebook* (1962), interpreted as a major contribution to feminist politics. A prolific writer, Lessing has written both experimental and realist fiction, as well as non-fiction and autobiography. Two volumes of her autobiography have been published: *Under My Skin* (to 1949) (HarperCollins, 1994) and *Walking in the Shade* (1949–62) (HarperCollins, 1997).
7 'Unexamined Mental Attitudes Left by Communism' in *Putting the Questions Differently: Interviews with Doris Lessing, 1964–1994*, edited by Earl G. Ingersoll (Flamingo, 1996).

the socialist alternative being available. That strikes me as decidedly odd. As far as I can see, there is now on the Left simply no serious thinking about economic alternatives to the current drift.

Now that communism is dead in Europe and the West, though, the things about Marx that are still interesting can be looked at without any Cold War considerations getting in the way. One idea I don't want to let go of is that those who possess large amounts of property and capital, as well as the power which comes through that ownership, tend to find extremely highfalutin rationalisations for their self-interest. As an historian of nineteenth century Germany or France, Marx interprets much of what happens politically through the self-interest of the large property owners. That often seems to me a useful way of understanding what happens in the world. In that small way at least my thinking has been influenced by Marxism.

✧

Most of us can name a handful of writers or books that have been influential at different points in our lives in giving direction to the development of our thinking. Which writers might you name?

The first thinker to influence me in a big way, as I've mentioned, was George Orwell. But more recently the writer who has illuminated most strongly what has obsessed me most of my life — human suffering under totalitarianism — and the writer whom I now most admire is Primo Levi[8]. Levi is an intellectual in the deepest sense. His sober description of this suffering will, I think, make his writing endure. And, for the extraordinary complexity of her thought, I would include Hannah Arendt[9] amongst the people I admire most.

---

8 Primo Levi (1919–87), Italian–Jewish writer who was also a chemist, managing a paint factory in Turin for the last three decades of his life, until his suicide in 1987. Sent to Auschwitz in 1943, his first book, *If This is a Man* (1947), recorded the atrocities he had witnessed with a striking mixture of detachment and human feeling. Although he wrote further about his wartime experiences in *The Truce* (1963) and *The Drowned and the Saved* (1986), and published novels, short fiction and poetry, it was his collection of meditations, *The Periodic Table* (1975), which won him the greatest acclaim.
9 Hannah Arendt (1906–75). German-born political thinker who fled Nazism in 1941, teacher at several American universities and author of such influential works as *The Origins of Totalitarianism* (1951), *The Human Condition* (1958), *Eichmann in Jerusalem* (1963) and *The Life of the Mind* (1977).

In the end, their enduring influence is often not so much a matter of who they were — Orwell, for instance, was a democratic socialist, but that's not why he endures. Orwell endures because of a kind of lucidity of spirit and a generosity of spirit, and also because of a love of country, qualities which may not have been particularly obvious when he was fighting his battles for democratic socialism against Soviet totalitarianism.

I'm surprised that Dostoyevsky doesn't appear in your list of writers who helped form your attitudes.

Well, in a way that's accidental. I've read a lot of Dostoyevsky, and he did in fact play a big role in my thinking. He's a very Russian figure, but there's something about him that slightly frightens me. As well as his novels I've read quite a lot of his journalism, *Diary of a Writer*[10] and so on. Although I find the novels sublime, and even the religious part of Dostoyevsky highly interesting (strangely enough, as I feel that I don't have a strong religious dimension), nevertheless, I don't like his Russian nationalism, his hostility to the Muslims or his fierce hostility to the Enlightenment. So I feel ambivalent about Dostoyevsky. If ever he became politically influential, I'm sure he'd be extremely dangerous. Orwell and Arendt are writers whose instincts I utterly trust, whereas, although I'm fascinated by Dostoyevsky's political ideas, I don't trust them. In lesser people, as it were, they're the sorts of ideas which come to no good.

Dostoyevsky is not a writer I could ever feel completely at home with. Ferocious anti-Enlightenment thinking is very dangerous in the contemporary world, and Dostoyevsky is one of the most impressive and ferocious anti-Enlightenment thinkers.

I take it that your own attitude to the Enlightenment is a positive one. Yet socialism is, after all, one of the inheritors of the Enlightenment.

---

10 Written between 1873 and 1881, *Diary of a Writer* is characterised by a kind of aggressive, mystical populism — orthodoxy and nationalism battling the evil forces of the West (principally atheism and socialism).

The Enlightenment developed in all sorts of directions. One is the democratic direction — the destruction of the sense of social hierarchy and also the destruction of the idea of religion playing a role in the governance of the State. In those senses I belong to the Enlightenment. More recently — and this, to some extent, is a change in me — I've come to understand that something like multiculturalism — cherishing diversity, withdrawal from the idea of social unity — is an extension of the Enlightenment. I feel strongly that the great fight against the Enlightenment has been *politically* malign. I think that Nazism or fascism is a battle against the Enlightenment. I'm influenced here by Ernst Nolte's book[11]. So, in the end I'm on the side of the Enlightenment. Despite all kinds of cavils, that's where I stand. I'm not comfortable with hierarchical or anti-democratic thinking, or with thinking that wants to place religion at the centre of politics, or that's suspicious of the kind of diversity which I think we've come to see the deep virtue of.

What if the diversity includes such things as Nazism?

I belong to the English tradition, which I think Australia has been enormously lucky to have inherited, and central to that tradition are ideas of representative democracy, parliamentary sovereignty and the rule of law — those are basic, from my point of view, and if diversity is not to be based upon this kind of political and legal structure, then it would be opposed by me. The diverse groups must accept some sort of core values. I think that's what communism and fascism have taught us: that to found good societies on anything other than representative, liberal and rule-of-law principles almost always leads to disaster. So my sense of diversity, which includes partly ethnic, partly sexual and partly racial elements, is founded on that English base.

✧

---

11 *Three Faces of Fascism* (1969).

One of Robert Manne's great strengths lies in his ability to apply an almost forensic eye to actual cases — the pro-communist journalist Wilfred Burchett, Helen Darville, economic rationalism, there are many examples. When he's 'on the case' with the whiff of humbug in his nostrils, his language seems to change, he can become (in a gentlemanly way) quite confrontingly rude. The gloves come off.

Well, sometimes it's humbug I smell, sometimes it's a pile of corpses. But yes, I think the best approach is to take a particular case which is in contention and move through it forensically — and I hope fairly. Rather than analysing the rather abstract question of, say, intellectuals cultivating communism (an approach which often doesn't get you very far, especially with sceptics), I've had an instinctual preference for taking a single case and going with it as far as I could go. In the case of Burchett[12], for example, it was very simple: I read a magazine article[13] claiming he was the Dreyfus of Australia, the innocent victim, in other words, of a conspiracy of the wicked. Well, I smelt humbug, falsity. And, more importantly, if a claim like that could be taken seriously, then there was something very wrong with our intellectual culture. It was the sort of claim I thought should be contested and shown to be false. It's a matter of accumulating evidence and then revealing it, while being fair to it. That's what an historian is trained to do: to come to terms with the evidence, wherever it might lead you. My aim was also to use the Burchett case to try to show in more general terms what was going on in Australian intellectual life in the mid-eighties. Interestingly enough, I wouldn't be able to write that article now. I no longer feel passionate about the issue in the same way, partly because I don't think intellectuals have the same illusions about communism they so recently had.

Is 'being fair to the evidence' quite the right expression to describe your approach? I think your fairness is largely rhetorical, isn't it? And that may be quite legitimate.

---

12 See 'He Chose Stalin: The case of Wilfred Burchett', reprinted in *The Shadow of 1917*.

13 Gavan McCormack, 'An Australian Dreyfus?' (*Australian Society*, August 1984).

Well, in Burchett's case, for example, it was important not to ignore the fact that at a certain point in his life he helped Jews get out of Germany. Fairness does not, in my view, mean sitting on the fence — the fair case may be a hostile case. What would be very unfair would be to leave out of a story positive elements which played a part. If I were to write about Burchett again, I might include something more about his particular kind of personal heroism, his plain physical courage, which I suspect is probably connected to his polemical dishonesty.

Another case which got to me even more deeply than Burchett's was the Demidenko case. I took it up because I was really shocked that a considerable part of the literary culture here was blind to the shabbiness of this young woman's very foolish and poorly written book on a subject that was at the very heart of the tragedy of my people and my family — indeed, of twentieth-century European history. Virtually nothing in Australian public life has unsettled me more than this case. It was a most peculiar thing — I've never felt like that about anything else I've written. I felt that until I had put my case as best I could, until I had revealed what was shabby about *The Hand that Signed the Paper* and astonishing about the misjudgment of it, I literally could not rest.

I want to stress how important it's been to me to understand the Nazi Holocaust. That's what I came up to university wanting to find out more about. And what I discovered was that what had happened in the Soviet Union under Stalin and what was going on in China under Mao was not dissimilar in its destructiveness to what had happened to my own family. I had no alternative but to break with the Left at that point. It seemed to me that anyone who had any sort of ambiguous relationship to what was happening in the Soviet Union or China had made a terrible moral mistake. I had been on the Left before this — in fact, I'd belonged for a brief time to the Labor Club at university, which was the furthest to the Left of all the groupings — close to the Communist Party — but I broke with them quickly. Nothing in my life has mattered more to me than my understanding of the Nazi Holocaust. It's the ground of my being.

Robert Hughes

' Look, I remember when I was a kid there were

no intellectuals in Australia, there were things

called 'pseudo-intellectuals' — do you remember

pseudo-intellectuals? Anybody you disagreed with,

dealing in the realm of ideas, was a pseudo-intellectual.

It's like when John Howard called me a

self-appointed cultural dietitian...

I've been puzzling over that phrase for ages.

The other thing, of course, about intellectuals in

Australia is that they're always self-appointed —

as if you were waiting for the Queen to come along

and touch you on the shoulder and say,

'Pouf! You're an intellectual!' '

ROBERT HUGHES — *polemical, pugnacious and very public — homing in on the Australian reluctance to grant intellectual status to others and suspicion of those who grant it to themselves.*

Perhaps Australia's most prominent expatriate intellectual, Robert Hughes is Time *magazine's art critic (with a regular readership of millions), as well as the presenter of two hugely popular television series ('The Shock of the New', based on his own book [1981], and, more recently, 'American Visions'), and the author of several worldwide best-sellers.*

The days have more or less passed when we were acutely aware of which Australians made their life here and which had to leave our shores permanently in order to lead a full life in their chosen field. (It's the ideas which still seem to have to leave our shores to be turned into realities, but that's another question.) The question of where you live simply doesn't much concern anyone any more. With the new technologies we can all be present everywhere, all the time more or less, as if physics and metaphysics have started to overlap.

In the postwar years, however, when the intellectual infrastructure in Australia was still underdeveloped, we were acutely aware of who left for the wider world and who stayed at home. In the arts area alone, all sorts of names come to mind when we start to think of who went away and never came back permanently: Clive James, Barry Humphries, Sumner Locke Elliott, Jeffrey Smart, Justin O'Brien, Sidney Nolan, Peter Porter, Jill Ker Conway, Peter Conrad, Germaine Greer ... And Robert Hughes was one of that legion who left Australia for Europe in the 1960s, although he moved on to the United States in 1970, and there he's stayed ever since.

Over the past 25 years or so, living in New York's SoHo district, he's made his name writing his influential, punchy columns in Time *and publishing his best-selling books, which range well beyond the confines of art criticism: popular history in* The Fatal Shore *[1987], the essay collection* Nothing If Not Critical: Selected essays on art and artists *[1990], his acclaimed study of Barcelona and its history [Barcelona, 1993], and his passionate, boisterous, very funny attack on public culture in America in the 1980s and 1990s,* Culture of Complaint: The fraying of America *[1993]. His most recent publication is the book of the television series* American Visions[1] *and he's working at present on the first major study of Goya.*

It's usually less the argument that wins you over in Hughes' books (in my experience) than the language: rich, physical, and somehow both fastidious and pungent at the same time. It's his language that packs the wallop. Which is not by any means to denigrate the erudition and experience he brings to his intellectual positions.

One intriguing aspect to his public thinking (about art in particular) is the question of what formed Robert Hughes as a thinker. Most intellectuals, after all, when you ask them, readily reel off names — Foucault, Dostoyevsky, Gramsci, Edmund Burke, even a particular book. Yet, when you read Hughes, you have no sense of a central, shaping figure of this kind.

FIRST OF ALL, I don't really think of myself as an intellectual — I'm a writer. Of course, the two do overlap, but I've always felt a little uncomfortable about being called an intellectual rather than a writer, a practical writer. Obviously what most formed me initially was my Catholic background, being educated by the Jesuits and, very luckily for me, being brought up in a house which had a fairly large, although by today's standards antique, library. So I was encouraged as a child to read pretty widely. Quite honestly, I can't say that in my teens there was any particular European intellectual I read who influenced me to any major extent. The exception might be George Orwell, who had a strong effect on my conception of style[2].

What is it exactly that the Jesuits gave you?

Firstly, a fairly strong theological training, based on Aquinas. Secondly (and this is rather difficult to summarise), the Jesuits were very good teachers. Their teaching at that time was very much based on subjecting propositions to logical analysis as well as on rote learning, committing texts to memory — the procedure which is now thought

---

1 A six-part BBC television series shown in 1996, and published in book form by Harvill in 1997.
2 Ian Britain, in his *Once an Australian* (Oxford University Press, 1997), suggests that both John Ruskin and Cyril Connolly, in their different ways, influenced the young Hughes (pp 181–82).

to be so destructive of the juvenile mind. Our education (in the early fifties) was also strongly based on the study of Latin and, to a lesser degree, Greek. One aspect of the Jesuits' approach to education that certainly resonated with my own family background was the practice of argument as contestation. We were encouraged to debate, to develop our faculties and to think on our feet when clashing in the debating hall and so on. That went very nicely with the fact that there were so many lawyers in my family.

What are the Jesuits like with humbug?

They're dismissive of it. It was a very anti-superstitious kind of religious training.

I ask you the question because it seems to me that one of your leading characteristics is a nose for sham and humbug. You like to identify what we might call 'the authentic' — Gaudí as architect, say, or Auerbach as expressionist painter — as opposed to 'the sham'. This isn't something that modern art critics much care to do because it implies a hierarchy of values, seeming to suggest that the world is not just made up of simulacra, that the Julian Schnabels and Jeff Koonses of the art world should not be taken as seriously as the Bacons or Rauschenbergs.

I don't think that the world *is* made up of simulacra. I think that what is interesting in the world tends to be real and resistant and open to common experience. I don't take a relativist view on this. Art that tries to probe the real, the resistant and the weighable interests me a great deal more than art which is just a sort of shuttle of transposed media images, although there are exceptions: for example, Robert Rauschenberg, whom I admire enormously and who does deal in media images — good art can be made from that. Of course, he's not Paul Cézanne, he's not engaged in a painful effort to find out the limits of the visual resistance of this rock, this stone, this creek bed or cottage. But what I like is that kind of patient head-butting quality that certain kinds of art have.

You're not afraid of what is normally called elitism. In fact, you've pointed out that in matters of art elitism does not mean social injustice or even inaccessibility. What does it mean?

Elitism in art simply means a preference for what you discern as the best within your own experience. I think one of the commonest human experiences is perceiving some things as being done better than others. We have absolutely no difficulty with appreciating the grace and skill and aggressive finesse of a great batsman, or with saying that this batsman is better at batting than somebody else who just got bowled for a duck. That doesn't mean you're engaged in some act of social or gender discrimination, it just means that you're legitimately enjoying the sight of something being done better than you sitting on the Hill could do it. This is one of the reasons, after all, that we watch sport.

I think this applies to art as well. A great interpretative pianist is likely, whether you're able to analyse the sensation or not, to give you a fuller experience in the concert hall than somebody who is mediocre. That's all I mean. There is this joy in watching articulate skill doing its work, in watching human consciousness go about its mysterious work. And to me this is one of the great pleasures of art and not one which is to be despised.

With sportsmen it's easily measurable in objective terms — Bradman gets a century, this sprinter runs 100 metres in so many seconds — whereas the reasons you prefer Rauschenberg to Schnabel are harder to pin down.

That's perfectly true. Yet with some work you have a feeling of dissatisfaction, you know that the work is pretending more than it can deliver on, that there's something stale, humbuggish and falsely rhetorical about it. The critic's job is to try to plumb down and find out why this is so, what produces these feelings. And it's not just a matter of introspection. You develop a nose, or rather an eye, for good drawing which is extremely hard to describe in objective terms. It's never possible to elevate it into something like a three-foot rule that you can apply to every drawn configuration, yet you can look, for instance, at a number of seventeenth- or eighteenth-century Chinese scrolls, noticing that the brushwork exemplifies what the Chinese call *ch'i* (which is a kind of vital energy present in the line), that an authentic kind of visual language is present — hard to define, but possible when you have some experience of it.

This is what you mean, presumably, by 'eyes with histories'[3].

Yes, continuous exposure to works of art of all kinds is vital. It's admittedly a rather vague kind of cultural science we're dealing with, but rule number one is that you must look at as much art as you can. Nobody walking in cold off the street without having seen much art before is likely to be able to understand why you or I are so moved by Goya's Black Paintings. To do that you need to expose yourself to a lot of art.

Your roots are not in the Academy in any real sense. In fact, you make the point that very few intellectuals nowadays are attached to the academy except as 'decorative hermits'[4], *Simon Schama*[5], *Robert Darnton*[6] *and Edward Said being obvious exceptions. You seem to come from standing in front of actual paintings.*

Well, you can stand in front of actual paintings in the academy, too. And there are people working in academe in America who do

---

3 From a reference in 'Art and Money' in *Nothing If Not Critical: Selected essays on art and artists* (Collins Harvill, 1990) to 'admirable' collectors and dealers 'whose eyes have histories . . . who buy from informed love rather than herd instinct'.

4 See Section VIII of Lecture 1 in *Culture of Complaint: The Fraying of America* (OUP, 1993). Hughes goes on to say that 'most contact between academe and the general intelligent reader seems to have withered, because overspecialization and the *déformations professionnelles* of academic careerism are killing it off' (p.68).

5 Professor of Humanities at Columbia University, author of best-selling studies in cultural history such as *The Embarrassment of Riches* (Collins, 1987) about the Dutch Golden Age, *Citizens* (Viking, 1989) about the French Revolution, and *Landscape and Memory* (HarperCollins, 1995) about the relationship between culture and landscape.

6 Professor of History at Princeton University and author of numerous popular books on eighteenth-century French themes, such as *Mesmerism and the End of the Enlightenment* (1968), *The Great Cat Massacre* (Basic Books, 1984) and *The Forbidden Best-Sellers of Pre-Revolutionary France* (W. W. Norton, 1995).

write for public magazines. Apart from the people you mentioned, there's Louis Menand[7], for example, who writes frequently on social topics for the *New Yorker*. One of the problems is that the American academic community is so large, it's such a huge industry, that in writing for a specialised academic audience you can permit yourself the idea that your audience is in fact a general one and the only one that counts. That may not be the case in Australia. Yet the way you write for a general or specialised audience is very different.

What I come out of is journalism. I come out of writing for the public right from the beginning — I don't mean that I was ever a police-rounds reporter, but I started writing criticism in my early twenties[8]. I was lucky, I suppose, in that I was doing this in Australia where my obvious defects would not be exposed too rapidly. So I've always thought of writing as an act by which you reach a general audience. For a long time I had an inferiority complex about not having any degrees, but I've lost that now because it would have been all too easy to suppose that the specialised audience I'd have written for constituted the whole world — a great mistake. In any case, I've always liked the idea of there being a general intelligent audience — not necessarily expert, but curious about cultural and other topics — residing within the readership of mass-circulation magazines or newspapers. Or watching television, for that matter.

How big is this audience — at least in America?

I have absolutely no idea. I doubt anybody has ever tried to measure it. However, *Time* magazine, for which I've been writing since 1970, sells about five million copies a week and the notional readership, allowing for the people who pick it up three weeks later while waiting for the dentist, is thought to be close to twenty million. Now, it would be vain to suppose that all twenty million turn to the art column — they don't. All the same, I think it would be reasonable to say that

---

7 Author of *The Future of Academic Freedom* (University of Chicago Press, 1996).
8 It was in 1962, when he was writing for *Observer* and *Nation*, that another expatriate, Alan Moorehead, told Hughes that 'if you stay in Australia the way you are, Australia will remain very interesting, but you are going to become a bore'. (Interview with Luke Slattery, the *Australian Magazine*, 12–13 August 1995.) At this distance, one might like to ask: to whom?

there are probably a million or a million and a half readers interested enough in art in America to read my column. Actually, it would give me the jim-jams if somebody were to make a serious effort to count the number of readers because it might turn out that nobody read my column and they'd fire me.

Do you regard yourself as a scholar?

No, but I hope to get my facts right. I'm not an original scholar, but I read widely and check my facts. In *The Fatal Shore* and also in *Barcelona* there is original scholarship to some degree. There I think I did make a contribution to scholarship, but the companion volume to the television series *American Visions* is certainly a secondary text. It doesn't even have footnotes or a bibliography!

✧

(At this point a passage was played from John Corigliano's 'Fantasia on an Ostinato'.)

In some ways I expect those variations on Beethoven and the pleasure we take in them illustrate one of Robert Hughes' strongly held views: that the more you know, the more you've seen and read and heard and experienced, the more attuned you are to what's there, the richer its meaning for you. This should seem too obvious to mention, but in recent decades, at least in the humanities, a suspicion has been lurking that this point of view is elitist, privileging those with access to resources or an expensive education. Certainly, in Australia many tertiary art schools now have an Art Theory Department but no Art History Department at all — strange, but true.

Robert Hughes has few kinds words to say about the uses of theory, at least in the post-modernist sense of the word. In fact, although he applauds the work of such complex and sophisticated thinkers as Simon Schama and other university-based scholars, he doesn't see the visual arts themselves as a strong source of intellectual ideas, unlike history or literature. I suggested that in this respect the visual arts might be closer to a form such as a dance.

I think they're more on the side of dance than of history. When we say 'the visual arts', we're talking about the actual making of paintings, videotapes, performance pieces, sculpture and so on, not all that superstructure of interpretation and teaching which is dependent on it. Obviously there's a lot of scholarship and intellectual activity (a great deal of it rather obfuscatory) that goes on around the visual arts, but you don't have to be a particularly deep conceptual thinker in order to be a painter. What you need is a kind of visual intelligence, which is a different kettle of fish. On the whole, works of art don't carry conceptual meaning in the way that trucks carry coal — or, for that matter, the way history books carry ideas.

All the same, when you write about works of art, you have to bring conceptual thinking to bear on the way you understand a painting.

Yes, you have to locate the painting within a common fabric of knowledge or social experience (to be rather vague about it). Every work of art contains its own history. (Every dish you eat in a restaurant contains its own history.)

Yet, at this particular moment in the culture we live in it's commonly held that, since the truth about history can never be known, there's more point in reading theories about history than there is in attempting to 'know' anything about the past.

Well, to paraphrase Henry Ford, 'Theory is bunk'. Anybody who is a relativist to the extent of claiming that the truth about the past is completely unascertainable and can be legitimately presented in accordance with his or her preferred version of it is, in my opinion, uttering nonsense. While it's true that the past is a foreign country and that it's impossible for you or me to will ourselves back in every particular into the mind-set of somebody living in the Dordogne in the fifteenth century, there's nevertheless plenty of evidence which is ascertainable and siftable and testable about the way people in the Dordogne in the fifteenth century ate, thought, acted, fought and so on, certainly enough to enable us to say that some statements about the people living there at that time are closer to the truth than others. The idea that as soon as something is past it dissolves in a kind of miasma of imperfect science strikes me as just so much relativistic nonsense.

So, by the way, does the idea that all experience is necessarily gender or racially derived, and that it's impossible for a man to write about the experience of women or vice versa, that it's impossible for whites to write about the experience of blacks, and so on. As far as I'm concerned, this is just a surrender to superficiality, it's a giving up of the ghost.

You have suggested that post-modernism and the theories associated with it are in 'entropic decline'.

Politically in America, yes. The academic world tends to be swept by currents of fashion. It can be a very conformist place, where you find that all the fish are pointing in the same direction. Long before the Berlin Wall collapsed, when the fundamental bankruptcy of Russian and European Marxism was revealed, a tremendous crisis occurred among *bien-pensant* Leftists in the academy. What could they turn to now? What followed (and I think it was very sad), because there was no longer any common core to hold radical desires together or in equilibrium with one another, was the dissolution of Marxist universalism into the particulars of gender and race, into the politics of race and sex. This was the crisis which the academy went through in the 1980s and from which it has still not emerged. The dream that somehow or other theory was going to exercise some effect upon real politics in the real world has gone up the spout.

After a while, theorising in this way becomes a sort of self-referential game, with few serious consequences outside the formation of more theories. It's a very poor substitute for older forms of historical — including art historical — analysis. One of the things that really bugs me about it all is the sameness of the language it produces. The young learn to write in a peculiar sort of colonial patois — they've even learnt to denounce colonialism in terms which are purely French colonial. When I come across the dread words 'discourse', 'hegemony', 'site' and so on in an article, my heart just sinks. Jargon is the enemy of thought.

Your language is at the core of the strength of what you write, it's language as much as anything else that seduces your readers. In fact, you told journalist Luke Slattery a couple of years ago that 'language is life itself'.

Well, language is all we writers have to work with. Why confine ourselves to a particular kind of artificial patois? I love the concreteness of language, I always have and always will. Language connects us to the world. With its enormous, sensuous vocabulary, it's like the sense of touch.[9] This is true of slang as well. One of the richest things in the world to me is slang or argot, including Australian slang, which has this wonderful kind of metaphorical weirdness about it. 'I saw him stamping around like a beaten favourite' — to me that's poetry. Since this sublime instrument is at one's disposal, one should learn how to play it.

You mentioned George Orwell's influence on your writing style.

He influenced me deeply. Orwell's rules about how to use the English language, such as always preferring the concrete word to the abstract, always preferring the Anglo-Saxon to the word with a Latin or Greek root — I've found these rules of great practical help. And never start a sentence with an abstract noun — it's better to start with 'and' or 'but'. The other thing you must do, of course, once you've written a sentence or a paragraph, is read it over to yourself, either mentally or out loud.

✧

---

9 An analysis of Robert Hughes' written style confirms his point about 'concreteness': his vocabulary and syntax are both calculated to excite his readers to pay attention and to reveal his own emotions rather than to demonstrate his mastery of or allegiance to a particular ideology and its codes (unlike much academic writing). His verbs tend to be 'physical' ('beat', 'shear', 'bawl', 'tar', 'grind', 'jam', 'starve' and so on), as does a high proportion of his adjectives ('goatish', 'mushy', 'vivid'), his text being peppered with colourful, often colloquial nouns ('gadzookery', 'claptrap', 'thuggishness', 'quack', 'duffer'). The effect is to invite the reader into his mental world as a curious equal rather than to lecture, intimidate or silence the reader.

Robert Hughes' prose is very persuasive. There's a kind of elegant, almost erudite larrikinism to it, which must have at least some of its roots in an Australian boyhood. This shooting-from-the-hip example of it is from an article which first appeared in the New York Review of Books *in 1989 on Jean Baudrillard's* America. *(It is reprinted in* Nothing If Not Critical.)

As the fifties wore on, it became increasingly apparent that America was merely a stage set for French Left-wing bigotry about *l'Amérique*. America was no longer an intriguing idea. It had withdrawn its original offer of revolutionary transformation. Russia now did that; and then, when the horrors of the Soviet utopia bulked too large for even Stalinists to ignore, Cuba was supposed to. A dozen years later this reluctance to look had become general. America, as all good *soixante-huitards* knew, was a bellicose caricature, an imperialist Hulk, a crass *société de consommation* nourishing itself on the flesh of the Third World. Its physical image had dwindled to two vertical features (the skyscrapers of Manhattan and the buttes of Monument Valley) and a horizontal one (the grid of superhighways). It was populated by oppressed blacks, the ghosts of slaughtered Indians, rednecks in pick-up trucks, hippies and Pentagon generals. Its culture was directed by mass media, and the only worthwhile things that came out of it were new rock and old movies. Once the revolutionary illusions of 1968 had gone down the pipe, French radicals — as Diana Pinto pointed out in 1982 in *Le Débat* — continued to comfort themselves with imagery drawn from what was left of American counterculture, so that 'in each case, the "interesting" America remained the one defined by its opposition to the Establishment'... No verification, no empirical reporting were needed to deal with such a place.

It's only against this background, that Jean Baudrillard's new book *America* can be savoured in all its remarkable silliness. Baudrillard, who taught sociology at Nanterre from 1966 to 1987, is regarded, as the jacket copy puts it, 'as France's leading philosopher of post-modernism'. As such, he has the badge of a distinctive jargon. Jargon, native or imported, is always with us; and in America, both academe and the art world prefer the French kind, a thick prophylactic against understanding. We are now surfeited with mini-Lacans and mock Foucaults. To write direct prose, lucid and open to comprehension, using common language, is to lose face. You do not make your mark unless you add something to the lake of jargon to whose marshy verge the bleating flocks of post-structuralists go each night to drink, whose waters (bottled for export to the States) well up between Nanterre and the Sorbonne. Language does not clarify, it intimidates. It subjects the reader to a rite of passage and extorts assent as the price of entry. For the savant's thought is so radically original that ordinary words will not do. Its newness requires neologism; it seeks rupture, overgeneralization, oracular pronouncements and a pervasive tone of apocalyptic hype. The result is to clear writing what the flowery blandishments of the valets to Gorgibus's daughters in Molière's *Les précieuses ridicules* were to the sincere expression of feeling: a parodical mask, a compound of snobbery and extravagant rhetoric.

And Baudrillard is not only the most *précieux* of all current *ridicules* but also the one who is quoted the most solemnly in Paris and New York, particularly among art dealers, collectors and critics ... His argument, in essence, runs as follows. Thanks to the proliferation of mass media we now have more signs than referents — more images than meanings that can be attached to them. The machinery of 'communication' communicates little except itself. Baudrillard is something of a McLuhanite; not only is the medium the message, but the sheer amount of traffic has usurped meaning. 'Culture' — he is fond of those snooty quotation marks — is consigned to the endless production of imagery that has no reference to the real world. There *is* no real world. Whether we go to Disneyland, or watch the Watergate hearings on TV, or follow highway signs while driving in the desert, or walk through Harlem, we are enclosed in a world of signs. The signs refer just to one another, combining in 'simulacra' (Baudrillardese for 'images') of reality to produce a permanent tension, an insatiable wanting in the audience. This overload of desire in a disembodied, media-invented world, is like pornography, abstract. Baudrillard calls it 'obscenity'.

In a tirade such as this (not without its own snobberies and rhetorical devices), the impact Hughes' writing has is scarcely due to any watertight argument or the force of his objections to one example of post-modernist thought — Baudrillard's champions are unlikely to be persuaded to abandon their allegiance to Theory on reading it. His writing has an impact because he communicates his objections with such verbal panache, such wit and such intimate knowledge of his enemy. His achievement in essays such as this one, in other words, lies less in original thought or lethal argument than in his success at giving permission to his non-specialist audience to resist orthodoxies and authority figures, if they're so minded, Right-wing demagogues such as Pat Buchanan and Jessie Helms as much as the Afrocentrists, the post-modern theorists, the fashionable therapy-mongers and the Manhattan art establishment. In short, he's a public intellectual with a very sure sense of what kind of intellectual anxieties his audience might have, what kind of faultlines (so to speak) they may feel stretched across. And this is arguably precisely what a public intellectual should have a sense of and analyse in public.

✧

Some public intellectuals see their role as to mould taste, others to enlighten or to articulate muddied issues. What aspects of their role would you highlight?

I think it's the public intellectual's role to give people a handle on the meaning of events in the world, to provide a thoughtful analysis which is outside the immediate scope of reportorial journalism. It's to argue opinions, to argue positions, to get into public fights — in a word, to make people think. And you do this by writing, by appearing on television, by lecturing, by being interviewed in the media. So the public intellectual has to be conscious, not only of the existence of the public, but of certain responsibilities, such as comprehensibility, towards that public — that's the principal thing. The public intellectual must not talk down. In fact, if he or she does, then he or she will pretty damn quick cease to be public. Now, in America the role of the public intellectual has become much more institutionalised than in Australia: there are now, for example, all these think-tanks, from the moderately liberal and to the very conservative indeed, whose job is to harbour thinkers (supposedly heavy thinkers) whose task in their turn is to secrete the basis of public policy debate.

All the same, when I think of the words 'public intellectual', I really think of somebody independent, who just does his or her job by argument, without significant back-up from corporations or from the extrusions of corporations into the intellectual realm ('foundations', as they're called). That's a role still worth taking on. In Australia, with its relatively small population, the independent public intellectual tends to be found much more in academe than in freelance public life. Look, I remember when I was a kid there were no intellectuals in Australia, there were things called 'pseudo-intellectuals' — do you remember pseudo-intellectuals? Anybody you disagreed with, dealing in the world of ideas, was a 'pseudo-intellectual'. It's like when John Howard called me a self-appointed cultural dietitian... I've been puzzling over that phrase for ages.

The other thing, of course, about intellectuals in Australia is that they're always self-appointed — as if you were waiting for the Queen to come along and touch you on the shoulder and say, 'Pouf! You're an intellectual!'

In Australia the kind of public intellectual I have in mind tends not to find much space between journalism on the one hand and academe on the other. In America it's somewhat easier, there's more space. It's inevitable: there are more magazines, more opportunities for freelancing.

Some theorists on the subject of public intellectuals feel strongly that they have a responsibility to give a voice to the voiceless, which is another way of saying to help society's oppressed.

It's probably true that a public intellectual has certain responsibilities in that regard, although, ultimately, the voiceless have to find their own voice — a public intellectual can't speak for them. You can certainly talk about them, of course, trying to give the broader public some understanding of or insight into their situation. At the same time there aren't so many voiceless people in American society today. They do exist, but there are also many people speaking for the traditionally voiceless now, even if this sort of activity attracts condemnation from the conservatives.

One of the problems you might see with creating a more confident intellectual climate in Australia would presumably be that anxiety you've often mentioned about our own provincial status and the purely local significance of what we think and do.

Yes, but I think that this anxiety is on the way out, I really do think that it's vanishing. There will always be some residue of what years ago was once called the cultural cringe, but my impression is that Australians are now a great deal more culturally secure and less uptight about their status than they were when I was a kid. As they should be. Writing in English, Australians are connected by a zillion filaments to other cultures anyway. In fact, the idea of a public intellectual who is purely provincial is, if not a contradiction in terms, at least highly undesirable.

The fact is, though, that publishing an article in the Age *simply isn't as 'significant' as publishing an article in the* New York Times *or the* London Times.

That's not necessarily true. It depends on how good the article is, how much to the point. It also depends upon what audience you're expecting to reach. An article in the London *Times* may not reach an Australian audience. However, this is a situation which, alas, is beginning to solve itself: I notice that more and more proprietors, such as Murdoch, are using syndicated reviews from their English magazines and newspapers in their Australian ones — it's a terrible pity. The main thing that made it possible for me to develop as a critic was getting work in Australia as a critic. If the art and book reviews at that time had been syndicated articles by Englishmen, then I would have had correspondingly less opportunity to write. I'm not advocating a rigorous kind of trade-union nationalism whereby only Australians get to review books in Australian papers, but the trend, due to the monolithic collapse of proprietorship, seems to be worryingly in the other direction.

How does the quality of our media in Australia strike you?

Australians are always complaining about the quality of their news-papers, but some of the newspapers look pretty good — particularly the *Australian* and, to a lesser extent, the *Sydney Morning Herald* and the *Age*. (In America at the moment the number of newspapers one feels one must read is down to about four.) All the same, the increasing monopolisation of media ownership, electronic and print, within (effectively) three pairs of hands, is a cause for concern, especially when you combine that with the assault on the ABC. One of the things I like about Australian argumentative journalism, as contrasted with what you find in American daily newspapers, is that some trace of the Australian irreverence towards the noble, the mighty and the influential, still remains in it. There's a kind of larrikinish wit which hasn't yet been squeezed out. Americans have never exactly been larrikins anyway, but in America this irreverence is being gradually squeezed out by the weight of the sense of official function. In fact, I like the way television interviewers in Australia are prepared to ask politicians hard questions, something which is becoming less and less common in the United States, where people like Barbara Walters ask questions which are as soft as pastries.

What, from your perspective, are the main issues for Australian intellec-tuals at the end of the century? You'd count the republic as one of them, presumably.

Living in New York as I do, I can't follow as a matter of course the issues particularly exercising the Australian public's mind from day to day. However, there are some obvious ones, such as the thorny questions arising from Australian racism and the fundamental questions about how Australians are to govern themselves, how they are to behave towards one another as members of one of the very few functioning multicultural societies in the world. And after all, on the whole, Australian multiculturalism rubs along in a pragmatic and mostly benign way, it hasn't turned sour in the way it has in America. The matter of the republic is naturally linked to those concerns, because arching over all of them are the still fundamental issues of who we are, why we're here, what we're doing here. There is no longer any single simple answer to the question of what it is to be an Australian. Perhaps there never was a simple answer, but any attempt to frame answers is certainly a good deal more complicated now than it was in my boyhood, when Australia was mostly Anglo-Irish-Scot, and Aborigines were disregarded.

Consequently, since the job of intellectual argument is to frame the context in which policy decisions can be made, rather than to frame those policy decisions themselves, I'd have thought that there's a very fruitful field in Australia at the moment for public argument about these topics. But Australians are naturally argumentative, aren't they? We love to argue, and so we should.

✧

In 1984, true to his principle of never shirking an argument, Robert Hughes let fly with a scandalous and now celebrated attack on the New York art establishment, centred in SoHo in Manhattan: his spoof on Pope's Dunciad *called* The SoHoiad or the Masque of Art[10]. *Like Pope, Hughes aimed his barbs at those who have earned his disapproval or contempt, at what he considers humbug, dullness and pretension.*

Close by the Hudson, in MANHATTAN'S town,
The iron palaces of Art glare down
On such as, wandering in the streets below,
Perambulate in glamorous SoHo,
A spot acclaimed by savant and by bard
As forcing-chamber of the *Avant-Garde*.
'Tis there, dread DULNESS dwells in sweats and glooms,
Gnaws her brown nails, and shakes her sable plumes;
FRIVOLITY extends her flittering hand
O'er the distracted, fashionable band,
And YOUTH sustains its present coalition
'Twixt vaulting Arrogance and blind Ambition,
Whilst rubbing shoulders with the newly-great,
Impartially selling *Smack* and *Real-Estate* ...

---

10 First published in *The New York Review of Books* in 1984, but reprinted in *Nothing If Not Critical*.

JULIAN SNORKEL, with his ten fat thumbs!
Ad Nauseam, he babbles, whines, and prates
Of Death and Life, Careers and Broken Plates
(The larger subjects for the smaller brain)
And as his victims doze, he rants again —
Poor SoHo's cynosure, the dealer's dream,
Much wind, slight talent, and vast self-esteem.

'Shall I compare me to Picasso? Yes!
Within me, VAN GOGH'S vision, nothing less,
Is wedded to the genius of TITIAN
And mixed promiscuously, without permission,
With several of BOB RAUSCHENBERG'S devices.
The market's fixed to underwrite my prices —
Compared to my achievement, JACKSON POLLOCK'S
Is nothing but a load of *passé* bollocks'...

And BARBARA WOOZE, in descants loud and long,
Rends her fair locks, and chants her *Willow-Song:*
'O entropy! O misery! Oh Hell!
G-d's dead, Art's dead, and I am far from well!'
Yet KAKOPICTA, Muse of Transient Modes,
Sweeps her slack Lyre, and charms the list'ning Toads ...

'... As once the tourist, 'midst the ruins of *Rome*,
Cull'd from the earth the decor for his home,
A cornice here, a herm or statuä there,
To prink the prospect of the dull parterre,
Cumbering his house with false Etruscan urns,
Such is the custom of our *Post-Modernes:*
Post-Modernism long ago took note
That when Invention flags, we needs must *quote:*
And when the cobbled-up quotation drops
To semi-literates and earnest fops
(American collectors), the convention

Is to extol it as a new *Invention*.

Thus to advance, but likewise to retard,

Is purpos'd by the *Post-Trans-Avant-Garde*.

So in our world the energies are spent —

What few remember, dullards may invent.'

David Williamson

‘ I'm not regarded as a thinker because

my thinking is in an area not really considered

the province of thinkers.

Thinkers think about issues —

the environment, social injustice and so on.

In the media's image of them they don't think about the

deeper philosophical questions, they don't think,

for instance, about David Hume's question,

‘What is the essential nature

of humankind?’ ’

B UT DAVID WILLIAMSON DOES. *Indeed, the question of what makes us human is at the core of almost everything Australia's most famous playwright has ever written, and by no means everybody likes his answers. As he points out, his very interest in such questions puts him at odds with some of the most prominent players in Australia's intellectual culture, particularly those of a post-modernist[1] persuasion.*

Other considerations no doubt play a part in the reluctance of the cultural establishment to acknowledge David Williamson as an intellectual. Unlike Europeans, we Australians rarely value our artists as thinkers — or the artist in our thinkers, for that matter. Any Frenchman or Russian, if asked to name his country's leading intellectuals, would almost certainly include several writers and poets in his list — indeed, in French, the word écrivain (writer) is almost synonymous with 'intellectual'. The artist's role in Australia seems to be very different. While we might sometimes look to artists for perception or wisdom, it's to scientists (social and physical) we turn for intellectual ideas.

David Williamson, however, is one of the few full-time writers we might indeed number amongst our leading intellectuals (although, in line with the curious Australian tendency not to consider someone whose ideas you disagree with as a true intellectual — they are 'pseudo-intellectuals' or 'jumped-up intellectuals' — many of his most ardent critics have been keen to deny him this status). David Williamson is passionate about the ideas which govern Australian lives, he's critically engaged with his own society, his plays are more and more often vehicles for intellectual argument across deep faultlines, and his public arena is vast.

One of those faultlines he straddles is the traditional one, lying between science and the humanities. In fact, the key to David Williamson's obsession with the nature and origin of what makes us human seems to lie in his intellectual formation in the late 1960s: at that time, just at the point when he was emerging as a playwright in the ideologically fraught world of Melbourne's Pram Factory and La Mama, David Williamson

---

1 For what I hope are understandable reasons in the context of a radio conversation for a general audience, terms such as 'post-modernism' and 'post-structuralism' are used throughout this chapter as shorthand terms covering a variety of philosophical movements which developed strongly in the 1970s as a reaction to the world-view of modernism. Charles Jencks, an authority on the subject, recommends *The Post-Modern and the Post-Industrial: A critical analysis* by Margaret A. Rose (Cambridge University Press, 1991) as 'an impartial, scholarly guide to all this'.

was, unusually, both teaching thermodynamics at Swinburne Institute of Technology and writing an MA thesis in psychology, and the tension between the scientist and the social psychologist in him has remained, as it has in our intellectual culture.

There are certain elements of our humanity (from a dramatist's point of view, perhaps the most interesting elements) which, as Williamson sees it, are rooted in something much more universal and objectively real than the mere intersection of cultural discourses.

THIS INTEREST OF MINE in what Hume called the most important question that could ever be asked stems from my experience as a psychology student in the late 1960s. Psychology was supposed to be a science, but it was in fact heavily infected with ideology. At that time the ideology was behaviourism. We were taught that, in the light of B. F. Skinner's[2] experiments with pigeons and rats, we human beings were infinitely modifiable. If we were put on the right reward schedule, we could be shaped to be anything the people giving us the food pellets wanted us to be. We were no more than blank sheets waiting to be written on by whichever ideologies wanted to control us. Now, this was thought to be an ideology of optimism: whatever was wrong with the world (violence, war, xenophobia, acquisitiveness, aggression, territoriality and so on) could be quickly wiped away by the right reinforcement schedules. Deft social engineering could make us perfect.

As the years wore on I began to realise that this was actually less a science than a utopian ideology directed at reshaping the world, and a terrifying one because, if human nature didn't exist, if we were just blank slates waiting to be written on, then we could be written on by anyone — the fascist right just as easily as the utopian left. I began to suspect it was all much more complex than that. Some time in the 1970s I twigged to the fact that the social sciences were trying to pretend that Charles Darwin had never existed. The horror religion had been faced with in the nineteenth century was still facing the

2 The Harvard Professor B. F. Skinner's school of psychology focused on patterns of responses in animals to external rewards and stimuli. He applied the results of his research with animals, using the reward technique, to human learning, radically influencing educational theories and methods in the United States and other Western countries. His best-known works are *The Behavior of Organisms* (1938), *Walden Two* (1961) and *About Behaviorism* (1974).

social sciences — they simply refused to believe any instinctual urges at all lurked in our psyches. They lurked in animals, right up to the chimpanzee, but not in us.

I came to believe there *is* a human nature. While we're a flexible species, there's nevertheless a bedrock there of 'humanness', the result of a long evolutionary history. Like every other animal, we're a deeply competitive species, competing as individuals or groups for the resources that allow us to survive and reproduce. Nationalism, for example, is an example of ferocious competitiveness between groups, and to pretend there's no predisposition towards tribalism in human beings is to draw the blinkers over our eyes in the most foolish of ways. And a bit of tertiary education isn't going to knock it out of us. Certainly, ideologies are powerful, influencing us and partly shaping us, but there are also basic instinctual predispositions in the human species which can't be ignored.

I'm not arguing a social Darwinist perspective, by the way. Modern biological research has established that sociability and the capacity for sympathy are potentials just as deeply rooted in us as egocentricity. We're always in oscillation between the egocentric need to further our own interests and the need to win approval from the family or group. Our sociability, our need to interact with other people is very strong. It's in the oscillation between the two that human nature provides us with drama, and my drama in particular is about those two competing needs deep in our nature: to grab what we can for ourselves, but to do it in such a way — disguising our selfishness from ourselves and others — as to retain the love and approval of our group.

You seem almost to have a bee in your bonnet about this question of what makes us human — in the broadest terms, genes or culture. Why? Why that question and not, say, getting the history of Australia right or exploited minorities?

I've *always* been obsessively interested in the wellsprings of human behaviour and human difference — why individuals differed from each other. Just after the War, you couldn't easily discuss genetics because of the association with Hitler and his claim that Aryans were genetically superior to other races (which bears no relationship to the arguments of contemporary researchers). The anti-nature, pro-nurture outlook persisted into the 1970s and I found I was working in a branch of science that was supposedly looking for the truth while ignoring half the evidence. So it did become a bee in my bonnet. Truth, after all, is what science is supposed to be all about. That's, in fact, what prompted me to write both *Dead White Males*[3] and *Heretic*[4]: I was profoundly irritated by the fact that the whole post-modernist academic structure was attempting to convince us that there is no such thing as objective truth, everything being just a power play between groups using the flexibility and deceit of language to push their own so-called truths down our throats[5]. Now, this view has quite a lot to recommend it: we know how ideologies have been used to distort the truth, we all know how slippery, evocative and emotionally affecting words can be, and we all know how they can bend us away from the truth. But that doesn't mean that there isn't a truth, or at least an approximate truth, out there. (The post-modernists never ask, by the way, where this ubiquitous drive for power comes from. Read Darwin if you want to know where the urge comes from — Foucault[6] has nothing to say on the subject.)

3 The Sydney Theatre Company (STC) production of *Dead White Males* opened in March, 1995. Brian Kiernan provides a useful account of the play's reception by both critics and audiences in his biography of Williamson, *David Williamson: A writer's career* (Currency Press, 1996). He also provides evidence of Williamson's conviction at the time that the play is more concerned with 'the difficulties and intricacies of male–female relationships in the mid-90s' than post-structuralist theory.

4 The STC production of *Heretic* opened in March 1996. Again, a useful summary of the play's production difficulties and reception can be found in Kiernan's biography.

5 Interestingly, in one of Williamson's first (unpublished) plays, a one-act three-hander called *You've Got to Get On Jack* (first performed at La Mama in 1970), a similar point is made: Jack, a grader-driver 'combines a primitive epistemology ("truth is what you feel") with absolute intolerance of his mates' or anyone else's views' (Kiernan, p. 53). Williamson remembers Katharine Brisbane's review of the 1971 production of the play as 'the first real encouragement [as a playwright] he ... received in print' (Kiernan, p. 68).

6 Michel Foucault (1926–84), Professor of History of Systems of Thought at the Collège de France, has been arguably the most influential of the French thinkers central to the development of post-modernist and post-structuralist thought in the humanities over the last quarter of a century. According to Michael Ignatieff, writing in the *Times Literary Supplement*, 'scarcely any philosopher working on the history of philosophy or historian working on the history of institutions, social science or sexuality can avoid confronting the challenge of Foucault's books'. His major works, in which he constantly returns to the theme of the conflict between desire and power, and the weapons, especially language, used in the battle, include *Madness and Civilization* (1961), *Discipline and Punish* (1975) and *The History of Sexuality* (1978). An introduction to his thought is available in *The Foucault Reader*, edited by Paul Rabinow (Penguin, 1991).

I believed, when I was at university, that the scientific method (the insistence on hypothesis, generation and then verification of the hypothesis by evidence) was also applicable to the social sciences and ultimately to the humanities — and I still do. Hypothesis support or rejection on the basis of *evidence* is the only way to increase the sum total of human knowledge. I still believe that science, although it's viewed with bitter suspicion by many in areas of the humanities and social sciences, is the only true path to ultimate wisdom. When I hear about some tribe's belief that the moon is a bowl of cheese ... well, the moon is *not* a bowl of cheese, their belief that it is is *not* as valid as the scientific view, and eventually that tribe is going to have to come to terms with that fact. In short, I retain a faith that the truths of science are the only real truths and that scientists are steadily coming up with answers to the questions the philosophers would have kept arguing about forever.

You don't write about what makes us human as a scientist, though. Your angle on these questions is a playwright's.

I've always been fascinated, not just by the wellsprings of our human-ness, but by human social interaction, the ways people use language to disguise from themselves and from others what their true motives are. Dialogue and language as a form of social manipulation and social power have always been an abiding interest of mine, as is clear from my early plays. In *Don's Party* [1971], in particular, the Labor Party supporters use language to disguise their avid interest in money — indeed, in most of the things the conservative parties are in favour of. As the night wears on, these baser motives of wealth and ambition emerge simultaneously with the sexual impulses.

And the conflict between the sexes has, of course, been an abiding interest of mine — it's an abiding interest of all drama, after all. In many ways, I believe, males and females do have different agendas, but in a relationship they also have common needs and common ground, so it's always a jostling match, and an intricate jostling match, fraught with all kinds of difficulties and intricacies, deceit and self-deceit. This conflict between the sexes is rooted in the male's biological predisposition to control the female's social and sexual life. (It's worth remarking that feminist biologists are now starting to assert the necessity for women to utilise feminist ideologies on a long-term basis and not to presume that a bit of kindergarten training in non-sexism is going to sweep male sexist tendencies away. It's better to fight against men with effective feminist ideologies, in other words, than to pretend their misbehaviour is about to disappear.)

In later life, while retaining that interest in the friction and attraction between the sexes, I've got more interested in the intellectual ideas that are currently fashionable in our society and how they have a bearing on social interaction.

As a matter of fact, I can agree in part with a lot of post-modern ideas. When I satirised Dr Grant Swain, for example, the lecturer in cultural studies in *Dead White Males*, I was satirising his *use* of ideology, but I wasn't saying that his entire ideology was erroneous. My point was that he was misusing his ideology for his own personal power — exploiting females, trying to control their sexuality to his own advantage — and that's human nature. While I can agree that the desire for power underlies much of our social behaviour, I'd say that insight comes just as strongly from Charles Darwin as it does from Foucault, and Darwin offers us an explanation. I'm fascinated by the theories of post-modernism because they're at least half-right[7]. They correctly focus on our pursuit of power, but fail to realise that the source of that urge for power is not societal, but comes from within.

In a nutshell, what I'm interested in is the interaction on a broad scale between human nature and ideology. What is human nature, what is ideology, and how do they intersect, negate and reinforce each other? Added to that is my constant interest in interaction and conflict between individuals and what shapes the nature of this conflict.

✧

---

7 Kiernan tells the story of an acquaintance accusing David Williamson after the premiere of *Dead White Males* of 'half-believing what Swain had preached, which Williamson cheerfully admitted' (p. 267). He also quotes a fax Williamson sent to Alison Summers in New York in which he says: 'A lot of the poststructuralism I give Swain has some power and the fact that he is the sleaze of the piece doesn't mean some of his arguments don't have power. It's Shaw's old argument about giving the devil the best ideas' (p. 299).

As Brian Kiernan, Williamson's biographer, has pointed out, there's an assumption in any satire about what is actually 'normal'. Hyperbole and distortion, in other words, imply some norm (loyalty, integrity, even monogamy). The gross displays of greed or rivalry we witness on stage amuse us because we agree they're gross. Some critics have suggested that David Williamson's notion of what is normal has become much more conservative than his radical early plays led us to expect[8].

Yes, I've often had that charge directed at me. Not only do I think it's untrue — if anything, the trend is in the other direction. I think if you look at early plays such as *Don's Party* or *The Removalists* [1971], you'll find they're very bleak plays indeed. At the time they were mistaken as Left-wing treatises. When it was first produced, *The Removalists* was seen as a savage Left-wing play about police brutality, about police beating up innocent working-class lads. In fact, it was bleaker and more pessimistic than that: the working-class hero was just as bad, venal, sexist and horrible as the policeman. Actually, I think the young constable (the one who actually does the damage, who kills Kenny) is possibly the most sympathetic character in the play. As far back as *The Removalists*, what I was saying was: 'Beware the dark human impulses, beware what lurks under the surface'. And what lurked under the surface of the sergeant in *The Removalists*, for instance, was very dark indeed: sexual impulses, but also the impulse to wield power, to dominate and to humiliate all those around him, including Ross. It was not your copy-book Left-wing play, as people in later years have realised, and neither was *Don's Party*. *Don's Party* was saying, 'Look, all these so-called Labor supporters, who are here to cheer on the victory of a Labor government, have no real commitment to social reform, have no real commitment to social equity, it's just their football team they're barracking for that night, and they're just as venal under the surface as the others'.

---

8 If 'conservative' is taken to mean 'opposed to radical change in the social order', a conservative gloss can clearly be applied to David Williamson in the specific sense that, like many others of his generation, he has come to doubt the *possibility* of immediate, radical solutions to problems such as greed, competitiveness and violence. Others of that same generation, of course, have pursued the goal of eradicating sexism, racism and inequality through social and linguistic engineering. If, however, 'conservative' is taken to mean sympathy for the Thatcherism of the 1980s and 1990s, then Williamson is just as clearly not conservative at all.

Those plays were misperceived at the time as being strident calls for social justice, whereas what they were in fact saying is what I've always been interested in saying: that there is a dark side to human nature, a desire for power, an acquisitiveness and a self-absorption — beware of it! Laugh at it if you will, laugh at the idiocy of those transparently self-aggrandising impulses, but beware! To the protagonists themselves, of course, these impulses seem quite normal — and that's where the humour comes from, of course, the audience seeing the sergeant justifying his violent behaviour in language full of self-righteous justification. If anything, as I've grown older, I think I've admitted into my plays more of the positive and pleasant side of human nature — the need to be compassionate, decent and sympathetic, for example, the side that calls out for justice. But the kick-off point for my satire is human nature as egocentric, acquisitive and sexist.

You were once described (accurately, I think) as storyteller to the Australian tribe[9]. Although your plays have enjoyed success overseas (perhaps proving your point about a common humanity), we think of you as a storyteller to us about ourselves. What stories do you think we're now ready to hear about ourselves? What issues still in solution are ready to be crystallised? The republic? The environment? Paedophilia, perhaps? What issues floating in the public mind are asking to be dramatised by a writer such as yourself?

I'm actually a little embarrassed by the tag 'storyteller to the tribe'. There are lots of storytellers to our tribe, and there are lots of different tribes within Australia who want to hear different stories. I'd hate to think I was supposed to be speaking for Australia as a whole — I have a certain audience that enjoys my plays, but I'm sure there are other people who hate everything I do. I'm just speaking with an individual voice to those Australians who want to listen to it.

You mentioned issues, but I've never been much of a social issues-

---

9 By John Dingwall, chairman of the Australian Writers' Guild, in a paper delivered at Perth Writers' Week in 1979.

type writer[10], and I've been strongly criticised for that. 'Why aren't you writing a play about the environment?', I've been asked. Yes, *Brilliant Lies* [1993] was ostensibly about sexual harrassment, but that was just the peg on which the play was hung. It was really more about the old uneasiness and enmity between the sexes, which has been a recurrent thread throughout my plays. At base I haven't been especially interested in examining particular issues as such, because that brings with it the suggestion that the playwright should then come up with solutions to the social issues he's focusing on. I've always avoided what one critic has called 'social studies-type drama', in which you seize on an issue, some wrong in society (urban poverty, say, or youth unemployment) and then write a play to dramatise the effect that social wrong has on your characters. In effect, you'd be lecturing your audience (which would be typically middle-class), they'd hear the voice of an authoritarian playwright who thinks he knows what's wrong, knows how to fix it, assuming a morally superior position to his audience. 'I know more than you do,' the voice would be saying, 'and, not only that, I'm also filled with much more empathy and concern about this issue than you bastards. So soak it all up, see what unworthy human beings you are, and go out of this theatre and make this country better.'

Well, I've always felt uneasy about that sort of role, because my basic position is that most problems are not easily soluble; a lot of them are terribly difficult and intractable, and I have no solutions to them. And the reason they're intractable is that our very essence as human beings is intractable and difficult. What I'm really interested in is looking at how difficult it is for us to live together harmoniously as social creatures, because our agendas are all so very different, so egocentric, and it's very hard to come up with harmony and happiness. What I want is for the audience to realise what's at stake. Even in terms of public policy it's vital we get a realistic picture of what human nature actually is. How naive we were in the 1960s with

---

10 In his Introduction to the Currency Press edition of *Heretic*, for instance, Williamson writes: '*Heretic* has been called a play of ideas, but it would be more accurate to call it a play of people who have ideas'. It is also generally true that in David Williamson's plays the focus tends to shift from the institution (the university department or the club) to the lives of individuals in that institution.

our accelerated learning programs and poverty programs. Social intervention by and large didn't work. In fact, the world is becoming less fair, less equal, and it's time we asked ourselves why.

I suspect that drama works best with a sense of enlightened pessimism, not with rational argument. Drama works best where you say, for example, environmental change is so hard to bring about because under the surface in every idealist there's a streak of self-interest. Town councillors will support environmental protection fervently until their patch of land is up for rezoning, when they'll suddenly decide that employment is much more important than the environment, and silently sell off their big parcel of land at a huge profit. I have the greatest admiration for the environmental movement — the world is facing environmental disaster, after all, and something must be done — but, when I sat down to write the play which had my first environmentalist in it, *Money and Friends* [1991], what I was immediately drawn to looking at was the self-interest lurking under the surface of public idealism in that area. A few of my environmentalist friends weren't too happy with the picture I drew of an environmentalist with a few venal qualities of his own.

So we're unlikely, I take it, to see a republican play, for example, or a play supporting land rights for Aborigines.

That's right. If I were to write a play about a land rights activist, for example, I'd be drawn to finding the flaws under the idealism. I'm not a deep cynic, I hope I'm just a realist. A relative of mine is working in the Kimberley area. Having gone there with the most idealistic of motives, he's since become aghast at the amount of venal behaviour amongst the power elites in the Kimberley region. Now, as a dramatist, what I'd want to say is, 'Beware the power elite that's telling you it's solving your problems — it's probably not. It's probably feathering its own nest.' As a satirist, I seize on idealists, scratch their surface and say, 'I don't quite believe your spiel'. It's not that there aren't any idealists effectively working for change, it's just that as a dramatist I don't find them interesting.

I've often been accused of satirising my own side, and in a sense that's been true. But then I've assumed that the Joh Bjelke-Petersens of the world are so blatantly self-interested, greedy and acquisitive that they're beyond satire. Why bother to satirise a figure on the far right when they're satirical figures as they are? But I've drawn fire for that.

✧

There must be difficulties, structural problems, writing about ideas for the stage. The audience can't go back over what's been said, for example, the ideas have to be starkly presented, and in the genres you work in (broadly speaking, the tolerant comic and less tolerant satiric genres) there's pressure to bowdlerise ideas — your characters can't have the kind of complicated argument you might actually have around a dinner table. How do you handle this problem of balancing what is immediately understandable surface entertainment (almost comic-strip humour at times) and depth?

The attempt to produce both intellectual depth and entertainment at the same time can be a desperate tug-of-war. At times I've been accused of going too far in the entertainment direction and not far enough in the direction of intellectual depth. But a balance can be achieved. In both *Dead White Males* and *Heretic,* I in fact ask the audience to grasp some quite complex arguments and intellectual positions (about cultural theory in the first and an argument between anthropologists in the second) in order to understand the drama.

Yet I agree there are problems — didacticism, for example. If all they do is spout ideas, the characters just become the mouthpieces for different viewpoints and have no life of their own, no discernible temperamental or psychological differences, none of those human qualities that make characters live as dramatic creations. Bernard Shaw ran into that problem all the time and didn't always overcome it. But unless the characters are complex beings, we're not interested in their ideas on the stage — it's not drama, it's a debate. What I try to do is structure my plays, often using satiric forms and even lapsing into farce, so that they inhabit the borderland between realism and satire, so that the audience is never quite sure what it's seeing: is it an absolutely accurate, realistic depiction of human behaviour or heightened, sharpened satire? I never quite know myself — it's somewhere in the borderland in between.

The basic problem for the dramatist is how to *distil* the ideas (and it *is* a process of distilling) in such a way that they're not trite, but still carry the meanings they need to in order to sustain the argument. When I was writing *Dead White Males,* for example, I read nothing but post-structuralism, Foucault and Derrida[11], for month after month, and I kept saying to myself, 'Underneath the verbiage, what's the essential idea? What's the simplest way this could be stated without losing most of what is being said?' I believe you *can* take a set of complex ideas and distil them to their essence while retaining, say, 70 or 80 per cent of what needs to be retained for them to be understood in all their power. You'll be criticised (quite heavily) for dropping the other 20 per cent of filigree, but if you're going to present them on stage, you've got to present the essence of those ideas, and I think the essence of what Foucault was saying, for instance, is quite simple — it's essentially what Nietzsche was saying much earlier. In Grant Swain, though, while I did make him a mouthpiece for Foucault's ideas in a distilled form, I also had to create a fallible human being, a character who was all too human, in a sense, someone whose carnal lusts, coming from deep in his evolutionary past, are still with him. Consequently, his ideology is at odds with his behaviour, and the audience spots that a mile off and takes delight in it.

There's always going to be some tension between theatricality and ideas. In my case that tension came to a head in the production of *Heretic*. We'd had a very successful production of *Dead White Males,* with Wayne Harrison directing it, and I think Wayne had had full scope for his theatricality with the appearance of Shakespeare in

---

11 French thinker whose philosophy is based on a critique of the ultimate metaphysical certainty characterising Western thought and Western theories of meaning. He founded the critical movement called Deconstruction, which particularly influenced members of the Yale school such as Paul de Man, but also critics and writers as divergent in their views as Edward Said, Harold Bloom, Gayatri Spivak and Eugenio Donato. Deconstruction appears to be derived from Ferdinand de Saussure's theories of the arbitrary nature of the verbal sign (although this is now contested), attacking the belief that a text has a fixed meaning, valid in any context, and thereby undermining such concepts as truth, identity, rationality and absolute oppositions (such as cause and effect or truth and lies). Derrida taught at both the Sorbonne (in the early 1960s) and the Ecole Normale Supérieure (from 1965). He came to prominence as a result of three works published in 1967: *Speech and Phenomena* (a study of Husserl), *Writing and Difference* and *On Grammatology*.

the dream sequences, and it was a very harmonious production. In *Heretic*, though, where I was dealing with Derek Freeman's opposition to the theories of Margaret Mead[12], I was pushing the theatre of ideas a little harder. For the audience to grasp what was at stake, there had to be a lot of exposition of ideas and in the end Wayne felt it was more than the average audience could bear. So he felt an enormous pressure to theatricalise and entertain, beyond the indications of the script, and our dispute came about, I think, because I was convinced he was pushing the theatricality further than was needed. He turned Margaret Mead into Marilyn Monroe, Jackie Kennedy and so on, whereas I thought she was an admirable, if mistaken, character, distorting science for what she thought were the very best of reasons. I wasn't sure that Wayne's theatricality was presenting her sympathetically, which is what I wanted.

✧

I wonder what plays you saw, what playwrights you were drawn to, when you first started to think of yourself as a playwright. Clearly, a writer is influenced by a myriad of things, but certain playwrights must have made you think to yourself, 'I could do that in my own way, that appeals to me, that's close to me'.

I think the influences when I was growing up were productions I saw of contemporary twentieth-century work, the macabre surrealism in the apparently realistic work of Pinter, for instance, in *The Caretaker*. I realised that these were not quite real people behaving in quite real ways, and the ways in which they were behaving said a lot about our inner emotional needs and the forces driving us. It struck me that

---

12 Margaret Mead (1901–78), an outspoken American anthropologist and campaigner on such issues as women's rights, race relations, nuclear proliferation, environmental pollution and sexual morality. The author of 23 books, mostly on the cultures of Oceania, it was her first book, *Coming of Age in Samoa* (1928, new edition 1968), which made her reputation as a cultural determinist. Not only her reliance on observation rather than statistical analysis, but also her radical belief that cultural conditioning alone accounted for sexual behaviour has been questioned by a number of anthropologists in the intervening decades, despite her eminence in her field (her position at the American Museum of Natural History and her presidency of the American Association for the Advancement of Science).

Pinter was distorting the surface in order to clarify what kind of creatures we are. I also saw Edward Albee's *Who's Afraid of Virginia Woolf?* and again was struck by the heightened reality of the way the characters were behaving. Albee was the first playwright I'd seen bringing Freud's subconscious into the conscious. Here were all these characters speaking out of the Freudian subconscious with a level of conflict which was above and beyond the real, but telling us something about the psychic forces underneath.

Going further back, I was always entranced and fascinated by Chekhov, Molière, Sheridan, Oscar Wilde, and satirists as far back as Aristophanes. I was always fascinated by writers who distorted and heightened surface behaviour in order to show us the venal, over-whelmingly egocentric forces underneath. Molière is superb at that, as is Chekhov in a gentler way.

I say 'gentler', although in fact Chekhov is a much more ruthless dramatist than most people give him credit for. They say 'gentle Chekhov' and talk about his 'love of humanity' and so on, but Chekhov's tragedies are actually heart-rending because nobody ends up emotionally satisfied, nobody ends up with the right person for them. And the level of egocentric behaviour in Chekhov's plays is quite profound: people talk about their own needs and wants over the top of other people talking about their own needs and wants. No one is hearing what anyone else is saying. They're all going round and round in their own little egocentric worlds. Chekhov is quite ruthless and cold in many ways. I was always fascinated by his plays; his was a strong influence on me, and the reason is again that in his work there's always the appearance of absolute reality or something close to it, while at another level there's a distortion — he makes his char-acters more egocentric than they would be in a real social situation in order to heighten the sense that we are all islands unto ourselves.

Seeing the productions of the early work of John Romeril[13] and

13 Romeril was identified with the Australian Performing Group from its inception, with most of his plays being performed at La Mama and the Pram Factory. Influenced by Brecht, his theatre is political, improvisational and often humorous. His best-known plays are *Chicago, Chicago, I Don't Know Who to Feel Sorry For* and *The Floating World* (all from the early 1970s) and the musical (with Alan John) *Jonah Jones* (1985). His latest play is *Love Suicides* (1997).

Jack Hibberd [14] was very important to me in the late sixties because it was liberating: it was saying, we are allowed to write about our own social milieu, urban Australia — we don't have to write about outback myths. Here at last was a group of dramatists intent on finding out what it is that's unique about Australian behaviour and Australian social patterns. That was a liberating force on me.

✧

Sydney Theatre Company director Wayne Harrison and theatre critic Katharine Brisbane both know David Williamson's work intimately, although from different angles. Each of them sees the value of what Williamson does in a somewhat different light. While both speak of his being almost 'uncannily' attuned to the Australian Zeitgeist and admire his remarkable ability to dramatise it entertainingly (an important skill in any public intellectual), Wayne Harrison stresses Williamson's transforming role, his ability to fashion the way we think about ourselves as well. He's vehemently opposed to the view that Williamson's plays are basically just entertaining comedies of manners.

Wayne Harrison

David Williamson is obviously an intellectual — he's an important contemporary thinker. You can't dismiss David simply because, on the surface, his work doesn't bear the marks of heady intellectual fare. He's often been criticised for being some sort of frivolous, naturalistic writer, but I've always argued that his work is anything but naturalistic. In fact, the entertaining way he uses his intellect to present arguments through recognisable scenes from our lives can be quite deceptive: these scenes can appear quite innocent, but they've been selected, organised and edited to reinforce his own complex intellectual positions. In fact, he's highly manipulative in his choice of material and argument to reinforce a thematic point.

---

14 Closely associated with the Australian Performing Group until 1976, Hibberd is the author of a large body of work, less political than Romeril's, exploring contemporary Australian stereotypes, myths, rituals and attitudes, often using satire, music and broad-stroke characterisation to jolt his audience into an awareness of its heritage and its absurdities. *Dimboola* (1969) is Australia's most frequently performed play, while *A Stretch of the Imagination* (1972) is generally regarded as his most important play.

There's always going to be a problem, though: theatre, in my view, is primarily an emotional experience, rather than an intellectual one. A play can have intellectual rigour informing it, but what happens in the theatre is first and foremost an emotional experience, as far as I'm concerned — which has led certain critics to call me an anti-intellectual or a populist. The very act of gathering in that space and giving yourself over to the emotional interaction on stage is in the first instance not an intellectual but an emotional experience. Part of David's success does come out of the intellectual component to his work, it's true, but his real success comes from the way he connects emotionally with his audience, from the strong identification that occurs between the stage and the auditorium as people submit to the storytelling and the emotional journeys of his characters. That's what makes him a great man of the theatre.

How is this ability to provide an emotional connection a 'problem'?

Well, David has made his reputation turning the everyday evidence of society into dramatic works. So when he decided to write *Dead White Males*, a play based keenly on his intellectual investigations, he set me a problem of how to represent those ideas on stage without boring everyone senseless. My approach was to come up with a highly theatricalised presentation, a production stripped of any naturalistic detail, combining the intellectual component with the emotional content of the family scenes. It's a problem not only David faces, of course, and it has to be confronted at the point of writing: how to turn the ideas into characters, voices, emotions and actions. Critics said of Tom Stoppard's *Arcadia*, for example, that it was a wonderful roller-coaster ride through Tom Stoppard's library, but was it theatre, was it dramatic art?[15] I would say that the point is whether or not the audience found it an exhilarating night in the theatre. In the case of

---

15 Author of a number of acclaimed and popular plays of ideas, such as *Rosencrantz and Guildenstern Are Dead* (1966), *Jumpers* (1972) and *Travesties* (1974), which, for all their intellectual brilliance, left some critics and theatre-goers wishing for greater engagement with social and political realities. His interest in 'pure craftsmanship' was modified in some later plays, such as *Cahoot's Macbeth* (1979) and *Night and Day* (1978), in which he explores themes of freedom and totalitarianism. Indeed, it has been said of *Arcadia* (1993) that it 'explores the nature of truth and time ... and the disruptive influence of sex on our orbits in life'.

Dead White Males, I think that together David and I succeeded in weaving difficult post-structuralist and liberal humanist ideas into a recognisable Williamson family situation. You always know when David is in top form and has hit the social or political button fairly and squarely: the plays go through the roof at the box-office. And *Dead White Males* is probably the most successful production he's ever had[16].

What do you see as the common area of intellectual concern in David Williamson's plays?

He is constantly trying to unravel what it is that makes people as complex and difficult as they are, to get down to the essence of what makes us human, what makes us moral, what makes us mistreat each other. He's a brilliant analyist of human behaviour, in the subcategory of the Australian male and the Australian female. Part of that process is examining the relationship between men and women. In the case of *Heretic,* for example, I don't think it's been fully appreciated yet that, apart from the intellectual conflict between Mead and Freeman, David was also looking at the history of the relationship between middle-class men and women in this country, that slice of gender relationships that David seems to know so well and write about so insightfully. In a number of absolutely key scenes he showed the evolution of that relationship across decades in an utterly simple but affecting way. In the character of Derek Freeman he showed how one man (who comes from my father's generation), very set in his ways, forced himself to change in his attitudes towards women, as he had to if he wanted to continue in a relationship with his wife, if he wanted to continue receiving her love, allowing her to grow as a person. It's a wonderful subnarrative in *Heretic*, and, I think, a great achievement of the writing.

David Williamson has survived as a playwright in a way most of his contemporaries from the 1960s and early 1970s have not.

---

16 Kiernan puts the total audience for the STC production at about 120,000.

David is more than a survivor — he's transformed himself from period to period, from decade to decade. He's still very much a person of the nineties, as much as he was of the seventies. That can only be put down to a talent or facility for being not just a reflector of public taste (although he's a very good litmus test of what the public mood is), but one step ahead of it. He's an interpreter of public opinion and taste, while at the same time fashioning it. There are very few people who have that ability. *Dead White Males*, for instance, as several critics have remarked, anticipated the mood change in Australia in the last part of this decade. The call to pause, to listen just one more time to what the older generation has to say about what's been happening in this country over the last fifteen years, the way it's been refashioned, the possibility that change has been too rapid, seemed to anticipate what was happening on the national stage, especially in terms of the change of government. It's not a matter of conservative or reactionary politics, it's a matter of an uncanny ability to give voice to nascent changes in the public thinking. He analysed what was going on in the country and then transformed it into a theatrical statement that had huge emotional impact.

✧

Katharine Brisbane, theatre critic and Williamson's publisher at Currency Press, emphasises his extraordinary ability to articulate ideas and views already informing the public consciousness, much in the spirit of Donald Horne's conviction that a public intellectual's business is 'to conceptualise for people something that's already floating around in their heads ... to crystallise it'. Katharine Brisbane, however, is not convinced that this ability qualifies a writer to be called 'an intellectual'.

Katharine Brisbane

If you think of an intellectual as someone who's leading us with new ideas, then I don't see David that way. I think his work is intuitive and emotional. To me he's much more like an actor in that regard than an intellectual. He has an actor's instinctual understanding and ability to enter the lives of other people, to imagine. He's an observer, with antennae for what the ideas emerging in the community are. His success has been due to the fact that he can capture and define issues, attitudes and prejudices that already exist in people's minds but have not yet been consciously grasped. So it was very exciting, particularly at the time of his early plays, to go to the theatre and recognise this and say to yourself, 'Goodness, he's right, and I hadn't thought of it'.

In *The Removalists*, for example, which had such an enormous success in the very early seventies, he defined a whole period of confrontation, he took the climate of the moratoria, the protest marches and the anti-censorship battle and gave us a metaphor in terms of the two policemen. But what he was really talking about is how we Australians see domestic life, our relationships with other people, in terms of confrontation. That was really the lasting quality which *The Removalists* offered us, way beyond our relations with the police and all the rest of it. He was really the first person to articulate that and that was very exciting.

In those plays of the seventies in particular you can trace the changes in our political climate, our uncertainty, and the speed with which change was taking place in Australia during those years. *What If You Died Tomorrow?* [1973], for example, was a play which on the surface was about a doctor called Andrew leaving his first wife, setting up what was once upon a time called an irregular household with another woman, and starting a new life as a novelist. But it was also about speed of change in the Whitlam period and about how frightened people became, how unsteady the structure of Australia was, and in retrospect you can see all that in the play now. Whether or not we could at the time, I'm not sure, but he did capture how we were feeling. David Williamson charts our feelings in a quite uncanny way, I think.

Of course, he understands his audience very well; he has a great instinct for what it's telling him and rarely goes too far beyond that. He's a public playwright and that's how public playwrights write. It's one of the secrets of his success: his work reflects what we're thinking today rather than advances it. He's stayed at the top of his profession for over 25 years by listening to and respecting his audience.

Would it be true to say that in recent years David Williamson's plays have become more conceptual?

There's certainly a growing concern with wider issues than just domestic ones. The turning point came, I think, with *Sons of Cain* [1985] and you see it again in *Brilliant Lies* [1993]. Since then I think he's consciously moved towards more global issues. Instead of relying on gut feelings, he's researched the issues and thought them through in a much more intellectual way than in his early plays. So there's a new quality. Something's been lost in the process — there was a great energy in those early plays — and something's been gained.

How would you compare him to other playwrights of ideas — Stoppard, for example?

Tom Stoppard is very different because he likes ideas for their own sake, he plays games with them. That's not what David is interested in. He's much more interested in the tribal voice, in interpreting Australians to themselves and other people. It's also worth bearing in mind that Stoppard writes for an audience which is very different from an Australian one. He writes for a university-educated audience which enjoys witty banter and the play of ideas for their own sake, regardless of the characters, whereas here in Australia I think we still have a working-class culture in a very important sense — having money and possessions doesn't make any difference.

Only two Australian playwrights come to mind as obvious playwrights of ideas: Dorothy Hewett[17] and Nick Enright[18]. Even then I'm not sure I'd call their work 'intellectual' — I don't think the theatre works that way. Theatre has to hit the audience in the gut first of all,

---

17 Her many plays, although they range widely in style from realism to rock opera, can be grouped thematically in two broad areas: those on sexual and family themes (such as *The Golden Oldies* [1967]) and those on the threat to the landscape and cultural heritage from development and 'progress' (such as *Fields of Heaven* [1982]).

18 From *On the Wallaby* (1982) to his recent highly acclaimed *Blackrock* (1996), Enright's theatre constantly presents the audience with 'issues': women's roles in the family (*Variations* [1982]), the treatment of women convicts (*First Class Women* [1982]), rebellion against social and political conformity (*St James Infirmary* [1993]) and in *Blackrock* a range of youth issues including parenting, peer group pressure and violence.

and it's only when it's on the page or when you're studying it at university that you're really aware of the intellectual mind at work. I think Enright *is* interested in working with ideas and pushing ideas forward — in fact, I think he's more inclined to push his ideas than Williamson is — but I think he's a clever enough playwright never to go too far. Hewett, of course, has always pushed the boundaries. That's why she's never made any money as a playwright and a lot of directors are frightened of her, really terrified of her plays. As a result she's mainly known as a poet.

Ideas plays are always a problem. To have a good idea for a play is, in my opinion, always a doomed enterprise. You have to feel a *need* to write a play, a need coming out of the emotions, rather than the intellect. In the 1930s and 1940s an enormous number of people tried to write plays about 'the outback' — the fires, the floods and the dust; they were almost all urban Australians, and the plays didn't work because they didn't spring from a real need to express how their authors saw life. Nowadays such people watch television and decide to write television pieces.

The other obvious problem with ideas plays is that they can so easily become polemical. Audiences detect that straight away. After all, if they want that, they can go to public lectures.

On the other hand, theatre is the perfect platform for ideas because it's always at the forefront of change, being so much cheaper than film. If you want to present important current issues in a dramatic form, you're unlikely to try to make a film about them simply because it takes so long and costs so much money. This is why alternative theatre is so vital. AIDS plays in backstreet theatres in America, for example, were tremendously important in finding acceptable ways to make the public face issues they didn't feel ready to face. From off-off-Broadway the plays moved onto Broadway, into the cinema and even became musicals.

The language in a Williamson play always appears, however deceptively, as utterly true to life. While we take pleasure in recognising it as 'real', I wonder if this apparent realism may not conceal at times, almost too effectively, the structure of ideas underlying the work.

David's plays are almost seamless, his art is hidden. He's a very elegant, economical writer — it's almost impossible to cut him, for example; very difficult even to isolate a quotation to demonstrate his humour or understanding of character, because everything's related in an intricate but hidden way to the development of the character and situation. As far as the apparent naturalism of the dialogue is concerned, David usually writes up to eight or ten drafts of a play and the earlier drafts are often more poetic. There were some truly beautiful passages in the earlier drafts of *Travelling North* [1979], I remember, which eventually disappeared. Perhaps his advisers — and David listens to a lot of advice when he's writing, you always write plays as part of a team — advised him against it, maybe there's a fear of losing a certain Australian quality. The point is that audiences respond wonderfully to David's plays and his most recent plays, which are plays of ideas, *Dead White Males* and *Heretic*, have been hugely successful.

Arts&Ideas

Deborah Jones

Shirley McKechnie

Adrian Martin

Catharine Lumby

Meaghan Morris

' We live in a society which is saturated with images and information.

However, since they're no longer located in

discrete sites, we don't have a

contemplative relationship to them.

Even if we're reading a philosophy book, the phone

still rings, the fax goes and so forth.

The skill of interacting with images and information today,

or the process of consuming them, is a

much more lateral one. '

Catharine Lumby

C ATHARINE LUMBY *has lightly, but with some precision, put her finger on the nub of the problem we are about to investigate: how does the intellectual culture work in the 1990s, particularly from the point of view of younger Australians? How are ideas disseminated through the various artforms and what sort of ideas are they? Many younger Australians (and Lumby stands at the more established end of Generation X), and especially those with a tertiary education in the humanities, clearly have a strong sense that the very words 'culture' and 'ideas' mean something different from what they meant to earlier generations, and that they reach people and invite participation in fundamentally different ways as well.*

Catharine Lumby's word 'lateral' is a key to the shift in perspective: it suggests that culture and ideas emerge in our minds as our gaze shifts from one conjunction of images and text to another, along connecting pathways of meaning. It has more to do with a response to surfaces than was perhaps the case a generation ago. Certainly, for many Australians, ideas are no longer just grand cogitations about what is real, why we exist or what surplus value is. Nor, obviously, are they disseminated overwhelmingly through written texts.

It was a mixed medium — theatre — which Deborah Jones, Arts Editor of the Australian, *first spoke about. There's a script in theatre, of course, but that's little more than the blueprint for what is experienced in the darkened auditorium. In another era plays were an established source of ideas in the old-fashioned sense of the word. But Deborah Jones is not at all sure that Australian theatre today is fulfilling an ideas function in either the old or new senses.*

Deborah Jones

I have found myself increasingly disappointed with Australian theatre, not so much with the presentation, but with the playwriting.

So it's not the productions of Chekhov or Molière that disappoint you?

No. We have directors like Barry Kosky and Neil Armfield who are wonderful at expressing in new and individual ways the ideas contained in such texts. However, at the risk of sounding terribly sweeping, I'd say that most Australian playwriting is extraordinarily thin when it comes to ideas. There's a certain facility for plot, it's true, but a plot was never an idea. The plays I see have a thin surface. Even at the level of looking at what character means, or how a character might relate to a given situation, or to teasing out strands of behaviour in a character, I find the plays I see poorly written.

What do you put this down to? Is it the Zeitgeist? Is it the contemporary fashion for circus and spectacle?

For a long time I think there's been an unacknowledged confusion between action and ideas in Australian culture. You can see it in our great love of sport. Now, I adore the physical achievements of a footballer or a gymnast, but they're not art. People speak of 'poetry in motion', but of course it's not. It may be beautiful, exciting and enormously satisfying, but it's not an idea. Just because something looks beautiful and is difficult to do, people think it has some intellectual power.

Are we, though, perhaps expecting too much of the theatre? In Russia in the nineteenth century, let's say, the theatre was one of the only arenas where you could publicly discuss ideas, but in Australia in the 1990s ideas can be discussed in the newspapers, on the radio, even on the Internet — we don't need the theatre for that any more.

There's no single well of public opinion in Australia now for theatre to address — there are small pools of it, sometimes just conversations between individuals. And it's also true that Australia has a rather thin history in terms of ideas in many respects. For long periods we looked to other people for ideas, and it was really only in the fifties and sixties that Australian playwrights started looking to their own culture for ideas and deciding that we actually did have a culture, and that there were ideas of our own to be expressed. In any case, my feeling is that those ideas have rarely been taken up with any great power in the theatre — in literature, certainly, but not in the theatre. I think it comes back to the confusion I spoke about before between action and ideas: it's thought that if you put a bit of action and a plot on the stage, that will be enough to make people bring their own ideas to the theatre — well, I don't think it is. I think theatre often talks down to its audiences in Australia. In fact, I think our audiences are hungry for new ways of thinking, want to go home and argue about ideas, yet often all they're offered is a nice night out.

Perhaps theatre should only be commentary on ideas. A play about Wittgenstein, for example, need not be like a novel about Wittgenstein[1] or a biography, in which you can detail his ideas and argue with them, including whole pages of quotations in your text.

A play about Wittgenstein is obviously not worth doing if you're just going to write a narrative about where he was born and went to school, what he wrote and how he died. That would be quite a pointless exercise. But this doesn't mean that theatre lacks the ability to discuss deep ideas. For example, one of the most intellectually stimulating plays I've ever seen is *Angels in America*[2] — it offered an enormous breadth of intellectual discussion.

Yet it wasn't pretending to be a film, or wanting to be a book or wanting to be anything other than a piece of drama in which live actors on the stage interacted with a live audience in a single physically enclosed place.

What about opera? Can opera still be a source of ideas, given that opera audiences have usually seen the opera they're watching many times before? Isn't it basically an emotional and musical experience?

For a great many people it is simply an emotional experience, I'm sure. The surtitles allow people to understand what's going on but reading them is a kind of a separate experience. The audience listens to the German or Italian on stage, while the ideas are in the surtitles above them — there's a certain dislocation. What is being sung on

---

1 As Derek Jarman demonstrated in his engrossing film *Wittgenstein* (1993).
2 Tony Kushner's two-part theatrical epic about AIDS (1992).

stage is meaningful, but is not heard as meaningful. It's a sensory rather than an intellectual experience. It's trickier in the case of an English opera when the words are clearly enunciated and the audience can listen to them straight from the singers' mouths. The feeling in the audience is always very different. Take Opera Australia's production of Britten's *Peter Grimes*, for example. Now, that opera does have something to say about human alienation, and, because it's sung in English, it strikes you in the head, the heart and the gut — in other words, intellectually, emotionally and viscerally. That makes for extraordinarily powerful opera.

What about dance, which is even less text-based? Can dance be a source of ideas?

Anyone who was at the Melbourne Festival in 1996 and saw the Nederlands Dans Theater would be in absolutely no doubt whatsoever that in the hands of masters such as Jiri Kylian dance can overflow with ideas. One of his works, based on primitive movements, was about ideas of relating to the land and the imposition of human beings on the landscape and so on. Now, the audience brings its own experience, its own reading and understanding to what it sees. An interpretation of dance is never as fixed as it is in the theatre or in literature. It has an extraordinary ability to explode outwards with meaning for an intelligent and interested audience.

All the same, all too frequently dance is just people stretching their legs, saying, 'Isn't this pretty?'. For me that's just gymnastics and has no particular power. Yet, what I might call the extended use of the body, the highly trained use of the body by dancers and singers, can suggest to the audience a greater world of experience, even if in an unlocated kind of way. The ability to negotiate the limits of the voice, for example, or to do something almost other-worldly with the body, evokes ideas of extending our powers beyond what this little frame we inhabit is usually capable of. As a rule, not being a terribly demonstrative people, I think Australians tend to look for this kind of physical demonstration in sport. But we can also find it in dance, most specifically, and in singing. It's a way of freeing ourselves from our own bodies. So, even though in themselves these forms might not be saying anything deeply interesting in terms of ideas, they can set the mind free, allowing us to bring something of ourselves and our ideas to the experience.

Deborah Jones modern sense of looking to the arts, less for argued concepts or informed discussion, than for some kind of private stimulus to rethink the self — and the conviction that this is important, that it's thinking of a vital kind — is something that finds an echo in the thoughts of almost all our commentators in this discussion.

✧

In Shirley McKechnie's opinion, we tend to think of 'ideas' too narrowly, and her approach to the relationship between action and ideas diverges from that of Deborah Jones. Shirley McKechnie is a former dancer and choreographer, now lecturing in dance at the Victorian College of the Arts. One of her main concerns is to reposition dance in the arts field in Australia as an art form offering the public a rich array of ideas, but not in the conventional sense of the word. Dance, in her view, differs from other art forms as a source of ideas.

Shirley McKechnie

It's fundamentally different in the sense that dance ideas are not composed of words. The ideas that choreographers work with, for instance, are ideas manifested in space and in time. That's where the ideas are — that's how choreographers think. I'm speaking about choreographers because it's generally the choreographers who are the creative artists, and dancers who are the collaborators, although in recent times dancers are more frequently being involved in the choreographic process. Nevertheless, it's the task of the choreographer to bring the ideas together, and the ideas they're investigating in the studio are fundamentally ideas manifested in space and time.

There is, of course, the notion that a dance can be about something or refer to something outside itself — *Swan Lake*, in that sense, is about a princess and a prince and good and evil. Many famous ballets are about things in that way, having a narrative base. Many dances are about mood or atmosphere. There's a kind of continuum: at one end of the spectrum is the totally abstract dance, the dance of pure form, which works like architecture or three-dimensional design in space — William Forsythe's work for the Frankfurt Ballet, for example, or Twyla Tharp's *In the Upper Room*; as you move away from that, you come to dances of mood, of qualities suggesting atmosphere and deeper poetic insights. The closer you get to character, the more narrative you have. These things frequently merge and co-exist, but the way in which you can talk about dance ideas is only in space and time. Dance exists in time like music and in space like architecture.

In more traditional societies one imagines that most of the people watching the dance — whether a corroboree, say, or a folk dance or fertility rite — understand the language being used. Isn't it a problem in our society that this kind of understanding or cohesion cannot be assumed? It's often quite possible that very few people in the audience, let alone society at large, have the skills to interpret what they're seeing.

They don't have the skills because they don't have the knowledge in the body. Knowledge in the body comes in early childhood: in indigenous societies, the children dance, they're dancing by the time they can walk, you can see them in videos and films watching the adults, trying to copy them. So, in some sense, the dance comes along with every other kind of language, it's parallel to the verbal and visual languages. In our society, the languages that are most particularly developed and valued are those of the verbal intelligence and the mathematical intelligence, and most of the other intelligences — the visual, the kinesthetic, the aural — are dismissed as being unworthy in our society. They've never been unworthy in indigenous societies, they were in fact the whole expression of the culture. (And by 'kinesthetic intelligence' I mean that intelligence in the body that allows you to understand the world through your bones, nerves and muscles, a survival intelligence in the natural world — you can't hunt or climb a tree or find your balance without it. And this is the material the choreographer brings into the studio.)

One of the important things to consider is the idea put forward in the last decade or so by cognitive psychologists and thinkers such as Howard Gardner[3] postulating a number of different kinds of intelligences. Gardner, for instance, has proposed that there are seven basic types, and he exemplifies them with people such as Einstein, Picasso, Stravinsky, Martha Graham, T. S. Eliot, Gandhi and Freud[4]. He says, for instance, of Einstein that he would never have passed the normal intelligence test at school — in fact didn't do very well at school, nor did Picasso, who was apparently quite a dunce. Nevertheless, Einstein could imagine himself sitting on a beam of light, travelling through the galaxy noticing what was happening to the bodies he was passing — you can't do that without what Gardner would call a kinesthetic and spatial intelligence. It was only later, after the thought experiments, that Einstein proved what he'd imagined with mathematical formulae, writing about it later still, quite sparingly, in words. So, when we talk about intelligences, the way people think and the way ideas are manifested in the arts, these kinds of ideas about multiple intelligences become very important.

Martha Graham, for example, Gardner identifies as a great exponent of kinesthetic intelligence: her work embodies kinesthetic ideas as well as referring to ideas outside that language (as in works such as *Frontier* [1935], about early American life and experience, and *Clytemnestra* [1958], drawing on Greek drama). But Gardner failed to see that Graham's real intelligence lies in her ability to use kinesthetic language to create choreographic ideas — she created a whole new symbol system, for example.

Let's imagine a ballet about racism and what happens when we're intolerant of difference. Wouldn't it be true that in our sort of society,

---

3 Howard Gardner, a developmental psychologist and researcher at Harvard University and author of numerous books on intelligence, creativity and child education, is best known for his ground-breaking book *Frames of Mind: The theory of multiple intelligences* (Basic Books, 1983) and, more recently, *Multiple Intelligences: The theory in practice* (HarperCollins, 1993).

4 See *Creating Mind: An anatomy of creativity seen through the lives of Freud, Einstein, Picasso, Stravinsky, Eliot, Graham, and Gandhi* (Basic Books, 1994).

language-based as it is, a ballet such as that is always going to be seen as a very secondary source of ideas — the ideas about racism that are really going to affect society will be the ones voiced in the media and in books. A ballet on that theme is always going to be seen as some sort of supporting act, surely.

Yes, I think that's absolutely true. What the dance can do, though, is to take the universal pattern from your particular instance — the universality of the marginalisation of the outsider, for example. It's been remarked that in dance you can't say, 'This is my mother-in-law', for example, you can only deal in universalities and then, through the imagination, move to the particular. In drama you move in the opposite direction, from the particular to the universal. The moment you try to deal with a particular instance of something in dance, you introduce dramatic ideas, and the dance becomes more dramatic than kinesthetic, although kinesthetic qualities will still be present. But it's no longer a matter of a pure form, it's now mixed media. And that's the direction many of the arts are going in, actually. Some artists feel that they can say more by bringing together forms from verbal language, visual language and kinesthetic language.

Indeed, we're sung to during ballet performances nowadays, and an extraordinary number of fashionable painters seem to include written text in their paintings. Is it a sign of distrust or a lack of assurance on the part of some artists that 'ideas' in the wider, 'multi-intelligence' sense are not quite enough to give a work of art its desired significance? This might be particularly so when significance is equated with social significance, as many commentators accept that it should be when discussing the public intellectual culture.

✧

Adrian Martin is known to many Radio National listeners and Age *readers for his art and, especially, his film criticism. He is the author of* Phantasms[5], *a book of essays examining the trends and oddities of*

---

5 (McPhee Gribble, 1994).

popular culture in the early 1990s, with particular reference to the dreams and drives underlying the culture as a whole. While he approaches these issues from his own idiosyncratic angle, he seems to share with our other speakers a much broader notion of what ideas are and of how important meanings are produced in technologically advanced societies than a critic would have done 30 years ago.

Adrian Martin

I definitely experience films as the source of most of my ideas. I read a lot as well, everything from magazines and film gossip to cultural theory, but it's primarily films which give me the stimulus for my ideas. What I mean by that is that, for me, the cinema (and I mean a certain kind of popular cinema — horror movies, musicals and action films in particular) provides energetic models rather than necessarily particularly self-conscious objects. These films are not necessarily made intellectually, with a whole lot of intellectual rationalisation, but it's in the energy of what they do, the energy of the way they tell a story, the way they put images and sounds together, the way they present actors and fictions, that unfailingly touches some nerve with me — about the state of the world, or the state of myself, or the state of relationships, even when those things are not being directly depicted or discussed in the film.

Horror movies are a good example. Horror movies are an extra-ordinarily philosophical form, whether they know it or not. All of our modern anxieties about our human bodies, for example, are there at every level in horror movies. Whether we go back to the classic sort of puristic horror movie, the original Draculas and Frankensteins, or go to the cruddiest zee-grade zombie movie in the local video shop, we unfailingly find in them some sort of unconscious representation of anxiety about bodies — it may be modern sicknesses, problems of sexual repression or sexual liberation, problems of how bodies negotiate each other in the social world, problems of death, problems of life — all of these things are played out in an extravagant, expres-sionistic and often unconscious way in these movies. And that is what I love in cinema.

There may be no thesis or moral in this kind of film, wrapped up for you in the final scene to be taken home and thought about — indeed, I'm least interested in movies which preach a moral lesson, but I am interested when they plunge me into the confusion of contemporary experience. They may do this in a highly metaphorical way: in a movie about zombies, for example, there may be no explicit mention in the film of modern diseases, say, but that is no doubt what's being played out unconsciously. And it's for that kind of 'vital drama' (as it's been called) that I go to the cinema.

Do you also read novels? When you mentioned what you read, you referred to magazines on the one hand and theory on the other. There's a huge area in the middle, of course — storytelling, poetry and so on.

I always get complaint letters when I say this on the ABC, but I'll say it again: I find it takes too long to read novels.

Too long for what?

Simply too much time. For me — and I'm not speaking for the world or anyone else — but for me it takes too long to read a novel. Movies fit better into my lifestyle. They give me an instant hit: they take two hours to watch and then I've got the rest of my time to think about what I've seen, connect that to other movies and to write my own stories — my reviews, essays and other pieces. I've tried to struggle through many great and not-so-great novels, often not getting to the end. I wouldn't deny they were great novels, but I am not a novel reader. I read essays, some poetry, short stories — the shorter the better — but not novels. It's movies that give me a concentrated experience.

Do you think you're representative of your generation in this?[6] Do you think there's a difference between generations in where they look for their ideas and understanding of what it means to be human?

---

6 According to a recent Roy Morgan survey, published in *Panorama* (December 1997), it is actually young Australians (aged between 14 and 17) who read the most novels: 71% have read a novel in the previous three months. The 25–30 age group is least likely to have read a novel in the previous three months (51%), while the average across the whole population is 54%.

I don't suppose I represent anyone but myself. Still, I think there's a vague generalisation you can make about the generations — certainly, a lot of my friends are deeply into audio-visual storytelling — film and television, basically — certainly more than they're into theatre, which these days is the most despised of the arts, the dinosaur of the arts. Theatre doesn't move fast enough, it's too static, quite apart from just the stagebound nature of theatre. Australian drama usually bores me to tears — David Williamson, Hannie Rayson[7], Tobsha Learner[8] and so on — even though they write plays of ideas, thesis plays, about the way we live. You get six characters representing six different types talking to each other: the cerebral, the sensual, the intellectual, a Liberal, a Labor supporter and so on. This sort of thing drives me crazy, it's too schematic and illustrative. I don't get this sort of thing in the cinema, either in the popular or the art cinema. Experimental theatre, whether Barry Kosky's or the lower depths of experimental theatre, does interest me. That's where you find the energetics of theatre, imagery and bodies.

The theatre is about words, of course. Do you have some suspicion·of words and their power?

I'm not suspicious of words as such, I love them, I spend a lot of time writing and speaking, and the power of individual words means a lot to me. I'm deeply suspicious of the self-explanatory, illustrative kind of language used, for example, in the dialogues in the 'great Australian plays' I was talking about, and in newspaper columns. I like language which reaches poetic levels: the great Romantic poets, hard-boiled detective novels, the surrealists with their strange little condensed stories, puns and games — I like these condensed forms, these flashes of illumination, these conjunctions of metaphor and wit. I like it when understanding is produced in a dynamic way, and I get that when I watch horror movies, action movies and

---

7 Melbourne playwright whose best-known plays are *Hotel Sorrento* (1990), *Falling From Grace* (1994) and *Scenes from a Separation* (with Andrew Bovell, 1996).
8 American-based playwright whose best-known plays include *Glass Mermaid* (1994), *Witchplay* (1995) and *Wolf: A dedication to Priapus* (1992). Her book of short stories, *Quiver*, was published by Penguin in 1996 and her novel, *Madonna Mars*, in 1998.

musicals, and also, say, when I read Nietzsche's aphorisms or Meaghan Morris's essays.

To what extent are you nourished by the Australian cinema, or do you find that it's basically film-makers from other countries who give you what you want?

For most of my life as a critic/cinephile, I haven't got a lot of energetic nourishment from Australian cinema. Much of it has tended to be in a relaxed, naturalistic groove, depending to a large extent on that model of the Australian theatre we were talking about earlier — bland thesis-films in which characters enact various social positions with a resolution to the conflict at the end. Of course, you can have very fine films made according to that model, I'm not opposed to naturalism as a model any more than I'm opposed to the nineteenth century as a time. But it's been more the exceptions which have excited me in the Australian cinema — George Miller's *Mad Max* movies, for example. Now there's a true Australian philosopher: George Miller, whether he knows it or not. When he made those *Mad Max* movies, he literally (and I don't want to sound cruel) didn't have a thought in his head. When he made the first *Mad Max* movie, he just thought, OK, I love action movies, I love a certain kind of American cinema, I want to see cars barrelling down the road and guys fighting each other dressed like punks. He'd taken in some of the energy of punk music and American cinema, and a dream formed in his mind of the first *Mad Max* film: the loner on the road, the cars and the oil and the fire, and off he went and made this extraordinarily dynamic and energetic film.

That film produced a lot of good critical commentary. The *Mad Max* films really tapped into something important in Australian life and culture, particularly to do with our car culture and everything cars mean to us — cars as escape, cars as the destruction of someone else, or yourself, the relation between you and your car, and you and your home, domesticity and the fraught domestic relations in Australian suburban life. All these things were played out in the highly expressionistic *Mad Max* movies, without a single character ever having to sit down and say: 'I have a problem with suburbia and domesticity. Now

I'm going to get in my car and burn down the road.' But it's all there.

Miller himself became actually more of a conscious intellectual when everybody started saying to him, 'Your movies have mythic significance, George. Haven't you read Joseph Campbell?[9] Haven't you read Jung, haven't you seen Kurosawa's samurai movies?' It's all there — the Viking legends, everything. He started to take all this in, and his movies, I think, became to their detriment much more self-consciously mythic. By the time you get to the third *Mad Max* movie, there's not enough of the energetic action-drama left, there's too much of the mythological symbolism and all the characters have become figures from a Joseph Campbell system of mythology. In *Babe*, for example, some years down the track, you very much have the edifying Joseph Campbell myth of someone sublimely struggling, suffering and overcoming. In a contradictory way, I find a film like that less intellectually stimulating.

Couldn't something similar be said about a lot of visual art at the moment?

Yes, I think it could. There the question revolves around theory and practice in the arts. There's a certain sort of utopian idea around, which I do not share, that all artists are theorists and all theorists are artists. So artists are invited on to panels to talk about theory and theorists are expected to knock off the occasional personal piece and call it ficto-criticism or a new kind of literary essay. Particularly in the art world, there's terrible pressure on artists now to be theorists.

Where does the pressure come from?

I think it comes mostly from the education system within the art world — the art colleges and arts schools. In these sorts of institutions you must not only demonstrate your painting skills, but be able to back them up with theory. You've got to not only walk the walk, but

---

9 Author of numerous works on mythology, religion and symbols, including *The Man with a Thousand Faces* (1975), *The Historical Atlas of World Mythology* (1983–89), *The Flight of the Wild Gander* (HarperCollins, 1990) and *The Way of Animal Powers* (HarperCollins, 1988).

talk the talk. I think that leads to lots of sort of absurd pseudo-intellectual and quasi-intellectual pronouncements, fuelled by nothing more than the anxiety to look like an intellectual if one is an artist.

Now, in popular cinema this pressure doesn't exist, or at least not to the same degree. Even in the privileged realms of art cinema, whether it's French, German or Iranian, I don't think directors are under any particular pressure to come out with an intellectual thesis about the films they make. Some try, like Wim Wenders[10], and fail miserably. You wish he would just say, 'My work speaks for itself' — sometimes that is the best thing for an artist to say, rather than discussing the work in a schematic, rationalised, reductive sort of way.

✦

Catharine Lumby's recent book, Bad Girls: The media, sex and feminism in the nineties[11], *in jumping into the middle of the debates about pornography, censorship and popular culture (so called), and feminist attitudes towards them, manages to tell us a lot about the ideas of a younger generation of writers, thinkers and public commentators about how the mass media work. In* Bad Girls, *and in her regular columns in the* Sydney Morning Herald, *Lumby looks at how they influence the way we think and why the ideas they bombard us with are not necessarily as trivial as we assume. This is particularly true, in Lumby's view, of television, which she sees as less hierarchical, less targeted at particular classes or age groups than the print media, which once dominated the public arena.*

Catharine Lumby

Hierarchies are dissolving. Television is a space in which everybody has to compete on the level of the image, and this has enabled a more genuinely democratic debate. Ever since the sixties, for example,

---

10 German-born director of such films as *Summer in the City* (1970), *The American Friend* (1977, and his first English-speaking film), *Paris, Texas* (1984), *Wings of Desire* (1988) and *The End of Violence* (1997).
11 (Allen & Unwin, 1997).

television has been telling people what their place is in an ideological sense, while at the same time giving them a vision of a different place. Television has actually made the domestic or private sphere public, providing a window out into the public sphere. So whatever women were being told their place was, they were at the same time getting a vision of a different place, a different space. The rise of television gave the 'barbarians' a tour inside the gates of the public sphere, the elite, democratic sphere. And with that have come demands that they have a voice. I think that there are now demonstrably far more marginalised groups visible in our culture, certainly in news and current affairs, than there were when paternalistic, educated, liberal intellectuals were dominating that sphere and speaking on behalf of those people.

Of course, what many paternalistic, educated, liberal intellectuals will say in reply is that the quality of the discussion has been impoverished, that the ideas being disseminated are trivial, that you can't hear the great minds arguing about the great ideas any more on television (except possibly on SBS).

That depends how you construe 'ideas'. Women's magazines, for example, have been derided in precisely the same terms women have been derided in. In fact, mass culture is often demonised by association with the feminine. It's criticised for its obsession with the body, with sexuality, with relationships, with food, with addiction — these sorts of subjects. It seems to me that to say that women's magazines are inherently trivial because they deal with these subjects is simply to say that we need to maintain a split between the public and the private, and that economics, politics and matters of state are over here and they're important, while issues pertaining to the personal, the physical and to relationships are over here and they're women's business, close to nature and should be reviled. Yet surely one of the great achievements of feminism and of a number of civil rights movements has been a revolution linking issues considered private to the public, bringing the private into public consciousness.

There's also a confusion between style and content. If you turn on a talk show, you'll hear the very embodiment of politics, and the fact that it's not being expressed in middle-class terms doesn't mean that there's no content or substance to what's being said. Rational, educated speech is not the only language which produces meaning.

People of your generation — I think you place yourself at the beginning of Generation X — take a particular view of how we receive messages in the kind of society Australians live in, how ideas are circulated nowadays. The multiplicity of places messages are transmitted from is something you're very aware of, presumably.

That's a broad question — 'messages' and 'ideas' can encompass everything from the book I happen to be reading to architectural facades to the television that's on in the corner. One of the big changes is that we live in a society which is saturated with images and information. However, since they're are no longer located in discrete sites, we don't have a contemplative relationship to them. Even if we're reading a philosophy book, the phone still rings, the fax goes and so forth. So I would say that the skill of interacting with images and information today, or the process of consuming them, is a much more lateral one, it's no longer just a question of bringing superior knowledge to bear on a text or image. Part of the skill of interpreting images and information today is interactive and intuitive. We read across texts. And, what's more, the various media texts we're surrounded by are constantly quoting from each other and recycling each other, lending each image a sort of half-seen, layered dimension. In other words, images and information don't stop at their own borders.

To give a banal example: one could be reading a Jane Austen novel, go to the movies and see the film of *Pride and Prejudice* and then later that night see the send-up of the Jane Austen fad on 'The Simpsons'. What I'm saying is that none of these texts operates discretely, they all interact with each other.

And this is different, you think, from 50 years ago?

I think it is. One of the things that's different is that these images and information are not locked away in universities or in books you have to have climbed a particular kind of intellectual ladder to have access to. They're out there in the broader community being accessed by many different kinds of people. Now, I don't want to appear too utopian about this, but it does seem to me that it's not simply people with university educations who have very sophisticated skills in reading, interpreting and playing with these images and information. Proof of that, I think, lies in the sophistication of many of these supposedly banal texts. You know, television is always sending itself up. You don't have to watch 'Frontline' to know that news and current affairs work to a formula. Comedians on commercial television have been sending this stuff up for some time.

It does seem to me sometimes that your generation is much better educated than earlier generations to look at, say, Parliament House in Canberra, which is underground and has a huge flagpole on top, and work out what what the message is. You're more educated to do this.

Well, some skills have been lost and some gained — the art of finishing a book, for example, as well as the skill of contemplation and concentration, have waned. What I'm focusing on is what has been gained. As in your example of Parliament House, I think we've learned to find value and meaning in a diverse array of cultural forms. We have a broader kind of literacy today.

What sort of connection do you see between ideas and contemporary visual arts?

Contemporary art has become a specialist area of our culture. It doesn't occupy the grand place it once did, when thousands of people flocked to see Manet's 'Olympia' and it caused an extraordinary scandal. Contemporary art is far more on the margins. People might flock to see a Manet retrospective, but contemporary art has a specialised audience, and that's partly because it often requires a specialist knowledge — it's not representational in the classic sense and it's often highly self-reflexive. That's probably partly because it's in competition with such a diverse range of visual forms: cinema, photography, television and so on. Yet some of the best art draws on and re-invents areas of popular culture and that, to me, is the most exciting kind of visual art.

A lot of it seems to be an illustration of art theory.

I thoroughly agree with you. In the eighties a lot of exciting ideas came out of the art world — post-modernism in Australia was intimately linked to the art world, for example — and there were magazines around such as *Tension*, *Frogger* and *On the Beach* which provided a space for debate about ideas. But ideas have moved on. Some of the most interesting theory now is about finding the extraordinary in the ordinary in everyday life, and there's a sense of ossification in some sections of the art world now with art ending up just illustrating theory, and it's hard to maintain an interest in that kind of work. Who's interested in disinterring the Heideggerian references in somebody's monochrome?

✧

Catharine Lumby's remarks about power relations and how modern theory makes a new analysis of those relations possible touch on an area Meaghan Morris is eloquent in. Meaghan Morris has come to occupy a prominent place in several spheres of our public intellectual culture, as a lecturer in art and media studies, as a film critic and as a writer, roles which came together to powerful effect in her influential essay collection, The Pirate's Fiancée[12], about feminism and post-modernism. In all these roles, Meaghan Morris has played an important part in shaping how a certain kind of public understands the culture it's surrounded by, even created by, the games that culture plays and the values it inculcates.

The term 'cultural studies' crops up frequently nowadays, but what is distinctive about its project, in comparison with that of other disciplines in the humanities, is not always clear.

---

12 *The Pirate's Fiancée: Feminism, reading, postmodernism* (Verso, 1988).

Meaghan Morris

Cultural studies draws on other disciplines. It looks at the ways people live — their art and artefacts, their religion, what they do for pleasure, how they work and so on. What's distinctive about cultural studies is that it focuses simultaneously on how ordinary publics respond to culture and on what we now call cultural industries. Culture has become an important part of our economy.

And the word 'culture' has several meanings.

That's right, and one of the major conflicts within cultural studies centres on what culture is and how we should think of it. The most common broad definition of culture is one Raymond Williams[13] came up with some 25 or 30 years ago: culture is a whole way of life. The culture is everything people do, how they feel about it, their relationships to other people, the atmosphere associated with living in a particular way. That's an anthropological definition of culture. The main conflict, or dynamic, in the field is between this kind of anthropological or sociological definition and aesthetic understandings of culture — the kind I have, in fact, being a literary critic by training.

So, in addition to art, opera and literature, which we might uncontroversially describe as 'culture', the term could also cover driving, city design, the use of parks, gardening, the popularity of certain breeds of dogs…

Yes, and the attitudes that go along with those things, as well as the mysterious social judgments made by people of one culture which people of another culture might not make — the differences between cultures are of interest.

And what is the relationship between cultural studies at the end of the century and classical Marxism?

---

13 Coiner of the term 'cultural materialism', Raymond Williams has written numerous books since *The Long Revolution* (1961) in the fields of literary and cultural studies: on the mass media, drama, the English novel and socio-historical philology. A key work is *Marxism and Literature* (1977).

It's obviously been influenced by classical Marxism, but cultural studies really got going in the 1960s at a point when classical Marxism just wasn't describing the world people lived in in Western societies, offering utopian programs that nobody wanted to take up. At a certain point, for instance, the question had to be put as to why the working class in certain developed countries had not acted in the way expected of it in classical Marxism. And so it was time to look at the world in a more wide-eyed way, asking questions about what was going on without starting from an ideological program that told us how to interpret it.

In cultural studies there seems to be almost a project to make people aware of how power operates in given situations — in shopping at the supermarket, say, or choosing what clothes to wear. There seems to be a strong emphasis on the uses and misuses of power.

Cultural studies is very much interested in power, it's true, partly because we've had to ask ourselves why culture as an industry gets entangled in all sorts of other social conflicts (to do with gender, race and sexual power and so on). But I think the interesting thing about cultural studies is that it also looks at power as something positive. It's a distinction that's hard to make in the English language, but in French it's easy because there are two words: *pouvoir* and *puissance*, which is the positive ability to get up and do something.

As well, cultural studies differs from a lot of traditional ways of talking about power — ways which now look pretty cranky — in that it always wants to ask how people use what they're given as culture — the conventions and manners — and how they can change, if they want to, the ways of living and social conventions they've been born into. So power is a preoccupation — but not an oblique or paranoid notion of power. If there's a dogma in cultural studies, it's that everybody probably has a little bit more power in their lives than they're taught to believe they do.

Women seem to have more presence and authority in cultural studies than in many other academic fields.

It might be just a generational fluke — cultural studies emerged at the same time as feminism — but I think there's much more to it than that. Cultural studies is necessarily interested in private life, because, if you want to look at a whole way of life, you can't think of culture as something that only happens in the public sphere traditionally dominated by men. Cultural studies heads straight for the kitchen or lounge-room and asks questions about the social relations and cultural events enacted there. Cultural studies makes sense of the kind of experiences women have had of culture — including high art. Cultural studies is also interested in the manipulation of gender roles, how gender structures our everyday lives, and especially in the fine detail of social encounters, say, the feelings that jump between people and so on. Of course, cultural studies is often criticised for being interested in the full list of politically correct subjects — gender, race, sexuality — but the fact is that these are major preoccupations of our era, along with emerging from colonialism. Our interest is in what these things mean in everyday terms for ordinary people going about their business.

In this connection it's worth remembering that cultural studies scholars who write on gender, race and sexuality in films, for instance, are following, and not leading, changes that ordinary people in society have brought about. In many ways cultural studies has ridden on the coat-tails of social change.

A lot of the writing in this area seems to be about representation and representational systems — film, language, television. Indeed, the television series 'Sylvania Waters' seems to be of more interest in some ways than the 'reality' of the suburb of Sylvania Waters.

That's true for a lot of us in cultural studies. I would have to admit it's probably true of me. But it's not true of everyone: sociologists working in cultural studies get angry with those of us who would rather watch television than go out and interview people. So let's clear that up: there are people who are interested in both.

Interest in 'Sylvania Waters', the TV show, connects to the new interest in representation generally in our society to the extent that we're all dealing with a new phenomenon: through television, the mass media, the Internet and so on, which convey huge chunks of writing from one part of the world to another, the audience for any single bit of imagery can be enormous and unpredictable to those who made the image. Now, this is something new in human history.

Once upon a time, literature and theatre belonged to a fairly small, select group of people, and they represented the rest of the world, including the peasants, foreigners and women, in the terms encouraged by their own view of the world. With the development of television, suddenly whole areas of society were, for the first time, starting to see how the other half lived. On television, for example, people could now see the lifestyles of the rich and famous with a detail and concreteness they'd not had before. In my own childhood, living around the back blocks of Maitland, we essentially had no idea whatsoever of life outside the Hunter Valley. How would you ever see it? So the mass media have completely changed the value of representation.

Some of the more glamorous spokespersons for post-modernism and post-structuralism can give the impression that, as far as they're concerned, we've reached a point now where we're living totally inside a kind of hyper-reality, totally inside representation, and that there isn't really much point any more in talking about the reality that is being represented.

Yes, and that's probably a good description of what it feels like to be a rich American academic. I mean, it is true that such a line gets pushed, but I think much more fuss is made about it than it actually merits. The more important and serious point is that, when we talk about the world, or paint a picture of it, or even film it, we're using some kind of medium with its own conventions to do it — language when we speak to each other, for example, conventions in painting, and so on. In our own experience in Australia, it took a long time to learn to 'see' Aboriginal art. The first settlers could not see it, because they didn't know the rules.

They couldn't 'see' Aboriginal bodies, either, in that sense.

No, they couldn't, that's right. You don't just naturally 'see' reality without its being in some way shaped by the expectations and the culture that you've grown up with. But that's very different from saying that reality is just images.

It does seem sometimes that cultural studies is almost (ironically) in complicity with commodity capitalism, in the sense that many of the more popular writers constantly seem to be focusing on its products: the films, the American sit-coms, the advertising, fashion, rock music — all those things that transnational capitalism is pumping out for us to spend billions of dollars consuming. In some ways, cultural studies seems to have ended up legitimising this kind of culture by paying it so much attention and glamorising it, while not writing about pet care or gardening at all.

That's often a justified criticism, I think. There's a fine line, I suppose, between the study of contemporary commodity capitalism, which is clearly a crucial thing to do — we do need to understand what sort of world we're living in, especially when it's changing as fast as it is — and legitimising the beast itself. It's obvious there's a whole new career path to be had in being young and cute and writing a book about Madonna — and then you get interviewed and you end up in the same magazines which interview Madonna. There's not much one can do about it, except point to the other interesting, serious questions there are to be asked about real life for the majority of people. (Personally, I never want to read another article about Madonna as long as I live. I am certainly interested in gardening, pets and going to the beach in a very mundane way.) From my point of view, the most interesting work is that which is not blinded by the light of celebrity.

The theories of such modern thinkers as Derrida, Foucault and Baudrillard are applicable to life in the twelfth century, presumably, as much as to this multimedia world we live in now.

That's absolutely right. There's no reason whatsoever why a field like cultural studies can't have an historical dimension — indeed, in my view it should have an historical dimension. If what you claim to be looking at is how a whole way of life hangs together and relates to other ways of life, then there's no reason whatsoever why the twelfth century or ancient Greece should not be a field in which it's useful and important for us to ask questions.

And it's happening, but at this stage mostly in traditional humanities scholarship, where classical scholars, for example, apply their reading in cultural studies to their own field of endeavour. David Halperin[14], for instance, worked as a classicist on homosexuality in ancient Greece and classical literature and then, after becoming interested in the work of Foucault, his own work reached a much wider, non-specialist audience. I'm hoping that in the future we'll see a lot more of this kind of crossover. For that to happen, though, people engaged full-time in cultural studies will need to become a little more tolerant of and interested in other people's work. That will happen as we stop feeling so defensive, when there's less scandal about what we do. Then it will be easier to respond in an interested, civilised, tolerant and passionate way to traditional work. When you're continually defending the validity of an area of inquiry that's 30 years old now — it's not some silly new passing fad — you get into a space of continual exaggeration, disagreement, violence and bad feeling, which sometimes slows down the process of making the changes that need to be made.

Who are the theorising intellectuals addressing? Who is their public?

Until very recently the answer was obviously 'other theorising intellectuals' — the same two or three thousand people. Over the last ten years or so, though, there have been two new developments: firstly, as English becomes the lingua franca of academics around the world, theory is no longer just the jargon of a few thousand academics in

14 Now teaching at the University of New South Wales, Halperin is the author of *One Hundred Years of Homosexuality* (Routledge, 1990), a book of essays reassessing contemporary sexual culture through a post-modern analysis of gender and sexuality in ancient Greek culture.

English-speaking countries, but is becoming a shared background in which people in European, Asian and African countries can communicate about all sorts of things which have nothing at all to do with theory; and, secondly, because of the new demand for usefulness in the academy, more and more theorising intellectuals need to find a variety of publics to address. For example, it's quite common nowadays to write an erudite article for the other 2000 theorising intellectuals, then a lively crossover book for a wider general audience interested in ideas (such as Catharine Lumby's *Bad Girls* or Adrian Martin's *Phantasms*), and then you might write a newspaper article on the same subject. It needs to be done. Academics have to start talking to a variety of publics in our society.

✧

Both Catharine Lumby and Meaghan Morris have contributed to The Retreat from Tolerance: A snapshot of Australian society *(ABC Books, 1997), edited by Phillip Adams, a volume of essays on all the topics arousing heated debate in Australia: family values, free speech, racial intolerance, censorship and many others.*

Peter Conrad

‘ It's hard for me to describe what a

public intellectual in England looks like

because there aren't any.

The only ones there are Australians. ’

Australian Peter Conrad, *Oxford don, prolific writer on quite a dazzling array of subjects, and a man who, on certain subjects at least, is not shy about stating his case with a directness that can stop you in your tracks.*

Between 30 and 40 years ago, a number of educated, youngish Australians went away and stayed away, making their lives, thinking their thoughts, writing their books, painting their paintings and taking to the stage abroad. Ostensibly they left because Australia was an infertile field for big thinkers and creative talents, or so we're often told[1]. But the reasons were probably more complex than that. With a mixture of envy and disapproval, we called them expatriates — not émigrés or overseas Australians, and certainly not Australo-Americans or Australo-Brits. And the more globalised we all become, the more old-fashioned 'expatriate' sounds.

It's often an unresolved relationship we have with expatriates — and they with us — with bursts of mutual interest and regular visits interspersed with periods of something akin to mutual disdain, if not hostility.

Peter Conrad, who teaches English Literature at Christ Church College, Oxford, and has written over a dozen books on subjects as various as opera, American celebrities, the television culture and Tasmania, as well as many hundreds of articles on music and other arts in the English press, is an expatriate from the same period as Germaine Greer, Clive James and Robert Hughes. When he escaped at the age of twenty from Tasmania to London, he felt he was setting off for the 'navel of the world'.

When I left in 1968, I had a very good reason for going: I got a Rhodes Scholarship to go to Oxford and in the same year I got my call-up papers to go to Vietnam. Given the choice between Oxford and Vietnam, I went to Oxford, having been generously granted a two-year deferral from my military service.

---

1 The tenor of Germaine Greer's remarks about Australia and Australians as quoted in Christine Wallace's *Greer: Untamed shrew* follows a typical pattern: as a physical environment Australia draws her, but as an intellectual environment it has nothing to offer. In the spirit of Barry Humphries' remarks about 'the stifling intellectual torpor' of Australia, land of sponge cakes, chenille bedspreads and oafish hedonists (as late as 1984 he stated that Australia had 'no Intelligentsia whatsoever'), Greer claims that Australians are 'a race of bumptious louts', saying she'd turn down any offer of a book promotion tour to Australia because there 'are not enough people there, for a start, but the main problem is not enough of them can read'.

In fact, it was about eleven or twelve years before I came back, and when I did return to Australia at the end of the 1970s, I remember thinking with stupefaction, 'Why did I ever want to leave?' But, of course, a lot of things had happened in the meantime: the Vietnam War, which was the low point in Australia's brown-tonguing of the imperial powers, had been shamefully lost and was over, and the Whitlam Government had succeeded in creating an Australian culture. People of my generation (the sixties, which I don't feel any need to apologise for, even though the political mood has changed so much since then) were writing books and opening restaurants, two essential ingredients for the creation of a culture.

But at the time it was necessary to leave, for personal reasons and just to get out and see the rest of the world. I'd had such a colonial childhood, which had left me with the feeling that the world was elsewhere, and that I existed at some sort of tangent to it. And you must remember that the mode of transportation has changed enormously: when I left in 1968, I went by ship to England and, because the Suez Canal was closed, it took almost six weeks to get there. When you had to go on that sort of voyage in the days before jumbo jets, once you got to England you had an investment in staying there for months or years.

Being a Tasmanian must have made a difference. You give the impression in Down Home[2] *that to live in Tasmania at that time was, for you at least, almost not to exist. You constantly needed confirmation, through a Royal Tour or some such event, that you lived on the same planet as everyone else, that you weren't just imagining yourselves.*

The strange predicament of being Tasmanian is that you have a double sense of alienation. (And I don't think it's any less of a predicament now, by the way, than it ever was — in fact, I think now it's more of a predicament, because the State is even more impoverished and sad than it was when I was growing up there.) When the Olympic Games came to Melbourne in 1956, I remember, I was eight

2 *Down Home: Revisiting Tasmania* (Chatto & Windus, 1988) combines autobiography and history.

years old, and my father encouraged me to make a scrapbook of the athletes — I was always cutting things out and he thought it would be better for me to cut out pictures of athletes than of film stars, so I did. And I remember him saying to me, 'You should do this, because they won't come out here again'. It was a chilling thing to say, like a *memento mori*, and doubly alienating: this global event was happening on the mainland and, living on the very edge of that space, I had no direct access to it — there was no television, so I couldn't watch it — and it was also the only chance Australia would have in anyone's lifetime to be on the map. Then there were the shaming things, such as no one ever putting Tasmania on the souvenir ashtrays of Australia. It always dropped off the pop icons of Australia, because it was physically and mentally detached.

I feel very grateful now to have been born in Tasmania — if you can be grateful for where you're born (as if you had any choice in the matter, or as if there were any point in having an emotion about it). But I now feel grateful for the chance to see the world from that strange extra-territorial angle. It was a very frustrating time to grow up there, but looking back on it, I wouldn't be without it because I think it formed my view of the world, for good or ill.

Tasmania may also have nourished in you a sense of the Gothic. There's an attraction to the sublime hovering around your writing all the time — to a mixture of delight and terror. New York, for example, where you live for part of each year, seems to both horrify and bewitch you with its dangerous beauty and beautiful dangers, while about Lisbon, where you are so much at home, your writing has less edge, is itself more comfortable.

That's uncannily accurate, I think, and the source of all that is the Tasmanian landscape. When the plane bumps down towards Hobart airport, and I see Mount Wellington surrounded by storm clouds like a headache, I think, 'This is my landscape'. I grew up in the shadow of that mountain, looking at it every morning. Some sort of Gothic Romanticism obviously comes from Tasmania.

The only imaginative charge I've ever had from Lisbon happened when a friend took me beyond the perimeter of the city into a hidden valley squeezed into a gap between motorways. It was overrun by gypsies and refugees living in tents and hutches and collapsed grand houses — they were almost like the banditi in Salvador Rosa's paintings of sublime Italy and its dangers. After wandering around this very dangerous place one afternoon, I wanted to write my novel — I'd found a city with a Gothic underworld in the middle of it[3]. I need a border where reality runs out.

Your attitude to England seems to have changed over the years, as well as your attitude to Australia. In fact, you've been quoted saying some rather depressing things about England — perhaps not quite as depressing as things you've said about Tasmania — but you've referred to the English as 'used up', for example, you've called England 'a forgotten island', which suggests that you see a change in England's status[4].

Yes, it's all back to front. Colleagues of mine at Oxford, for example, will accept invitations to conferences in Australia, thinking they might catch a few weeks in the sun at someone else's expense, and they come back agog at what's happening in Australia. Things have moved into reverse, history is having its revenge. I remember when I was first at Oxford being abused by a fellow student in the beer cellar in my college for quoting Oscar Wilde on the subject of fox-hunting. This bloke had just come back from beagling in the afternoon, so I quoted, with all the wit of a twenty-year-old, the line about 'the unspeakable in pursuit of the uneatable', and he said, 'Bloody colonials coming over here quoting our literature at us'. In those days there was a real sense of condescension and contempt towards Australians. Nowadays it's absolutely the reverse. Australia is a fantasy land for the English. They now have a sense of inferiority with regard to us which we once had with regard to them. It's very satisfying to see how history deals with these old empires.

---

3 *Underworld* (Chatto & Windus, 1992), set in a valley inhabited by criminals and the dispossessed in the middle of an imaginary metropolis.
4 In an interview in the *Sun Herald,* 14 October 1990.

The English tabloids seem to retain a disdain for Australia, though.

Well, the English are a thwarted, envious race of people, and they get more so as their social, economic and historical fortunes decline. We are the tabloids' fantasy inferiors. Meanwhile, it's the people who are reading those tabloids who are saving up for a holiday on the Barrier Reef — or at least dreaming of one.

I'd like to understand the nature of your connection to Australia. Do you have any sense of responsibility to Australia (if that's not too strong a word)? Do you desire to be read by Australians, for instance? Or is that no more important to you than being read by Alaskans? Do you have any sense of bringing the metropolis back to Australia?

I have mixed feelings about it. I'm actually desperate to feel I have some connection with it still. One of the most gratifying experiences in my life was when I went back at the behest of the BBC during the Bicentennial year to put together a radio documentary about contemporary Australian writing, which I did mostly in Sydney and at the Adelaide Festival. It reduced me almost to tears of gratification to find that a lot of the people I talked to had read things of mine, knew who I was, and felt that I was engaged in the same activity they were engaged in. It pleases me enormously when a piece of my writing is anthologised in Australia, as has happened quite a lot in the last few years.

On the other hand, I find the way the word 'expatriate' is hung around your neck ritually the moment you arrive back in Australia galling. I hate it. It tells you something about the abiding insularity of Australia — it's as insular as England in its way, although on a somewhat grander geographical scale. It's a sign of lingering social immaturity, which I hope people will grow out of very shortly. British people live all over the world, Americans live all over the world, yet the British and Americans don't think of those who happen to live elsewhere as expatriates. It's a strange label, because there is a certain contempt and rejection in it, as well as a certain envy in the Australian context, perhaps. It's a label we have to stop using about one another. Australians were always a people who prowled all around the world, we've always been a nation of great travellers and wanderers, because until a very short time ago we were all aware that we lived on the fringes of the world, and that there were lots of things out there to go and explore. So why continue to label people in this way?

As for re-importing the metropolis to Australia, I actually feel now, when I go back to Australia, that I don't have anything much to contribute here. I mean, this country has a real culture. It takes its writers seriously, it gives them prizes, it gives them money to write their novels, it allows them a public forum to air their ideas in, it trusts and reveres them as the creators of culture and the re-creators of the national image. So I don't have any kind of condescending metropolitan feeling about the country at all.

✧

Someone with an informed interest in Peter Conrad's writing, and in that of other Australians of Conrad's generation who made their home in England and America, is the Melbourne historian Ian Britain, author of Once an Australian: Journeys with Barry Humphries, Clive James, Germaine Greer and Robert Hughes[5]. *Ian Britain thinks that this generation of thinkers, performers and cultural commentators — intellectuals, in short, of one kind or another — have quite a lot in common.*

Ian Britain

I call them 'word children' in my book, because to an extent I see them as verbal refugees from a culture that they at least imagined did not appreciate words, word play and what you could do with words. I think, however, that there's an element of myth, or self-myth, about their position as 'word children'. I'm not sure Australia was as inhospitable to intellectuals in that period as they suggest. They did feel a compulsion to leave, but I think it was for reasons that were

---

5 (Oxford University Press, 1997).

not altogether to do with the intellectual cultural desert that they perceived in Australia.

To some extent I think they were all in flight from their families, and I think part of the reason that some of them haven't come back lies in not wanting to confront their families and what they left, if only out of a fear they'll find out that they weren't as bad as they thought. I think you can see this most obviously in the demonisation of the mother in Barry Humphries' autobiography[6]. In Robert Hughes' case it had more to do, I think, with his relationship with his elder brother, who at that time was turning into a brilliant lawyer and became for Hughes a forbidding father figure (his own father having died when he was only twelve). So I think there's something of an individual, personalised psycho-pathology in these people that led them to leave, as well as general cultural factors.

Quite a few of these people have been involved in some kind of show business — you might even say that Robert Hughes, with his television appearances, is a showbiz personality, and the point has been made about Germaine Greer that she is an actor through and through, even thinking of herself as an entertainer in some senses. How seriously do we regard them as intellectuals, in the sense of really listening to what they have to say and being changed by it?

I do think of them as intellectuals, but I think of them as covert, or closet, intellectuals, who have needed to lace their intellectualism with showbiz. I describe them as intellectuals because they're all remorselessly and restlessly analytical, almost from the cradle. Barry Humphries describes in a memoir of his childhood how he delighted in a copy of Robin Hood that he received as a young child, going into an endless sort of cadenza of analysis over this. Now, of course, one can't necessarily see this as what actually happened when he was a child, but it fits that relentlessly analysing mode these people seem to share. Similarly, in Where I Fell to Earth[7] Peter Conrad talks about a nursery rhyme about Baby Bunting and the rabbits intoned to him

---

6 *More Please* (Viking, 1992). Demonisation of the mother is also an important motif in Germaine Greer's writing and public conversations, as Christine Wallace has documented.
7 (Chatto & Windus, 1990). An account of Conrad's 'life in four places': Oxford, London, New York and Lisbon.

by his mother, and this leads him on to a five-page analysis of the rhyme. Again, one can't say that this is how Peter Conrad thought at the time, but it shows the kinds of seeds of an intellectual frame of mind which were germinating even at that age. These were relentlessly curious people.

They're also all extremely erudite and scholarly. Barry Humphries more than the others disguises his intellectualism with showbiz, but it's very much there. The roots of his acts on stage can be traced back to all sorts of theatrical and literary traditions in which he is highly versed — the tradition of seventeenth-century masque, for instance. And I think Dame Edna bears some relation to Dame Alice in Chaucer's *Canterbury Tales*. There are all kinds of literary allusions and references in his work which we're not meant to get.

So, while these are people who are very intellectual in their orientation, perhaps not all of them are intellectuals in the sense of living for or living by ideas. That's probably true of Robert Hughes and also of Clive James, who uses his regular Saturday night television shows as a way of subsidising his interest in ideas — if you want to look at the intellectual Clive James, you go to his reviews in the *New Yorker* or the *London Review of Books*, dazzlingly erudite pieces on all sorts of topics his regular Saturday night viewers would have no idea of. In other words, if anything, Clive James wilfully sets out to disguise his intellectualism. That could be an Australian trait.

✧

If many Australian males feel safer dressing their intellectuality up as something else, Peter Conrad makes no bones about living for and by ideas, writing book after researched book on a bewildering variety of topics. Yet, even he, as we shall see, has had to 'perform' in order to gain acceptance.

Given that he now spends part of his year in the United States, and writes illuminatingly about America, Peter Conrad seems the ideal person to ask about the differences, as he sees them, between public intellectuals in the United States and Britain on the one hand, and 'down home' in Australia on the other.

Peter Conrad

It's hard for me to describe what a public intellectual in England looks like because there aren't any. The only ones there are Australians — the Germaine Greers and Clive Jameses. There aren't any public intellectuals in England because this is a culture which, uniquely, I think, has no conception of the intellect and certainly no respect for it. It's a deeply anti-intellectual country. It's a country which is owned by the people who live on the land, in the grand houses, and they are kind enough to permit the rest of us to live in it as well, so long as we don't make too much of a fuss. But it belongs to them, they are the definers of it, and they defined it for their own purposes such a long time ago and are so completely content with their definition of it that they see no reason for any kind of debate about what's going on in it. All this at a time of real ferment and transformation, when England must consider whether it's part of Europe or not and the very survival of this little country is at stake. In contrast with Australia, there's no one here to conduct or participate in the debate.

There are no public intellectuals in England. The only use that the English have for the figure of the intellectual is as a sort of learned idiot, a buffoon, an eccentric. You might have seen one of my Oxford colleagues, Emrys Jones[8], in Al Pacino's film about Richard III a few months ago. This is a man who looks like Spiderman, with a full repertory of twitches and mannerisms and quirks and speech impediments. It was brilliantly filmed by Al Pacino, with Emrys Jones as a ludicrous figure, spouting unintelligible things about Shakespeare, obviously unable to talk to a camera, probably unaware who Al Pacino was, accustomed to talking to his equally cobwebbed colleagues. It's summed up in a television program here called 'Mastermind', where they find people with crazy special subjects — last week, for instance, there was a woman who'd suffered from anorexia offering anorexia nervosa as her special subject, together with a dispirited, wan, middle-aged woman who was the world expert on the children's fiction of

---

8 Noted Shakespeare scholar, author of such books as *Scenic Form in Shakespeare* (1977), *Origins of Shakespeare* (1977) and the *New Oxford Book of Sixteenth Century Verse* (OUP, 1992).

Roald Dahl. And these people are sat down in a black leather chair and battered with questions about this or that little bit of intellectual minutiae they've made themselves master of. They're set up as slightly crazed, socially maladjusted, psychologically maimed people who know a lot of things, who are clever, but who are to be pitied for their cleverness.

One indication of the lack of public intellectuals in this country is the way the English use the word 'clever': it's one of the most opprobrious adjectives of all, to be called 'clever' is the worst insult. The idea is that if you're clever, you can't possibly be well-born, because if you had an estate and a grand house to live in, you wouldn't need to assert yourself in this rather vulgar way, to raise your voice in public and show an interest in ideas.

I just don't think that the figure exists here. And in a way that's good: when you think of the intellectual history of Europe, especially over the century or two since the French Revolution, you see a continent which has done its level best to destroy itself and the rest of the world with it, all as a result of intellectual activity. The two World Wars were wars of ideas, fought between people who were fanatical about certain intellectual propositions. And the English distance from all of that helped to ensure that the world was not destroyed by ideological fanatics.

The scene in the United States is slightly different, above all because of the Jewish intellectual tradition. There's a whole class of prophetic intellectuals in the United States, people who fled to the United States to escape extermination, like Hannah Arendt and Bruno Bettelheim[9], but also people like Reinhold Niebuhr[10] and Lionel Trilling[11], who really had a sense that they were speaking to the nation, and did so in the full awareness that the nation was listening.

9 Bruno Bettelheim (1903–90). Austrian-born psychologist, concentration camp survivor, director of a school for emotionally disturbed children and author of such widely read books on child psychology as *Love is Not Enough* (1950) and *The Uses of Enchantment* (1976), as well as *The Informed Heart* (1960) about the Nazi camps.

10 Reinhold Niebuhr (1892–1971). Religious thinker, political activist and teacher at Union Theological Seminary, New York. His works include *Moral Man and Immoral Society* (1932) and *The Nature and Destiny of Man* (1941–43).

11 Lionel Trilling (1905–75). Critic, professor at Columbia University and author of essays combining social and political ideas with literary scholarship (for example, *The Liberal Imagination* [1950] and *The Opposing Self* [1955]).

The United States, unlike Britain, is aware that it was created by an idea, and that founding idea needs constantly to be revised, refreshed and reinterpreted. I doubt that Britain was founded by an idea, although the beginnings lie so far back in the murk that it's impossible for us even to imagine them. Presumably it was just the coming together of a few tribes who grunted at one another and decided to live with one another once they found they couldn't run one another off this little patch of land. This is a completely different proposition from sending the Founding Fathers across the ocean in the eighteenth century and having them sit down on a new continent and talk about the right to life, liberty and the pursuit of happiness. And that founding moment, which is a moment of intellectual self-definition, is actually happening in Australia round about now, I think. It certainly didn't happen at the moment when Australia was colonised, because it was just being used as a social sanitary-disposal area by the British. Now, when that colonial heritage is being shed, comes the moment when the country decides what kind of place it is, and when intellectuals help to make that decision.

That's the thing that I admire intellectually about the United States. The problem there, however, is that most of these prophetic figures I mentioned (the Hannah Arendts and so on) are from an earlier generation. The hideous, corrupting thing that's now happening is that the public intellectual is shading into the celebrity, and has become absorbed into and corrupted by that culture, which has no time to listen to the elaboration of ideas, which only wants sound-bites, and is less interested in what people say than in how they look. They're just hustled across the television screen in 30 seconds. So the intellectual is probably bound, in the end, to become there, as in Britain, just a sort of hired buffoon. Gore Vidal, for example, a person of extraordinary intelligence, in order to get himself a public forum in the United States, has to turn himself into a clown on television talk shows.

What sort of effect do you think current intellectual fashions in the humanities are having on intellectual life in Britain and the United States?

A really baleful effect because they make everyone so doctrinaire. Fixed, *parti pris* positions are adopted, the party line is parrotted, and this becomes oppressive, faceless and dictatorially uniform, especially in American universities. It's the death of thinking, the death of the intellect. Yet what's wonderful about the human brain is that it's a real box of tricks, capable of changing the way we think of the world, of considering the world from ten or twenty different positions, like Picasso taking a face apart and putting it together again in a completely different way. The whole excitement of thinking is in the fact that you can be surprised by your own thought processes, and the thing I've always treasured in the thinkers and writers I've admired is their capacity to surprise me. Diaghilev's remark to Jean Cocteau, *Etonne-moi* ('Astound me'), was pretty good advice, the invitation to be original and idiosyncratic (and also to show off, which wasn't quite so good), to look at the world in an unrepeatable way, out of your own experience of the world, from your own angle. The death of all that comes with everybody falling into line, everybody obligatorily quoting everybody else, deciding on the doctrine in advance in that horrific, self-congratulatory way that's so common in academic discourse. Much academic writing I find unintellectual and unreadable. It's a pseudo-intellectualism, it's a summarising of the party line in order to secure tenure. It's part of the industrial structure of the profession now. In a way, I think universities are contributing to the death of the intellectual tradition.

✧

Peter Conrad's intellectual profile in Britain clearly has something to do with the magic mixture of academic knowledge and a flair for classy journalism. In Conrad's case, according to Ian Britain, it's a very particular mixture with Australian characteristics.

Ian Britain

Although Peter Conrad is the most prolific of the expatriates, in a way he's the least public of them. He obviously doesn't dabble in showbiz in the way the others tend to do. He's careful not to theatricalise himself in the public arena. He's done a little television, a little radio, but where he's been most public is in his journalism. From very early on, when he was in his early twenties, he was writing reams every week, in the *Times Literary Supplement*, the *Observer*, the *New Statesman* — his bibliography of articles is absolutely daunting. To that degree I think he's been very public, but it's not in that obviously vocal, physical way that the others have performed in public — or, in a sense, been court jesters.

What sort of ideas does he traffic in?

'Traffic' is probably a good word. I think he's interested in transmutations and cross-currents in the arts. In a way, it's an embodiment of himself, someone who has transmuted his own identity, someone who has drawn on an extraordinary cross-current of interests in painting, in opera, in literature, in history, in architecture, all of which he wrote about in his first book, *The Victorian Treasure-House*[12] and then again in his book on New York[13]. He really has the most eclectic, polymathic range of interests, comparable even to George Steiner's as a cultural journalist. And that's what I'd call him: a brilliant cultural journalist.

His range is quite dazzling. He doesn't have the seriousness, the earnestness or the sort of political commitment of a Steiner or a Susan Sontag, he lacks the gravitas of the American or Continental intellectual. There's a showbiz side to his prose, he's a scintillating skater. I often don't want to look too deeply into what he's saying because I'm carried away by the dazzle of a tossed-off epiphany. Once you engage with it too deeply, you start having all kinds of reservations about it, especially if you're a scholar like me who wants to research every last phrase.

---

12 (Collins, 1973).

13 *Art of the City: Views and versions of New York* (OUP, 1984).

Would you describe this lack of gravitas as an Australian characteristic? Despite his rejection of Tasmania and everything Australian early on, do you think there is actually something very Australian about Peter Conrad?

I think there's something Australian in the need to show off, to scintillate and to dazzle in a way that doesn't impinge too heavily on the reader or the audience. You can even sense it in his book about Tasmania where he talks in detail about the difficulties his family faced in having a prodigy in a working-class or middle-class household. Perhaps his other books, too, are trying to negotiate the tension of being born into a milieu that didn't really appreciate the intellect by providing some sort of confection to cover it up.

Australian intellectuals seem to be constantly tense about the way the public regards them, regards anyone it thinks has tickets on themselves — particularly male intellectuals. At some level they seem to feel they must keep saying, 'Oh, well, I don't take myself too seriously, so you mustn't take me too seriously'.

To a degree, I think that's right. And it leads to this sort of clownish quality that I've mentioned, although I see Peter Conrad more as a mischievous imp than a clown.

❖

Of all the subjects Peter Conrad writes on — American architecture, the slums of Lisbon, Tasmanian history, English literature, American superstars — the one he writes on most famously is music and opera. In Richard Osborne's review of his book The Song of Love and Death: The meaning of opera [1987] he was called 'the most literate and stimulating purveyor of operatic table-talk since Bernard Shaw'[14]. While music and opera are obviously the occasion for voluminous intellectual activity, there are questions to be asked about how a man whose life is governed by the intellect experiences music.

---

14 *Times Literary Supplement*, 29 January 1988.

Peter Conrad

The attraction of music for me is as a vacation from the possession of an intellect, and the reason is that I recognise it as something I'll never be able to understand. I mean that partly in a technical sense, but I don't regard any technical ignorance of music as a disqualification because I think that the most precious thing about music is the fact that it makes an emotional impact, a visceral impact and maybe even a spiritual impact on us, taking us into regions where the rationalising mind is running a long way behind. There's a great fascination and a great challenge, for me at least, in intellectualising these things, precisely because I know that their ultimate power lies beyond the reach of the intellect.

It's a chastening thing, though, for someone who lives most of the time in his head — someone whose existence is really headquartered above the neck, who looks at the body as basically a bit of an imped- iment he has to process food through — to look at people whose bodies are thinking, if you see what I mean, whose minds go to the tips of their fingers and toes. I have in mind great dancers, violinists, pianists or singers — really great singers, who can act as well as they can sing, people like Callas or Domingo (when he was good), or John Vickers. People who don't just produce a noise supported by the diaphragm, resonating in cavities in the head and then coming out of the mouth — their whole bodies are convulsed and galvanised by the effort, their whole bodies are working, their bodies have become vessels for an emotion.

This is a bit like the envy of the etiolated European for the noble savage, because it's a kind of primal existence these people have. As Yeats once said about a dancer, 'Her body thought'. And there's a wonderful line in one of Wordsworth's poems about an idiot boy who gets lost in the woods and is taken home by his horse, which knows the way to go, and Wordsworth says in this *faux naïf* ballad, 'You see, it was a horse that thought'. I just love the spectacle of the thinking body. To be presented with people whose toes can think, whose calves (like Nureyev's) can think is absolutely wonderful.

Or whose fingers can think. I remember once having dinner with the pianist Alfred Brendel. Most of the time, as we were eating, our hands were on the table, manipulating our knives and forks, but in between courses, his hands would disappear under the table into his lap. And I looked around at one point to see what he was doing, and there his fingers were, thinking in his lap. He was just doing exercises to make sure that they were still as nimble as they needed to be to play the Hammerklavier Sonata. I thought, 'Here's a man whose synapses extend to the very end of his arms'. It's in this that the attraction for me of music and the performing arts — the very notion of performance — actually lies. There's a mystique to it precisely because it will always remain unintelligible to me. I'm consoled by the thought that there's something in the world I won't be able to intellectualise or understand.

Opera is a little bit different though, isn't it? An opera can be about something in a sense in which a nocturne can't — it can tell a story and link us with bodies of ideas.

That's true, although I wonder why it is, for instance, that people are so infatuated with something like Wagner's Ring Cycle. Is it because it's a parable about the decline of civilisation, or is it because, as Nietzsche said about music, it really is miming the annihilation of the human being physically, exposing you to this great ocean of sound that consumes you and washes you away, allowing you, in a way, to experience your own demise? I tend to think that the ideas in opera are a bit of an alibi for the emotional stuff that's going on. It's like something T. S. Eliot said about meaning in poetry being a bit like the piece of meat that the burglar gives to the guard dog to keep it quiet while he breaks into the house. In other words, poetry is doing its real work on you emotionally or narcotically, spiritually or hypnotically, but the busy little rationalising mind needs to be given an excuse to keep it quiet, otherwise it'll think it's wasting its time.

I agree with you, though, about the intellectual content of opera — I think it's important to uphold that. I'm often struck by the thought that the grand tradition of European drama, starting with the Greeks, goes through opera in the eighteenth and nineteenth centuries when very little fine drama was being written. The dramatic spirit migrated into opera in the sense that drama was a communal experience. And what drama was doing was staging a kind of ritual, which was not just the ritual of getting dressed up to go to the opera, drinking champagne and looking at the singers through opera glasses. It was the ritual involved in the summoning up of collective communal energy — taking a lot of strangers, and by the force of music, by exposing them to this song of love and death, making them realise that this is a world that none of them had really understood, that they're all afloat on an ocean of passion and turbulent emotional forces. This great sense that drama is communal, that drama is a ritual, is something that was kept alive by opera at a time when pieces in the theatre were just pretending to be conversations between bourgeois householders in a room with the fourth wall removed.

My veneration of opera is also connected with its religious aspect. Opera is the form in which the gods were kept alive — the old, violent, volatile, classical gods who were the embodiment of passions, furies and frenzies. The Western world would have forgotten about those aboriginal gods if it hadn't been for opera, and to a lesser extent dance. In the twentieth century it's done more by, say, Stravinsky's 'Rite of Spring' than opera.

Nowadays the pagan gods are also kept alive by bands like the Rolling Stones or U2 or even, perhaps, Michael Jackson.

I suppose Michael Jackson is a strange kind of Ovidian metamorphic figure, a divine figure, with his cryogenic dormitory and his mutation between genders and races. Yes, pop culture certainly keeps the gods alive. It can transform an overweight Las Vegas singer like Elvis Presley into a god after his death, with sightings at suburban shopping malls. Popular culture is certainly a factory of myth. There's a class and age difference, though. This pagan frenzy is kept alive mostly for the young, but the time comes when you no longer know the names of the bands and it's no longer appropriate for you to go to the stadium concerts. For older people and people with different cultural backgrounds it's just music, and above all operatic music, that keeps all this going, gives us the blood transfusion we probably all badly need.

✧

You always seem to me to write meditations in some form or other, even when you're writing about such unlikely subjects as Joan Collins or Robert Maxwell[15]. You don't seem very interested in story, that very old-fashioned sort of linked narrative, for example, preferring to examine something until a meaning can be drawn out of it to be shared with us. That's a meditative approach.

Yes, I'm not very good with stories, even as a reader. I don't review novels on principle because literary editors always expect you to give a synopsis of the story, and I often just don't get it. I find the stories in films a bit hard to follow as well. Basically, I'm not very interested in stories because, after all, they all come out the same way in the end, don't they.

What are you preoccupied with, then, as a reader and a viewer?

I think what preoccupies me is the sense that a work of art is able to change the world, to replace the world with a replica of it, filtered through an individual imagination. It's something Nietzsche talked about. He said that we were given art so that we would not perish from the truth. What I am fascinated by and what I suppose I'm trying to do is to change reality from something which is just destiny, as it were, something you were given, to something which you can make or re-make. So, in talking to Joan Collins, say, or Robert Maxwell, I meditate on them in the sense that, while asking them questions and pretending to listen to their answers, I'm watching them in order to see what I can make of them, to see how I can turn them into characters, how I can recreate them myself, instead of guessing what's going on inside them.

---

15 See *Feasting with Panthers, or, the Importance of Being Famous* (Thames & Hudson, 1994).

You make them tell us more than meets your eye — that's what you do. And you do this through seduction, as far as the reader's concerned, I think, seducing us with language. When we read Peter Conrad, what we're always aware of (as when reading a poem) is your language and the way you're gauging all the time the exact impact of this or that word, this or that neologism, your acute awareness of register, your vocabulary, your way of weaving a spell over us with your language — it's almost more important than the subject you're writing about.

It's certainly as important. If it were more important, if I did it in a calculated, knowing way, I think I'd have gone over the top into mannerism and narcissism. But, yes, I suppose I am a kind of cultist of language. Once again, it's a sort of mysterious power which is inside one, not unlike the possession of an operatic voice. Great singers often talk about the voices they have inside them as if they were strangers resident inside their larynxes, whose behaviour they can't really control or understand. In a way I feel a bit like that about language. I mean, it's kind of wonderful to open one's mouth and to be not quite sure what's going to come out because of the spontaneous, improvised nature of thinking. When it works well, I have the excited feeling that I've surprised myself because something has happened on the page which I'm not directly responsible for.

I had the good fortune, of course, to grow up in a culture with its own virtuoso slang and its own wonderful, brawling rhetoric — vocally and verbally a very ebullient culture, as it still is, unlike the English, with its pinched understatements. Like the United States, Australia is one of those places where the English language came into its own, escaping from propriety and going to bed with dialects and slangs to become a great creative phenomenon, a phenomenon which, in its turn, creates those who speak it.

Your values and way of life seem to me to be the luxuries of a single man in some ways. As I listen to you, or read you, I'm put in mind of Auden and Isherwood. The freedom constantly to reinvent yourself, to surprise yourself, to be eccentric, to travel all over the world, is the freedom of the single man.

I always felt a sense of great affinity with that pair, I must say, and especially with Isherwood, and there's some truth in what you say, although not only single people have that freedom. It's the luxury of idiosyncracy, really, that's what being single affords you. And, of course, I was a single child. My sharp edges weren't rubbed off by siblings. But it's the oddities of what you are, I'd have thought, that make you an interesting, valuable and useful witness. I just work with what I've got.

Dennis Altman

❛ In some ways the greatest anti-intellectualism in

Australia comes from intellectuals themselves,

who tend to be overly critical and unsupportive of

each other, far more concerned to identify with

the latest trend from overseas than to foster

genuine respect for local achievement.

Those Australians who define themselves in

some ways as intellectuals tend to be either

apologetic or aggressive about it. ❜[1]

THE GENERATION OF AUSTRALIAN *intellectuals who grew to maturity soon after the Second World War, going to school in the forties and fifties and to university or escaping to England or America in the sixties, seems to have formed a very particular perspective on the world. It's a perspective on politics, individual freedom, rights and knowledge that sometimes seems little appreciated, let alone respected, by the generation educated in the eighties. Indeed several of the writers and thinkers taking part in this series — Helen Garner, perhaps, David Williamson, Robert Hughes — have found themselves caught up in a rather acrimonious dialogue with a younger generation with very different experiences of the world.*

Dennis Altman, one of Australia's most influential public thinkers, is a public intellectual in the grand tradition, moving in and out of his area of expertise to help mould society's views on areas of moral and political concern, especially in the fraught area of sexual politics. He is in the fortunate position, as he acknowledges, of belonging quite firmly to the generation born during the Second World War (and still feeling a bit shaky after three decades of seismic shifts), while, as Professor of Politics at La Trobe University, being constantly involved in real conversations with real students whose priorities, expectations, political consciousness and sense of national identity are entirely different from his.

The seismic shifts Altman's generation experienced — or 'changes in consciousness', as he calls them — and his reactions to them are recorded illuminatingly in his recent political biography (his words) Defying Gravity. *It's a very Altmanesque book in the sense that the political issues he writes about are always viewed from a personal standpoint, whether they are American politics, gay liberation, the Vietnam War or Labor rule in Australia in the eighties and nineties.*

WHEN I BEGAN *Defying Gravity* I actually thought I might call it *Generations*. Then I discovered there's already a large number of books out there called *Generations*. As one gets older, there's a growing sense that certain shared experiences and perceptions are indeed generational. There's a frustration, too, with those younger

---

1 Dennis Altman, *Defying Gravity* (Allen & Unwin, 1977).

people who seem totally unaware of things of enormous significance to those who lived through them, with those 22-year-olds who think they've discovered something nobody else in human history has ever thought of. At the same time I try to recognise that I was probably at least equally insufferable myself at 22, doing exactly the same thing.

The changes I'm really interested in are very much bound up with my own life (which is why I wanted to write in an autobiographical vein in *Defying Gravity*), and they're also bound up with the fact that much of my adult life has involved travel — indeed, what you could call the failure to be an expatriate. In fact, I played with using the word 'expatriate' in the title as well. At least the epigraph is a quote from Christina Stead[2], an expatriate from a previous generation, who really did feel by and large that to be either an intellectual or a creative figure was almost impossible in Australia — you had to expatriate yourself. Yet our generation actually changed quite rapidly — at some point we no longer felt the need. Of course, there are many people — including some younger than me — who still do feel the need. All the same, I see a growing sense that you *can* 'make it' in Australia, and this new sense is related, I think, to the fact that Australia has opened up in all sorts of ways — it's a much more diverse, tolerant, accepting and complex country than it was in the 1950s.

How have attitudes to homosexuality changed since the 1950s in this more tolerant and accepting environment?

The real shift came with a general loosening of attitudes and judgments in the late 1960s, the period Donald Horne called 'the time of hope', out of which came the beginnings of the gay movement, first with CAMP Inc.[3] (founded in 1970) and then Gay Liberation. It became both important and possible to 'come out' as gay, not only as a political act, but also as a way of linking one's sexuality to the rest of one's

2 'I only feel really happy when the pilot says we're at thirty thousand feet. I want to defy gravity ... The leading human trait [is] the attempt to defy the forces of gravity.' (From an interview with Candida Baker [ed.] in *Yacker: Australian writers talk about their work* (Picador, 1986).
3 A comprehensive account of the founding and activities of CAMP Inc. and the changes in homosexual subculture over the succeeding decades may be found in Garry Wotherspoon's *City of the Plain: History of a gay subculture* (Hale & Iremonger, 1991).

life, a theme I deal with to some extent in my novel *The Comfort of Men*[4]. During the 1970s a whole set of social and economic changes made for the very rapid growth of a visible gay world, particularly, of course, in Sydney, where Mardi Gras has become an internationally known event. In some ways, though, gay and lesbian politics lagged behind these changes — Australia was slower than every other significant liberal democracy apart from the United States in decriminalising homosexuality.

And how much significance do you give to current 'queer' theories?

Less than their proponents do. I'm sympathetic to the queer project, but it seems to me caught between on the one hand wanting to deny the importance of identities while on the other creating a particular style and set of intellectual assumptions which are just as narrow as the identities it critiques. A lot of queer theory seems to me a post-modern reworking of much that was central to gay liberation, which would be fine if there was greater awareness of this among queer theorists themselves. In any case, as I've written with boring frequency, queer theory seems to me useful as an aesthetic term but has not all that much to do with everyday life or politics.

Australia may be a more diverse and tolerant country than it was in the 1950s, but is it a more significant country? You say that you can 'make it' in Australia now (which you can), but part of the problem in the fifties and sixties, surely, was that we felt that what we did wasn't significant unless we did it in New York or Paris.

And we still feel that, of course, because in one sense it's absolutely true. If you publish a book in Australia on an Australian theme, it's enormously difficult to persuade anyone outside Australia to pick it up, unless the theme is very exotic or plays to overseas images of what Australia ought to be, like *The Thorn Birds*. But a book about Australia as we experience it will have problems finding an overseas

---

4 (Minerva, 1994).

market. I go into bookshops in places such as Singapore and Kuala Lumpur, where you can buy all the latest novels from the United States and Britain, but only those Australian books which have been published in New York or London. So to some extent, yes, what we do here still lacks significance.

On the other hand, two things have happened: firstly, it's less clear now than it used to be that the centre of everything that matters is in fact the North Atlantic — I mean, we're increasingly aware that all sorts of interesting and exciting things actually go on in other parts of the world, and that's related, naturally, to the huge economic boom in East Asia. A lot of that switch in focus is trade- and investment-driven, but, nonetheless, it's also made us aware of potential cultural interaction.

Secondly, electronic communication means that there's less of a sense of any centre at all. I mean, there was a time when I used to regularly read the *New York Review of Books*, it used to be very important to me. Now I quite frankly find it very boring. It reflects the concerns of an ageing group of largely New York Jewish intellectuals and their upper-class English mates in Oxford and Cambridge. When you've got electronic communications and you're in e-mail contact with people all over the world, you don't actually need to know the latest pronouncements from Balliol or Harvard about eighteenth-century literature.

I think we've re-imagined Australia hugely over the past decade or decade and a half. In the first place, we've had to re-imagine it in terms of its ethnic composition. When I was a kid in Hobart, my parents spoke English very well, but with an accent that was both unusual and a matter for some embarrassment. Needless to say, it's not like that any more. The sheer number of Australians who are first- and second-generation migrants and not of British origin has revolutionised this country — and it's much more than being able to go and have a cappuccino everywhere, or having 120 different ethnic restaurants to choose from, or holding ethnic festivals every weekend. It has to do with a real change in our understanding of who is an Australian. There's still room for more change, of course — I understand that Ramsay Street in 'Neighbours' remains resolutely Anglo-Celtic in a way that's actually quite unrepresentative of most of urban Australia.

In the second place, I think we've had to re-imagine the relation-ship between all non-indigenous (including the older Anglo-Australians) and indigenous Australians. When I was growing up in Tasmania we were constantly told that there were no Tasmanian Aborigines, they'd all died out. (They hadn't been 'killed off', but had 'died out'.) And we were taken to see their images in the Tasmanian Museum. Now, of course, there are thousands of people in Tasmania who consider themselves Aboriginal because they've discovered their Aboriginal ancestry. The debate about the relationship between immigrant (in the widest sense) and indigenous Australians is a continuing one.

In the third place, we've had to re-imagine our place in the larger world, and that's really our place vis-à-vis Asia. Again, when I was a child, there was still an emotional tie to Britain, there were still all those maps with their splotches of red — there was a strong sense of being linked to Britain. Indeed, the first time I went overseas, our ship stopped at all those red dots on the map. Then, as the British Empire collapsed, we transferred our allegiance to the United States and, although the American alliance remains, over the past fifteen years or so we've increasingly had to imagine ourselves as part of Asia–Pacific, we've had to re-think and become much more sophisticated about how we understand what Asia is and what our links to Asia might be.

So I think Australia is a much more exciting place now than most other developed countries because of these three changes — the huge national debate about who we are and our relationship to the rest of the world.

There have been big changes in the notion of political activism as well over the last two or three decades.

That question is usually put to me in nostalgic tones. 'Of course, *your* generation were activists', people say. 'Aren't you upset and depressed by today's students? They're so apathetic, they're not out in the streets.' Well, I think that's a rather superficial way of looking at it. There was certainly a period in the history of all Western countries — let's say from the late sixties well into the seventies — when there was a great deal of political activism. It was one of those periods in history when there really was a seismic shift; all sorts of things moved at a basic level and they've never gone back to where they were. Crucial issues beginning with the Civil Rights movement in the United States and the Vietnam War in Australia provided the impetus and the focus for large-scale street activism in those years.

In the 1990s the response to the sorts of changes we're living through is less obvious, I think. It seems to me related to the nature of global change: we're caught up in a global economy and it's increasingly unclear against whom we should protest. I think, too, there's a real cynicism about what happens if we change governments — in the end it doesn't really matter if John Howard or Kim Beazley is prime minister because the major decisions are not made by them. The major decisions are the result of large-scale flows of capital, trade and investment, over which we seem to have very little say. In that environment, combined with declining economic security, it doesn't surprise me that there's much less willingness to go out and protest. Partly it's seen as less effective than it once was and partly people don't have the sense of security. We tend to forget that the counter-culture in the New Left was essentially made up of people who had grown up believing that without much effort they would always be OK — there'd be jobs, there'd be security, there'd be housing. It's fine to say 'I'm going to go and live in a squat and be counter-cultural and communal' if, in fact, you have an alternative. The situation facing a lot of my students today is very different: it's one of real concern that they won't have either a job or the sort of basic security net that my generation used to believe was part of what a rich country automatically provides its citizens with.

❖

When, in 1964, Dennis Altman went overseas on his first significant trip abroad, a would-be expatriate as many of his generation were, he didn't in fact 'join up the red dots' in a headlong rush towards England — he made his way to the United States. And the United States has been a major theme of his, central to his life and ideas and career ever since.

It's where, as he says, he became an adult, it's where the challenge to work out a middle way between diversity and cohesion could be experienced at its most dramatic. And this is something he wrestles with constantly: how to conjoin human solidarity, as he puts it, with a respect for difference. It's no doubt a basic tension in any civil society, and precisely the kind of puzzle to exercise the minds of public intellectuals.

Although we're all well aware of similarities between the United States and Australia, Dennis Altman is also articulate on the subject of the significant differences between us.

Here I've become quite conservative. I would argue that we have to understand history, and the history of the settlement of the two countries is enormously different. There are similarities of course, such as the dispossession of the indigenous peoples, but there again the differences are huge because it took a lot longer and a lot more explicit fighting for the white settlers to dispossess the American Indians than was true in Australia, where it was done brutally and in a sense more efficiently and faster.

I think there are two huge differences in our histories of settlement: one is that American settlement came with a very strong rhetoric of political and religious liberty, particularly of course in New England, and the whole evangelical and messianic tradition of the United States really flows from that. The idea that this was the society in which men would be free — and when they said 'men' they meant men, let's have no illusions about it — and the argument that the United States was, to use the words of the eighteenth century, 'a beacon for all mankind' had nothing in common with the dumping of convicts in New South Wales.

The second difference is that our equivalent to slavery in this country was the convict system. In some ways it was probably just as brutal, but it wasn't sanctified by race. Consequently, on becoming free, convicts and their children and grandchildren became indistinguishable from everybody else. Indeed, their great-grandchildren could claim convict ancestry as a mark of honour. In the United States slaves, because they were marked by race, even after they were free, retained an extraordinary stigma. The extent of racism in the United

States is terribly hard to get across to those who haven't experienced it. When General Colin Powell was speaking in Sydney in 1997, he pointed out that even today he, the man most Americans would have wanted as president in 1996, can't buy a house in very many suburban areas in the United States. He could have added he probably couldn't hail a taxi on the street in New York City with much success.

Now that's a very different history from ours. When you add to that the continental size of the United States, the expansionism, the fact that by the end of the nineteenth century it was one of the major centres of the world industrial revolution, and throughout this century has been one of the world's major military powers (now, of course, the paramount one) you have two very different kinds of societies.

I think we tend to forget what a huge part the military plays in American life. Large numbers of major cities and communities depend on it for their existence. Luckily, we're an insignificant country with a very small military — something very much in our favour, I think. We're not militarised in that way, we are not a major world power, despite our occasional dreams of glory, from H. V. Evatt through to Gareth Evans. I wonder if our current Foreign Minister is smart enough to have dreams of glory — but maybe that's all to the good.

However, in certain ways, rather unfortunately, we're giving up some fine Australian traditions. I have been amazed and shocked by the ease with which we have, for example, privatised public utilities — electricity and gas, particularly. Ten years ago I would have said that what differentiated us from the United States was in part a much stronger belief in the need for public ownership of basic utilities — well, I've now been proven wrong.

Certain basic differences remain, all the same. Individualism is not as central to our sense of ourselves as it is for Americans — and there's both a good and a bad side to that. On the whole it's good because it means that there are limits to how far we are prepared to do away with any sort of social security system. I think it's bad where it means no protection for individual freedom of the kind they have in some areas in the United States, through institutions such as the Bill of Rights.

Despite a certain disenchantment with the United States, you are fasci-
nated by that country and its history, and it has obviously influenced
you in many ways. I wonder if the source of your fascination lies in the
tension you've been speaking of between individual rights and the
possibility in America for collective action on a large scale.

I think the answer would be more autobiographical. The real answer
of course is that I went to the United States at a particular age (21)
and the United States was the place where I first really became actively
homosexual, where I developed a particular sort of both political
and personal identity, and that I've constantly gone backwards and
forwards to the United States, and a great deal of my personal life and
my career have been bound up with it. That's the real answer and
anything else I might say would be a rationalisation.

It's also true to say that all of us live in the shadow of the United
States. I believe it's enormously important for us Australians to
understand the United States, even if we wish to reject large parts of
its culture. In fact, I get very impatient with that particular kind of
Australian snobbery which makes it acceptable to boast about having
been to Chad, Malawi and Tierra del Fuego but never having been to
the United States. People will tell you with great pride that they've
never set foot in New York, and for some reason you're supposed to
be impressed. Given that New York has a much greater impact on
how we see the world than Chad, Malawi or Tierra del Fuego, I'm
not impressed, because it's important, I think, to work out the
answer to your earlier question about the extent to which we're
being Americanised, and in order to do that we have to understand
America. Contemporary culture, intellectual life and the real sources
of power in the world — economic, political and military — are so
bound up with the United States that we can't escape it. In my own
case it's become a love-hate relationship: the more I get to know it,
the more I reject it. For all sorts of classic psychological reasons I
need it as an object both to hate and to love simultaneously.

In order to talk about your intellectual development, let's go right back to
your childhood. You've written that you were precociously intellectual as

a child, that you were a very 'serious little boy' (one of the common euphemisms for children like you) and that there was very little Australian input into the development of your thought.

What really struck me when I was thinking about my childhood for *Defying Gravity* — and I made a very conscious decision not to write *The Education of Young Dennis*[5] — was how dependent I was on British books: Enid Blyton, the Biggles and William books, and then as I got older — and I almost blush to admit this — P. G. Wodehouse. And it was true in a larger cultural sense as well: I remember my involvement in the university revues in Hobart (I first went to university at the age of sixteen, I was far too young), writing scripts which most commonly were parodies of Gilbert and Sullivan. We were most influenced by things like 'The Goon Show' and Tony Hancock — it's interesting how little else there was to influence us. There was very little Australian literature around, and virtually no Australian movies, although there was, of course, Australian radio: the ABC and 'The Argonauts' were an important part of my life — as they were for many people of our generation.

On the whole, though, the influences on us were heavily British[6]. In a way, it's particularly ironic because my parents were not British. My mother was Russian, although she'd come to Australia quite young, and my father had come as a refugee from Vienna, an enormously cultivated, upper-class, well-educated Central European, with a great knowledge of literature and music. Even so, he very quickly started reading British books and was drawn into the overwhelmingly dominant British picture of the world.

Up to a point this picture is still true. When Australians play Monopoly, they still don't think it's odd to be buying and selling Park

---

5 A reference to Donald Horne's autobiography *The Education of Young Donald* (1967; Penguin, 1988), in which he describes in great detail his early childhood in Muswellbrook, NSW, his withdrawn teenage years in Sydney and his encounter with a heady intellectual world at Sydney University in 1939.

6 It is interesting to compare Peter Conrad's account in *Down Home: Revisiting Tasmania* of growing up in Hobart during approximately the same period (Conrad is five years younger than Altman): Conrad places much more emphasis than Altman on the 'two termini' of his imaginative life, Britain and America, with American cultural influences reaching him principally through the cinema and, in the late 1950s, television.

Lane and Mayfair, even if most of the people playing have never been there. It really only makes sense to us in terms of the sort of childhood experience so many of us had — that world of petty snobberies, starting with Enid Blyton, through Agatha Christie and ending with E. F. Benson. Today, of course, we watch 'Absolutely Fabulous' *and* 'Blue Heelers'. It's only begun to change quite recently.

In the case of film, the influences must have been much less British, but I don't remember film as having an enormously important role. Certainly I went to the movies, but maybe because already I wanted to be a writer and was fairly introspective, and because it was words that were really the crucial thing for me, it's what I read which had the most impact on me, and what I read was overwhelmingly British. And that needs to be matched with what we were taught formally at school: we did British constitutional history, for example, that was how we began the study of Australian politics. (I understand the intellectual argument for doing that but, pedagogically, nowadays that would be a crazy approach to take.) So I know in some detail the histories of the Tudors and Stuarts, for instance, and that's been important, obviously, in forming how I see the world.

By the 1960s, however, when you were an undergraduate, your intellectual world must have broadened from that British base, for all the parodies on Gilbert and Sullivan.

As an undergraduate in Tasmania, my reading was pretty eclectic. I don't think I adopted any particular intellectual position. That was part of the problem I had in writing about those years — I'd love to have been able to say, 'I discovered Marxism at the age of eighteen and when I was in Melbourne I rushed to the International Bookshop, bought the *Collected Works of Marx and Engels* and spent the next ten years studying them.' Nothing like that happened to me. It was a strangely non-ideological education if you like, in which I did politics, history, a bit of French and a tiny bit of psychology, and my reading was drawn from all over the place.

When I went to the States as a graduate student at the age of 21, my reading again was fairly eclectic, but I was also exposed to

American liberal thinking in a number of ways. Sitting in on under-graduate courses, which they encourage overseas students to do, I actually learnt a lot about the American political system. Just living there, though, and asking questions, one became very conscious of the American liberal tradition which is a much more articulated, ideological view than the Australian liberal tradition.

Then, of course, there were certain individuals who influenced me, the most famous being Hannah Arendt, who'd come up to Cornell to teach a seminar. And what influenced me most in my encounters with Hannah Arendt were the discussions we had about the Vietnam War. At Cornell University during those first two years in the States were some of the leading critics of American intervention in Indo-China. I was enormously influenced, for example, by George Kahin[7] (well known to anyone in the field of Southeast Asian studies) The longest and most intimate conversation I ever had with him, rather like the longest, most intimate conversation I ever had with Hannah Arendt, was precisely around not just opposition to the war, but whether or not it was proper for me as a non-American to be active in the anti-war movement at Cornell. Obviously it was exciting for me at 22 to have these extraordinarily important figures taking this question seriously — there's something remarkably democratising about being involved in political movements which made this possible, it was a question which meant something to them as well. I wouldn't have had an intimate discussion with Hannah Arendt about the thought of Heidegger, say. It would have been absurd, because there'd have been no way of pretending we were equal.

I'm interested in knowing how you related to what we might call the Grand Narratives that were around at the time — two which immediately come to mind are Marxism and the general area of Freudian thought.

Engagement with those specific ways of thought came later. As an undergraduate I was not particularly exposed even to Marxist or Freudian thought — or as a graduate student, for that matter. When

---

7 Professor of Southeast Asian Politics at Cornell University, author of *Intervention: How America became involved in Vietnam* (1968).

I went to my first teaching job at Monash University at the end of the 1960s, I was taking fourth-year seminars where I was basically teaching my contemporaries. I was far too young. Often they knew much more and had read much more than I had. From that point on I started becoming aware of Marxism and Freudianism. I think it came from an awareness of people like Marcuse[8] and Gramsci, both of whom subsequently influenced the way I thought quite strongly.

I've never really believed in Grand Narratives — that is, I've never believed that there's a single explanation or a single account that makes sense of the world or human society. I was very attracted to certain elements in Marxist thought to do with the nature of power and the relationship between power and ideology — that's why Gramsci was so attractive. I was also intrigued by psychoanalysis, and that can no doubt be partly explained autobiographically. After all, I was having to deal with the fact that I was homosexual at a time when that was still regarded as something terribly strange and aberrant. And, interestingly enough, my reading of Freud was an enormously positive and reinforcing one. (According to the gay American stereotype of Freud, he was one of those nasty people we can trace homophobia back to. This is because historically American psychoanalysis became increasingly homophobic, not, in my opinion, because of what Freud had written, but because of particular developments within the United States.) When I encountered Freud, I was influenced by the reading of Marcuse, and of his *Eros and Civilisation* in particular. I also moved to Sydney in 1969, catching the tail end of the Push[9], and it was the Push which had brought to Australia the ideas of people like Wilhelm Reich[10], who, like Marcuse, tried to synthesise Marx and

---

8 Herbert Marcuse (1898–1979). German-born American political philosopher whose attempts to synthesise Marxist and Freudian thought made him popular with American radicals in the 1960s. In *Eros and Civilisation: A philosophical enquiry into Freud* (1956) he rejected any simple identification of civilisation with repression, stressing the sociological implications of Freudian concepts.

9 The most complete account of the libertarian network of anarchists and bohemians called the Push, and its influence on Australian intellectual life in the fifties and sixties, is Anne Coombs' *Sex and Anarchy: The life and death of the Sydney Push* (Viking, 1996).

10 Wilhelm Reich (1897–1957). Austrian psychoanalyst who considered regular orgasms for men and women promoted mental health, and who in the 1920s to 1930s attempted to combine his sexual theories with his Marxist beliefs. Expelled from the German Communist Party, he eventually migrated to the United States where his theories gained some popularity. His works include *The Function of the Orgasm* (1927) and *The Sexual Revolution* (1939–45).

Freud. Marcuse was actually much more attractive to me than Reich because Marcuse's approach was extraordinarily positive towards homosexuality. Consequently, Marcuse gave me a strong sense of personal justification, and I drew heavily on him for my first book, *Homosexual: Oppression and liberation*, which came out in 1971. Reich, by contrast, was quite homophobic, and ended up as a Right-wing nut — a not uncommon fate for émigrés to the United States. Still, it was that libertarian Push tradition in Sydney that introduced me to Freud, and we read and discussed him in the fourth-year seminars I taught at Sydney University in the early seventies.

One of the things people forget when they talk about the gap between academic and intellectual life, by the way, is how much you can in fact learn from teaching. As I talk to you, for example, I'm conscious of the fact that a lot of what I know about theory comes from being pushed by smart students and having them read things with me. (And I'm not a theorist, I have a magpie approach to theory, picking up a bit here and a bit there, putting it together in the nest. If it looks good, then that's fine, it's something to be used, but it's not something to be venerated and worshipped.)

When you say 'theory', do you mean theory with a capital 'T' — Foucault, Derrida, post-modernist or post-structuralist theory?

No. Theory existed long before the Left Bank. It is almost impossible to escape some kind of theoretical framework. The dominant one in my life is a certain sort of liberal understanding of the world based on Western rational, liberal thought, strengthened in my case by my American experiences. After all, liberalism is overwhelmingly the ideology of the United States, it's almost unchallengeable.

That's all theory with a small 't'. There's also capital 'T' theory based on a conscious reading of particular cultural theorists. In point of fact, John Locke was actually a more important theorist in the development of my ideas, in framing my picture of the world, than Michel Foucault, despite the fact that I've read much more Foucault than Locke (whom I had to read for a politics course). The problem is that almost everybody in the modern world is influenced by theory

— who is not in one way or another a Marxist and a Freudian? On the other hand, very few people are *consciously* influenced by theory, consciously read theory or are consciously aware of where they draw their theoretical ideas from. And so we go through waves, don't we? The people you referred to are the current wave of fashionable theorists. I'm old enough to remember a different wave that passed over us 20 years ago, and I expect to live long enough to see the next new wave. And in 30 years time somebody will undoubtedly say, 'My God, there were once these fabulous people called Lyotard, Deleuze and Guattari writing all this marvellous stuff which is now forgotten', and space for 23 PhDs and six post-docs will be immediately created.

What point were you at intellectually when you sat down to write your first book, Homosexual: Oppression and liberation?

At that time I was very much caught up in the romanticism of the protest movements of the end of the sixties and the beginning of the seventies. I'd come across enough contemporary neo-Marxist and Freudian theory by then to be able to put some sort of theoretical gloss on what was going on. What was really influencing me most strongly, however, was the exuberance of being caught up in the early stages of the gay movement in New York[11]. This was largely accidental: I went to New York in August 1970 on leave and literally fell into the early gay movement there. It was terribly exciting in the way an involvement in new movements can be. I guess it was the living through it that gave me the impetus to write. Then there were the literary influences — that generation of older homosexual writers such as Isherwood[12], Baldwin[13] and Vidal[14]. Through their writing they helped me find ways of being in the world, they had a huge

---

11 See *Homosexual: Oppression and liberation*, revised edition (Serpent's Tail, 1993).
12 Christopher Isherwood (1904–86). English novelist and playwright who emigrated to Southern California in 1939. He is best known for his novels about expatriate life in Berlin in the early 1930s (*Mr Norris Changes Trains* [1935] and *Goodbye to Berlin* [1939]), but also for the largely autobiographical works illuminating homosexual themes, *A Single Man* (1964) and *Christopher and His Kind* (1977).
13 James Baldwin (1924–87). Black American novelist, playwright and essayist. His best-known works include *Go Tell it on a Mountain* (1953), *Giovanni's Room* (1956), which described homosexual desire with a frankness unusual for the period, *Another Country* (1962) and *The Fire Next Time* (1963).
14 There is a discussion of all three writers and their impact on Altman in *Defying Gravity*.

impact on my life. It's not generally recognised that it was less writers like Kate Millett[15] or Herbert Marcuse who were the really significant influences on me, than fiction writers such as Isherwood and Baldwin. They're in fact theorists, too, of course — they theorise, although perhaps not in the language we're accustomed to. In Baldwin's novels, for example, you find a quite explicit description of how he sees American society working.

It's unusual for people in your position (professors of politics, let's say) to refer to fiction as often as you do as a source of ideas and inspiration.

Doris Lessing remarked in *Under My Skin* that 'fiction makes a better job of the truth'[16], and I think that's very true. I think that most positivist sociology actually tells us very little about the world. What it does is order the world. It's like a very sophisticated filing system that rearranges what we already instinctively know. Literature, on the other hand, helps us understand how other people see the world, takes us into other people's understandings of their world. It also intuitively makes connections before the social sciences make them. I know this sounds irrational, and I'm actually a highly rational sort of person, but I do believe that in terms of coming to understand the interconnections between things that aren't obviously related, literature is actually the most useful kind of writing — which is one reason I wrote the novel.

Fiction also reaches a tremendously wide public, which is important to me — I'm a populist, I believe in being read by the widest possible audience. (Of course, I also write academic articles and I've published at least one academic book, *Power and Community: Organisational and cultural responses to AIDS*[17], which is therefore virtually unknown — although I think it's actually quite a good book. Its British publishers consider publishing an ancient craft and don't see why the public should easily find its products!

---

15 *Sexual Politics* (Doubleday, 1970, and reissued by Virago, 1985) introduced the term with which Kate Millett, a political activist, writer and artist, defined the politics of power relationships in society based on sex.

16 (HarperCollins, 1994), p. 314.

17 (Taylor & Francis, 1994).

Still, as far as I'm concerned, one writes to affect both people and politics and therefore wants to reach as many people as possible. Fiction can do that, but so can non-fiction: I'm thinking of books such as Michael Harrington's *The Other America,* which, when it came out in 1962, literally put the question of poverty on the political agenda in the United States.

And it's true of your own books, Homosexualization of America *and* Homosexual: Oppression and liberation, *as well as of Francis Fukuyama's* The End of History *and perhaps even John Ralston Saul's* Unconscious Civilization *or* Voltaire's Bastards.

Well, in the end, that's what intellectual life ought to be about, surely — changing the way people see the world, and as a consequence of that what they do in the world. Not many people probably read the books themselves, but the books are picked up by the media (as happened with *Homosexual* in 1972) and are talked about in front of a wide audience. I actually feel quite comfortable with that: I think the publicity machine is a legitimate part of the way in which writers reach the public. In the case of *The First Stone,* for example, I suspect that much of the public comment came from people who either hadn't read it or were reading into it what they wanted to believe rather than what Helen Garner was actually saying. (Not that it's always clear what Helen *was* actually saying.) Nonetheless, *The First Stone* became an event, it's impact on public debate was immense. Now that's what I think intellectual life ought to be about.

Let's talk, then, about the nature of this public space where words change the way people think and act, and also about how intellectuals go about occupying it. It seems to lie at the conjunction of a number of other social spaces, and clearly entry into it is not a democratic process.

Wherever that space lies, certain people obviously control the entry points. In other words, there's a relatively small number of gatekeepers — the features and literary editors of the three or four major newspapers, for example, a handful of columnists, and the producers of a relatively small number of radio and television programs. These are the people who decide, for instance, whether a certain book is important or not, and who seem to reach a concensus among themselves about which issues are worth discussing and which aren't.

No one really knows why one book takes off while another doesn't — why Annie Proulx's *The Shipping News*[18], for example, took off without much pressure from the gatekeepers — but I don't think quality has anything much to do with it — quality doesn't necessarily win out in the end. And winning prizes such as the Booker plays a part, as do scandal and luck. I was extremely lucky, for example, in that I published my first book at a time when the gatekeepers were keen to open up discussion about sexualities (and specifically about homosexuality). In this context I was essentially turned into a public figure by the book review of *Homosexual* in *Time* magazine (and it wasn't even a very good review, but there was enough cultural cringe here for any kind of review in *Time* to count), and also by my appearance on the now-defunct current affairs show 'Monday Conference' on ABC television — Bob Moore's program. I was on air for 50 minutes and that was a big event.

Luck of this kind can be imprisoning, of course. The problem for me is that that first burst of publicity has defined me ever since. It's now very hard for me to break out of the way in which the media have constructed me. People often ask me why I don't write more on other topics for the media. What they don't recognise is that the media won't publish my writing on other topics. No one rings me up offering me $1000 to write a big story on the republic, for instance. In fact, the republic is a subject I've offered the press articles on, but they weren't interested — they wanted me to write something about the Mardi Gras. So there are both advantages and disadvantages in being taken up by the gatekeepers.

One of your academic referees once described you as an intellectual rather than a scholar. What do you think he meant?

---

18 The winner of the 1994 Pulitzer Prize and the *Irish Times* International Prize.

I don't think it would be unfair to say that it was Neal Blewett, who was then Minister for Health, who wrote that. He'd also been a professor of politics, so he was rather a good person to have as a referee. I think he meant that it's ideas rather than primary research which are my first interest. And I think that's largely true. What he meant by scholarship, presumably, was the meticulous compiling of data, the putting together of unknown bodies of knowledge to open up something that, until that point, had been unknown. Intellectual work, on the other hand, is more about working with material that's already out there, building something new out of it and making it accessible to people who otherwise wouldn't know about it. By and large that's what I do. I don't spend very much time in libraries or in archives. I never have, although that's not to say I don't think that kind of work is terribly important — for some purposes it obviously is. Again, I'm more like a magpie building its nest, plucking things from here and there. I read widely about any discipline whatsoever — I'm just as likely to quote a thriller as I am to quote the latest in French theory, and I try out of that to build an understanding of the world. I suppose this approach reflects my basic feeling that the world is a very complex, messy place and that no one discipline or theoretical framework can actually explain it.

Some people might see that kind of differentiation between the scholar and the intellectual as elitist: below stairs there are people beavering away in libraries compiling statistical analyses, while above stairs Dennis is chatting about the subjects that have been researched below stairs.

I don't see it as elitist, although I understand what you mean. After all, people make a conscious choice to be scholars. And I think there's a role for the dilettante in our society, as you have argued.[19] There are also people who manage to combine the two, such as Manning Clark, who was both an intellectual and a scholar. He increasingly used his enormous prestige as a scholar to intervene as an intellectual, and to

---

19 In the essay, 'Loitering with Intent: Reflections on the demise of the dilettante', first published in *Australian Book Review*, March 1997, and reprinted in *Streams of Light: Best antipodean essays*, edited by Morag Fraser (Allen & Unwin, 1998).

intervene in a range of areas which were increasingly not directly related to his scholarly knowledge.

All the same, I recognise that it's quite difficult to do, and that certain kinds of scholarship can be enormously demanding and time-consuming, requiring the mastery of a number of languages and years of hard slogging through archives. I admire people who do that. Perhaps there's a sense in which I'm not willing to invest in that sort of concentrated, dedicated work. What I try to do is to read the world (in the modern sense of 'read'), and that I do constantly, finding things in all sorts of unexpected places — and that goes back to the earlier point on literature, and not always with a capital 'L', either. Agatha Christie is as useful to us in understanding the world as Jane Austen, although she may not write as well. What I do is research, but not, I admit, in the classic sense of sitting in the Mitchell Library seven days a week.

The Australian settler myths you referred to brought with them a certain kind of anti-intellectualism — the kind of intellectual you're now describing didn't, after all, have much of a place in settler society. Yet you appear very optimistic about the place of intellectuals in present-day Australia, you don't seem to see it as a bleak scene intellectually at all.

There's a great *New Yorker* cartoon of two French peasants sitting in a hut somewhere in remote rural France, and one of them is saying to the other, 'Did you see the discussion of Deleuze in the latest *Le Monde*?' There's a widespread illusion in Australia that everywhere else in the world there's a vast and vibrant intellectual culture that we're deprived of. Now, of course, because of size there's obviously going to be more intellectual life in Paris, New York and London than in any Australian city, because they're vast metropolitan centres drawing on the whole world. Once you allow for scale, though, I'm not at all persuaded there's more intellectual support there than there is here.

And I think one can reverse the argument, too: over the last 30 years what has been striking about Australia is the extent to which there's been support for certain kinds of intellectual work. In fact, some of the most interesting intellectual discussions going on here have traditionally taken place on radio — radio is a very strong part of our intellectual tradition, compared, say, to the United States, where there's an absence of real public broadcasting. (That's why I'm so concerned about the recurrent threat to Radio National: it's one of the few areas outside of the universities where genuine intellectual work has been possible.)

On the other hand, in the United States, because of the size of the market, you have a much stronger possibility of paying freelance essayists well. The old *New Yorker* could afford to pay someone to spend a year writing one long article — well, it's a pity that's impossible in Australia, but it is. The *New Yorker* is supported by advertising revenues from a society vastly bigger than ours.

So, no, I don't think we're anti-intellectual in Australia, although I think we're suffering from the sorts of pressures being felt everywhere in the world at the moment: in the interests of efficiency and productivity, institutions such as the universities, publishing and broadcasting, which have traditionally been the main space for intellectual life, are under threat. Our productivity now has to fit certain bureaucratic criteria. But I don't think the situation is worse in Australia than elsewhere, and I certainly don't think our culture is particularly marked by anti-intellectualism. For instance, I find the number of self-professed intellectuals, people like Evatt, Whitlam, Dunstan and Carr, who have led Labor parties in Australia, quite fascinating — not Liberal parties, interestingly enough, but Labor parties, which are, or at least used to be, the party of the working class.

How do you account for the difference between leaders of the two parties?

Well, the Liberal Party is basically the party of the status quo — unsurprisingly, that sort of party doesn't want to ask too many difficult questions. Politics is an awkward place for an intellectual, but a Conservative party is likely to be an even more awkward place because it will be even more discomfited by the sort of hard questions an intellectual will put. Re-imagining is not what a Conservative party is likely to be interested in. Look at the leadership: there can be a kind of messianic re-imagining in Conservative parties — Jeff Kennett re-imagines Victoria regularly, in what some of us think of as night-marish forms: casinos and freeways and no social support — but rarely, I think, any intellectual re-imagining. Now, while it's true that there are problems for intellectuals on the Labor side, there's at least some scope to discuss ideas, especially on the part of people dissatisfied with the status quo and therefore more open to fresh ideas.

On the whole I'd say there's been more respect for intellectuals in our history than we like to believe — and that belief in itself is very much a part of Australian life. I think interesting questions are raised, for example, by Evatt's rise to power as an intellectual figure at a time in our history which we usually think of as particularly barren intellectually. Why Evatt? Why Whitlam? Why didn't Whitlam's intellectual arrogance turn people off? Within the Labor Party his intellectual stance won him great respect. For that matter, the only real challenger to Whitlam during his time as leader of the Labor Party was Jim Cairns, another intellectual. But then, while we're very good at recognising what we're bad at, we're not very good at recognising what we're good at. We need to re-think the importance of the part played by intellectuals in Australian history.

Helen Garner

' I was looking at "The Muppets" last week and

the two little piglets came in, and somebody asked them

a difficult question, and one of them said to the other,

'I didn't know there was going to be a test'.

And as soon as I hear the word 'race' or 'gender'

come out of my mouth, I start getting that

breaking-out-in-a-sweat feeling that there's

going to be a test, and I'm going to fail it. '

D ESPITE HER LITERARY PROMINENCE, *Helen Garner is oddly hesitant about the realm of the intellect. In a 1992 conversation with cartoonist Michael Leunig[1], for example, she said that 'the intellectual, inhibiting [self], this bothersome self' has to be 'disarmed', in order, presumably, for an artist to be truly creative. And to Ramona Koval on Radio National in 1996 she said that she wasn't interested in talking about her religious beliefs because 'that always seems so intellectual[2].*

The supposed conflict between 'artist' and 'thinker' has been rehearsed over centuries, of course, but in Helen Garner's case, given the social impact of both her journalism and works such as Monkey Grip *[1977] and* The First Stone *[1995], her unwillingness to be cast in the role of intellectual, let alone public intellectual, seems to grow out of the particularly Australian embarrassment with intellectual pretension. 'Embarrassment', she told Michael Leunig in the* Art Monthly *conversation, 'is a key thing in the Australian consciousness'.*

Yet right from the beginning in 1973, when she 'caused a stir', as she puts it, by discussing sexual matters openly with her students at Fitzroy High School in Melbourne, Garner's stance on issues of public concern has been a public one. In her newspaper and magazine articles, her fiction, her non-fiction and in media interviews she's never been shy about speaking her mind. Her ideas on social issues in Australian society, particularly those affecting women's lives (institutions, violence, social justice, society's demands in conflict with private needs), have been informed, complex and widely listened to. Although her arguments have not always carried the day by any means, they have influenced public opinion in Australia over many years in the classic public intellectual mode: in book after book she articulates widely held but unformulated ideas on matters of public concern (such as gender politics and sexual harrassment), freeing up the public discussion of these ideas and points of view and confronting Australians with questions about what kind of society they wish to live in.

Does Helen Garner feel that her intellectual side is in some sense at war with the creative or intuitive side to her nature?

---

1 'A Kind of Reality' (*Art Monthly*, no. 56, December–January 1992–93).
2 'Books and Writing', 5 April 1996.

IT'S PROBABLY MORE A feeling of being intellectually ill-equipped and inadequate. University was a strange time for me. I went to university without knowing why I was going, I just went there because I was Miss Clever Clogs from The Hermitage, and it was assumed by everyone around me that I would go to university. I felt I was on a track leading to the university. When I got there, I was so wild with freedom that, although I could spend my time merrily reading all sorts of books as well as poetry (I was studying Arts), I didn't really read or think deeply about anything.

The critical training I was given in the English course was, I now realise, heavily Leavisite, but I couldn't think of anything more boring than reading Leavis[3]. At the same time I think I'm deeply dyed with what I dimly recognise as a sort of a Leavisite approach to literature — that is, I'm interested in moral questions and I really do think that literature can enrich people. This seems to me a fairly straightforward proposition.

Can or should?

Well, to step sideways, I have a friend who once remarked to me that for her there are two kinds of writing: the kind that gives her energy and the kind that takes energy away from her. Some writing makes you feel feeble, stupid and bored, while other writing fills you with an enthralled feeling about being alive, about wanting to experience things and understand them. Now, I don't think that's a bad rule of thumb.

During those years, the early sixties, when you were studying English and French at Melbourne University, did you feel in some way intimidated by the intellectuals you encountered?

---

3 The influence of British literary critic F. R. Leavis and his journal *Scrutiny* was marked in both the Melbourne University and subsequently the Sydney University English departments in the late 1950s and early 1960s. Leavis's ideas were characterised by a dogmatic ranking of 'great writers', with D. H. Lawrence at the top of his contemporary list, partly based on the estimation of a writer's moral worth, an admiration for pre-industrial societies, an anti-theoretical bias and a preoccupation with metaphysical subjects. His most influential works were *The Great Tradition* (1948) and *The Common Pursuit* (1952).

I was terrified at university. I was terrified of the sorts of people I met there. In fact, I remember the first tutorial I ever went to: the most striking student present was the extremely well-read and opinionated young Patrick McCaughey[4] wearing a hand-knitted, daffodil-yellow sweater and beanie — and this was terrifying. You see, as I said, I was Miss Clever Clogs from a rather minor school in an even more provincial town than Melbourne. When I got to the university I was aghast at how ignorant I was and how ill-equipped I was to deal with tutorials. The very idea of tutorials filled me with such dismay that I basically wagged them for years. In fact, I was lucky to crawl out the other end with a degree at all. Actually, a rather disobliging Melbourne University academic once said to me, 'Oh, I enjoyed such-and-such a book of yours very much. I vaguely remember you at university, so I wondered if you were headed in that direction when you were there. I went back and looked at your thesis. There was no sign of it at all.' I was rather stunned by this, but I'm sure she was absolutely right.

What was the thesis on?

I'm not even going to tell you.

Do you think that as a defence against intellectualism of the kind you found intimidating you started to value and to develop some other side to yourself? And if so what would be a good word to describe it?

Contact with people is terribly important to me — the more direct the better. As I get older (and I'm now 54) I notice that I've become one of those middle-aged old ducks who try to strike up conversations with strangers. In fact, this becomes more and more fascinating to me as I get older: I sit next to someone on a bus and immediately I'm dying to talk to them — or not so much to talk to them, but to ask them things. I want them to tell me about their life, how things seem to them, what

---

4 During the 1980s, the flamboyant McCaughey was the Director of the National Gallery of Victoria. He then moved on to the Wadsworth Atheneum at Hartford, Conn., at the same time holding a Visiting Professorship at Harvard. He is now Director of the Yale Centre for British Art at New Haven, Conn.

they make of things. And I've noticed that while older people respond willingly, young people are very guarded against this sort of approach. They think, 'Oh who's this batty old thing?'. It's so disappointing.

And do you like these people in buses to tell you stories?

Not so much stories, I suppose, as personal testimony. Perhaps 'testimony' has too legal a ring to it — I like people to say 'I', I like to say 'I' myself. In other words, I'm most comfortable with people speaking directly about their own experience. It's generalising that makes me anxious (and this is part of my intellectual anxiety as well), although as you get older you feel more confident, I think, about generalising from your own experience. Otherwise, you'd be trapped inside some kind of narcissism. For example, when I said to Ramona Koval that I didn't like talking about my religious beliefs because it always seems so intellectual, the word I would underline would be 'beliefs': it fascinates me to converse with people about their religious experience, but as soon as you start talking about beliefs, the 'I' goes out of it — well, not necessarily, I suppose, but things start to get nailed down.

I'll never forget once driving through a country town in Victoria, and stopping to stretch my legs in a park. There was some sort of religious festival going on in the park and there was a sign up saying, 'It's not enough to do good or to be a nice person to get into heaven, you must believe' — and then there was a list of six points you had to believe in. I was deeply enraged by that sign. And I've never forgotten it.

Interestingly enough, in your famous piece in Cosmo Cosmolino *about visiting the crematorium, what stays with the reader, and what presumably stayed with you, is the perception you had at a particular moment which altered the way you saw the world — and the self.[5] It's the record of a*

5 Garner actually first described watching a cremation in an article entitled 'Death', published in the *Age* in August 1986 and republished in *True Stories* (Text Publishing, 1996). However, it was the description in the novel *Cosmo Cosmolino* (McPhee Gribble, 1992) in a chapter entitled 'A Vigil' which captured the public imagination. This novel is important in any consideration of Garner's role as a thinker and of the meaning of the word 'ideas' in her work, in the sense that, as Kerryn Goldsworthy puts it in *Helen Garner* (p. 1), it brought the old labels of stylist, realist and feminist 'slightly unstuck'.

moment, an actual experience that mattered to you and which you wanted to pass on to us that makes the writing so powerful, not any sense that you were exploring a set of beliefs through your writing. On the basis of Cosmo Cosmolino *we might presume that you think about religious ideas quite a lot — what is true and what is not true, for example — when you're shopping, sitting at home or on a bus.*

Oh yes, I do, a lot.

Isn't this vaguely embarrassing in the kind of world that you live in?

Yes, it is. In fact, it's so embarrassing that when *Cosmo Cosmolino* came out a few years ago, the response to it unnerved me a great deal. Doing the publicity for it, trying to discuss what I thought I was doing in it, had a very bad effect on me. I felt that by speaking publicly in the way you have to in those situations, across a table with a stranger, I somehow lost the lively contact that I'd had with the deep things I'd experienced and from which that book actually sprang. I remember being at the Adelaide Festival that year, doing publicity for the book, sitting in my hotel room and having a feeling of the most appalling desolation, and thinking that the exterior work that I was having to do to introduce this book to the world had actually separated me in a very painful and desolate way from what the book was about. And I've never really re-established that connection. It's only in saying this to you now that I realise that I hadn't even articulated it to myself before. In a sense, that's the trouble with relying so much on experience in my writing. Maybe it can't be kept alive. Maybe, as time passes, *things* turn into ideas. Perhaps that's why memory is such a strange thing, and everything turns a bit dry and thin and mental. Every now and then, though, a certain smell, say, might come back to you, bringing with it a tremendous rush of sense memory.

The mental — that thin, high little note of the mental — seems to sail away on the top of the great sounding depths of murky, rich, purple and red experience. And that's what I'm always trying to get down to.

You're on record as saying you think of yourself as a Christian but they probably wouldn't let you in. Would you still put it like that?

Oh, I think some of them would let me in all right, although now I wouldn't be so interested in choosing the word 'Christian'. At a time in my life when some might consider I was having a nervous breakdown, the only thing that I could find to help me which had a form I could make use of was the Christian ritual of communion. I still feel very strongly about that, it still means an enormous amount to me. A friend of mine once said he'd crawl over broken glass to get to the table, and I've certainly felt like that at times. It's still there as an enormous resource for me — the fact that you can crawl to the table and be given something to eat and something to drink, and you can be blessed. That's the core of it for me.

What do you mean by being 'blessed'?

It's a word with godly connotations, but one of the most telling uses of it for me was in something the cellist Pablo Casals once said: every morning when he gets up he goes to the piano and plays a little piece of Bach and it acts as a blessing on the house. Why is Bach the obvious choice? There's the formal immensity of his music, of course, but there's also something magisterial and impersonal about it. In Mozart's music, I suppose what you also feel is the frolicsome nature of his person. But clearly the idea of blessing has also got something to do with fathers. I remember when I was reading the Bible from front to back, in one of the books in the apocrypha, I was struck by the story of a young woman who leaves home to go out into the great wide world, and her father blesses her and says, 'Go out into the world now and let me hear nothing but good of you all the days of your life'. And when I read that kind of thing I feel like howling. I don't know why it touches me so deeply, but then, to understand that, I'd have to go into my family history.

You said that at one point in your life (between Postcards From Surfers *[1985] and* Cosmo Cosmolino, *I take it) some might consider you were having a nervous breakdown. Why did you choose that word?*

I mentioned that word because it came up in a review of Kerryn Goldsworthy's book about my work. (Scott Fitzgerald might have used the word 'crack-up'[6] — I'm a great fan of Scott Fitzgerald.) I'd never thought I'd 'had a nervous breakdown' until I read a review by Peter Craven in which he discussed things I'd written in the period of my life leading up to the writing of *Cosmo Cosmolino*. It actually seems to me the clumsiest of all my books, the one where I was least in control of the material. It's like a gawky, ugly child, which is why I've got a special tenderness for it. Of all my books it's the one that seems to disconcert people the most. The people who like that book are the people who aren't embarrassed by the idea that there might be something more than this world. And there aren't as many of those around as I thought.

In *Cosmo Cosmolino* I gave the main character, Janet, experiences I'd had myself. At a certain point in my life I experienced the presence of a strange being which came and stood by me, right in the room I was in. Now, I never turned around and saw this thing, I don't know what it looked like, and I don't know if there was anything there that could have been seen by the human eye, but this experience had a very, very powerful effect on me. Now most people, I suppose, given the nature of our culture, would say, 'Oh, you were having a crack-up'. People around me to whom I dared to mention this thing, looked frightened — frightened of what was happening to me, not frightened of the thing. And one critic at least has described this sort of being as something out of a vulgar schlock-horror movie[7]. It was a reaction which surprised me at the time. Those things are so hard to write about, especially when you have a history as a realist and all your writing has been realist, representational or naturalistic, concentrating on relations between people and the physical world, things seen and experienced by the senses.

✧

---

6 F. Scott Fitzgerald has a short story called 'The Crack-up' in a collection of short stories of the same name and edited by Edmund Wilson (1945, new edition 1993).

7 Jenna Mead, describing the apparition in *Cosmo Cosmolino*: 'This shimmering phallus reads like something monstrously vulgar from schlock horror rather than any unsayable truth...' ('Politics, Patriarchy & Death', *Island*, no. 53, p. 67).

Although even Garner's most passionate opponents would agree that her writing has been influential in the creation of public opinion, especially on what might broadly be called feminist issues, in recent times, in the wake of the publication of The First Stone, *some commentators have spoken not only of betrayal, but have gone as far as to call Helen Garner a traitor. What was it she stood acccused of having betrayed?*

I think I'm seen as having betrayed young women, in particular, because I did not back them against a powerful institution. I let the side down — and it's definitely a team story. Yet there are a lot of people who *don't* think I've let the side down. As you can imagine, since *The First Stone* came out, I've lain awake at many a 3 a.m. Even now, almost two years later, there are times when I still feel deeply anguished about the whole matter. It disturbs me greatly that I've caused pain to people who have already been through a dreadful experience. Indeed, the whole experience — the alleged incidents, the court case, the writing of the book, the attempt to stop the book in the courts, the brouhaha that broke out when the book was finally published — it's all been highly traumatic for *everyone* concerned. Yet the anguish radiating out from the central night in question doesn't radiate out to the entire world. At a certain point, outside the epicentre, as it were, the anguish turns into a series of propositions that people can contemplate — calmly or emotionally, but without hatred and rage. And I cling to that.

I think that one thing that made some people very angry in the book was that it *didn't* take a side — it was actually hard to pin down my attitude towards the things I was writing about. That to me is one of the achievements of the book: I didn't set out to say, 'Right, roll up the sleeves, let's see who is the guilty one in this story'. I think that would be a grotesque way of approaching any story. But it does enrage people when you say, 'Wait a minute, let's look at it *this* way . . . And now what if we look at it *this* way? . . . Then again, there's *this* angle . . . ' Some people don't like that.

When you put it like that, you make it sound exactly in tune with the times — that sort of many-voiced writing is precisely what post-

modernism has given us permission to do. It seems paradoxical that many of the most ardent supporters of transgressive, polyphonic writing have been amongst your most ferocious opponents. Actually, one of the things that makes some people sceptical about your intellectual status is that you don't appear to have any kind of manifesto.

No, I don't. Nor do I feel any obligation to have one. I'm not a polemicist — that's not my job, nor is it the kind of person I am. What I am is a writer. Up until recently, I think I've thought of myself mostly as a fiction writer, but now, of course, that's changed. I don't exactly know where the hell I am at the moment in that regard. I'm repelled by the idea that I should have to have a manifesto. My usefulness, not to mention my enjoyment of life, would be severely compromised by any idea of having a manifesto. I hate that sort of thinking where you whack down a grid on top of whatever happens and try to force it into a shape that suits your beliefs.

In one of your public conversations you said: 'What makes you think I have a frozen position on this?'. It was a wonderful moment, because, as I remember, you were actually speaking at the time to someone who operates quite well in the world of frozen positions. After all, frozen positions make things easy for us: we know then what colour every- body's stripes are, what vocabulary to use — in other words, when people adopt frozen positions we know how power works in their world. It can be very unsettling if someone says to us, 'What makes you think I have one? What makes you think that in ten days time, or ten months time, let alone ten years time, I may not see things completely differently?'

That's one of the things that make me really sad about *The First Stone*, you see. I feel that I offered myself to the people who didn't want to speak to me — the two young women who brought the charges against the Master of Ormond College, for instance — in good faith. I think that because they had frozen positions they couldn't imagine that anyone could approach *them* in good faith — especially since I'd written a letter of sympathy to the man they were accusing. In fact, I'd have been very open to whatever they had to say. But I think they imagined I was simply going to use whatever they might say to me to bolster my own overarching, hostile views. Well, there's nothing I can do about that now, it's all too late. History has rolled on.

The First Stone, whether one applauds it or not, still stands, I think, as an intellectual act of great cultural significance. It was the kind of intellectual statement which said, 'This is how I reached the conclusions I did' — only one kind, but a valuable one. Kerryn Goldsworthy (who is not by any means uncritical of The First Stone*) makes this point about 'positions' in her survey of your work: 'From* Monkey Grip *onwards, Garner's work has been illuminating faultlines in feminist theory — the places where, in actually trying to manage their lives and their language, women must choose amongst conflicting theories and strategies ... Victim or agent? ... "Equality" feminism or "difference" feminism? Politics or the psyche?'[8] Are you happy with the word 'faultlines'?*

I love it. In my experience (and I'm sure in other people's as well) many things that happen in our lives hurt us deeply. And in order to move on and not become obsessed by the pain, I think we sometimes have to back up a cement-truck and pour a large amount of cement over whatever has caused pain. And then we can move on. Now, in middle age, looking back at those points in my experience, I see the concrete breaking up and the old pain seeping out of it. That's the sort of faultline I'm interested in: when the concrete breaks up — the concrete of the desire to avoid pain, that frozen concrete — what comes out through the cracks is very interesting to me indeed.

Kerryn Goldsworthy actually identifies what she thinks the two plates are which have drifted apart: 'social order and sexual desire, and the domestic spaces in which that tension is released or resolved'.[9] (An old theme, of course, very like the classical 'duty versus passion'.)

I think she's right. I have a very strong sense of order, I like shape and I like order. (So I can't bear the tropics, all those trees and creepers

---

8 *Helen Garner*, p.6.
9 Ibid., p. 29.

joined in one ghastly mass. The first time I ever visited the tropics and saw that, it deeply disturbed me — I prayed to be transported straight to Scotland. I like separate trees.) By the same token, when I look back over my life, I see that it's been the most appalling mess. Life has been a tremendous struggle between those two forces of order and the desire to smash things (or to smash things on the way out towards whatever it is that's desired).

You grew up in and wrote about an era when people were supposed to be able to explore their sexuality and their passions in a very free-ranging sort of way. Yet, as we grow older, it dawns on us that actually the world doesn't work very well if everyone behaves like that, and most people drift into an arrangement with much more fixed rules. Along the boundaries of that arrangement there's going to be tension. There's a wonderful sentence in Cosmo Cosmolino, *for example, where Janet says, just after the break-up, 'To see a couple of any age lean towards each other across a restaurant table caused Janet's stomach to fracture like an egg.' (It's quite a painful sentence to read.) Here fracture seems to come from the recognition that, although part of you might want to explore desire in many selves, another part of you wants something very established, old-fashioned and settled.*

Nowadays it distresses me when I hear about couples breaking up. 'Coupleness' is not just a matter of marriage or men and women, it's something much deeper. To me it's an image in the Jungian sense of the linking of the masculine and feminine principles inside us. I think the desire for the resolution of struggle, for the reuniting of things that have been parted by force, is very strong in us. The resolution is only fleeting, of course — it's like trying get a handle on the unconscious, you can only do it fleetingly. Perhaps it's more like a headland obscured by mist. Occasionally the mist blows away and you say, 'Oh! Now I get it!', and then whoosh! the mist is back, and you're searching for the headland again.

Jung is quite important to you, isn't he?

Well, he has been in the past, partly because, at the point of my famous nervous breakdown — and note that I'm only using that word as of today — I went to an analyst who was very much interested in Jung. I don't think he'd describe himself as a Jungian, but he had been strongly influenced by him. There's a lot of imagery in Jung which I've found gratifying and useful — ideas presenting themselves in an intensely useful way, helping me to make sense of what I experience. I greatly value them. (Perhaps this is my 'intellectual' side.)

You don't mention in your writing many other 'great thinkers' — creators of systems of thought. You might have a throw-away line about Camille Paglia, say, but you don't seem interested in guru figures.

No, I'm not looking for a guru. That might be because the sorts of people I admire don't have systems of thought. The people who are important to me as writers are more likely to be novelists or fiction writers — Chekhov, for example, who has a view of the world but not a system, or Janet Malcolm[10]. Perhaps I'm drawn to writers who are useful to me at a given moment in what I'm working on. What I really learnt from Janet Malcolm was to give full credence to the tiny incidents that occur between two people when they meet — she draws meaning from the way somebody cooks lasagna, for example. (If I hadn't read Janet Malcolm, I'd never have written that passage about the old man putting the lid back on the biscuit tin in *The First Stone*[11].)

You're talking here about a way of writing, a way of dealing with material, rather than the influence of a thought-system — and perhaps we've hit here upon one of the areas of confusion with regard to your writing. One of the problems your writing presents for the reader is actually contained in the title of your selected non-fiction book True Stories: *here truth (very much the domain of the intellectual) sits beside stories (which can be either 'true' or fictional, but are 'art'). I think what confuses your public to some extent is that in your non-fiction you still use fictional techniques*

---

10 Author of *The Silent Woman: Sylvia Plath and Ted Hughes* (with a new afterword, Picador, 1994).
11 p. 189.

— *your language, your constructions, your characterisation. So your readers aren't always sure of the contract they've signed with you.*

I know what you mean, but I'm still amazed. Where does the contract reside? What sort of dryness or dullness would make it trustworthy? Do people think, 'This is just too interesting, I can't trust this, the people in it seem like characters in a novel'? Perhaps it's an Australian thing — little of our non-fiction, until recently, has been known for its sparkle or its attractiveness as prose. And perhaps no one believes in such a thing as a true story any more.

The question of research certainly raises doubts. Non-fiction is researched. What you do is present us with a story which represents conclusions you may have come to gradually over a long period of time. The work you've done — the research, the scholarship, the reasoning — isn't obvious. The thinking and listening you've done aren't obvious on the page. What you write is in the now.

I recognise your description of my work. The now *is* where I'm comfortable. I'm no good with the then, and I'm even more hopeless with the future. The now is where I feel at ease.

My point is that some might accuse you of bad faith, either because they can't quite define what faith you wrote in, or because they've mistaken it for something else. To take an uncontentious example, in 'Three Acres' in True Stories, *the story about a woman alone in a house in the country, a long way from anywhere, you actually explore some quite difficult ideas about women alone, about the sense of threat a woman might feel in that situation, whether it's rational or irrational, how to react rationally to the things that happen to someone completely alone, miles from any-where — all sorts of quite complex and subtle things based on a lifetime's experience, conversations and observations, yet we can read it as a Chekovian short story — it even has a gun in it. It's difficult to work out what sort of 'true story' this is.*

All I can really say is that in general I don't sense this as a problem. What did strike me as a problem was people talking about *The First Stone* as a novel. People would say to me quite thoughtlessly, 'In your novel *The First Stone* . . .'. I even started coming across it in the fiction section of bookshops. The booksellers would explain that their customers always looked for me in the fiction section, but it unnerved me at the time because I saw it as the direct result of the announcement by one of the severest critics of *The First Stone* that I'd divided her character into six separate characters, which I had in fact done for legal reasons.[12] Perhaps she'd hoped that this would discredit the book's *veracity*. Now I suspect that people called it a novel less as a result of her revelation as of what you spoke about earlier: they weren't sure what the contract was.

In your non-fiction, in particular, you show a strong interest in the relationship between individuals and institutions — well, your career in some ways started with a fraught relationship of that kind at Fitzroy High. The First Stone *comes immediately to mind, of course,* True Stories *opens and closes with a piece about hospitals, and then there are the morgues and crematoria, marriages, even the cruise ship in 'Cruising'. . .*

I adore hospitals. There's an enormous amount of both eros and *thanatos* in hospitals. (And I always enjoyed reading about the hospitals in Elizabeth Jolley's writing.) You see, the institution gives a frame to everything. I doubt I'd be as interested in watching a home birth (especially one that went well) as I was in watching the birth of twins at Penrith Hospital, which I've described in 'Labour Ward, Penrith' in *True Stories* — that was a thunderous experience for me. Perhaps the bursting through of a grid is what can happen in an institution, as at the crematorium. There was this square box with a human body in it, with everything controlled by the squareness and the block shapes, but what happened was that a bomb of life and glory went off in me inside that square room, where I'd expected to find control and an ending.

---

12 Presumably a reference to Jenna Mead. Mead's fullest account of the Ormond College affair and her reactions to *The First Stone* can be found in her essay in *Bodyjamming* (Vintage, 1997).

The institutions I'm drawn to are obviously the ones where extreme things happen. In the same way, popular culture is drawn to police and detectives. In police stations people go through extreme experiences, there's chaos and wild, driven human behaviour, and the police are the people through whom society attempts to regulate and resolve chaotic behaviours. So everyone loves detectives — there's actually an 'eros of the detective', I think.

Let's talk for a moment about eros. You've called it 'the spark that ignites and connects' (in the Jungian phrase), and it's characterised your writing ever since Monkey Grip. *You've also spoken about how eros can move through the intellect while not being itself intellectual[13]. Now eros might fear being choked by intellect, fear the loss of its particular kind of magic to intellect . . .*

That's true. But I don't think that intellectual writing kills that spark, the current running between writer and reader — and whoever is being written about as well. I think the best kind of intellectual writing nourishes it. Just off the top of my head: George Steiner. Now, his arguments are often difficult, yet there's always that sense in his writing of a sort of simmering liveliness, so that you come away from reading something of his feeling enlivened. This gets back to what I said earlier about books that take away energy and books that give it.

One thing, though, that you'd have to say about George Steiner is that he's certainly no amateur. In some (quite positive) sense of the word, it seems to me that your kind of intellect is an amateur intellect.

Yes, I think that's true. I'm not 'a thinker' in the sense that Steiner is. I mean, obviously my work involves thinking, but thinking of that deeply intellectual kind is not my skill. My major skill is picking up the vibe of a given situation. It's the vibe that's the most important and valuable thing about it to me. Another word for it might be the erotic charge — 'erotic' in the broadest sense, of course. It's not issues

---

13 Garner discusses these ideas in 'The Fate of *The First Stone*' in *True Stories* (pp 173–74).

as such that interest me — take race and gender, for example. I was looking at 'The Muppets' last week and the two little piglets came in, and somebody asked them a difficult question, and one of them said to the other, 'I didn't know there was going to be a test'. And as soon as I hear the word 'race' or 'gender' come out of my mouth, I start getting that breaking-out-in-a-sweat feeling that there's going to be a test, and I'm going to fail it.

What do you expect of a public intellectual?

The first thing that comes to mind is that a public intellectual ought to be able to write in such a way that you want to read what they say, and that's actually very rare. Perhaps that's just my cast of mind, my desire to listen to stories rather than arguments. But it's wonderful to be gripped by something as *writing*. And a public intellectual, as I see it, not only grips you in some deep way, but spins you around, spins around the way you look at the world or your immediate environment so that you get a different fix on it.

✧

Kerryn Goldsworthy, a lecturer in English at the University of Melbourne for many years and author of the illuminating short critical monograph on Garner's work in the Oxford Australian Writers series, knows both Garner and her work very well. I asked her how resistant she thought Helen Garner was to the realm of the intellect and its institutions.

Kerryn Goldsworthy

The impression I get from the things Garner has said in interviews and her own writing is that she trusts her instincts more than her intellect, and that she trusts the realm of the instinctive even more more as she gets older. There's overwhelming pressure to define things in terms of binaries, so she talks about trusting her instincts as if that were somehow in opposition to trusting her intellect.

Ideally, I think, you refuse to see those things as being in opposition to each other, using them instead to inform each other. And, in fact, I think Helen often does that, particularly in her non-fiction on public issues — you can see it in a lot of the pieces in *True Stories*. Some of her best writing, I would say, grows out of moments where she brings her intelligence to bear on something that she's felt instinctively.

Given this mix, can we still speak of Helen Garner as an intellectual?

Helen has a mediating function which is crucial in a public intellectual. I mean by that the function of transmitting ideas, making them available, making them comprehensible to large numbers of people. In that respect I think Helen has a very important role to play.

She certainly has a very good nose for which issues are worrying the public, often at a not very clearly articulated level, issues she can cast quite a penetrating light on.

Yes, and some of them, the most memorable pieces of this kind (including *The First Stone*), have been about public institutions — schools (State and private), hospitals, the morgue and so on. She's very good at dancing around among the private human moments that happen in those places and the wider public issues, including why those institutions are there and who administers them.

Why does Helen Garner 'ideologically madden people', as you once put it?

Because she refuses to line up. She makes people uneasy. And it's partly because so many people felt so strongly and positively about her earlier work that they felt betrayed when she stopped toeing the party line. You know, there was a Michael Leunig cartoon in the *Age* not long ago about problems with child care, which seemed to be blaming women. One letter to the editor said something like, 'Does this mean I'm not allowed to like him any more?'. Well, I think that was the reaction of huge numbers of women who had loved Garner's work, regarding her as ideologically on-side, and then suddenly felt completely betrayed by the fact that here she was obviously not toeing the party line. Righteous indignation is a drug, and it's a great deal easier to become indignant than it is to sit down and ask yourself why you're reacting the way you are.

One of the points you make in your book is the difficulty we might have in describing Garner's style as 'intellectual', and it's partly because, as you say, the thought processes are hidden.

Yes, people miss them. Because she was for so long an avowed minimalist, her art consisted largely in leaving things out. Care has to be taken in negotiating the gaps. Helen Garner is one of those writers who, insofar as she writes about ideas, does not take the easy way out. Margaret Drabble, for instance, seems to me to be more and more simply creating characters who talk about ideas — that's what I mean by the 'easy way out'. Garner, on the other hand, will take the single issue, the single image, as paradigmatic of something broader that's going on, writing about the issue or image in an almost plastic way. Her approach to the representation of ideas is oblique, in other words, rather than straightforward. For example, even in her non-fiction, there's a really strong sense of the numinousness of the physical world. An object or place will be invested with huge significance of some kind, or the suggestion will be made that this significance exists. And, of course, that significance is going to be related to ideas — religious, political, whatever. Garner's one of those writers who make the reader do a great deal of work. She won't take your hand and lead you through logical processes — in fact, she's not very interested in logic, as she's said. Or she wasn't when she said it!

Doesn't Garner also shy away from recognising any chasm between the techniques of fiction and the techniques of non-fiction? In the slightly murky area where artist and thinker overlap, the matrix of ideas she writes out of is turned into both fiction and highly crafted non-fiction. This seems to cause problems in interpretation for some readers.

That's right. In Garner's work, when it comes down to hard-line questions about what's true and what isn't, many readers experience difficulties. That was one of the things about *The First Stone* that got her into most trouble. *The First Stone* was the story of Garner's reactions, step by step, to what she encountered in investigating the events at Ormond College. People tended to misread it as a straightforward statement of her position, whereas in fact in one paragraph she'll write 'I felt this', and in the next paragraph she'll examine her reaction and say what was wrong with it. She was pilloried for having said 'I felt this' in the first place, as if that was a fixed position.

✧

A long-time friend of Helen Garner's is the writer Drusilla Modjeska, author of Poppy *[1990],* The Orchard *[1994] and co-author of* Secrets *[1997]. Modjeska by no means accepts Garner's dismissal of her intellectual status.*

Drusilla Modjeska

Helen wouldn't call herself an intellectual, she *demurs* from the title. Now, why is that? In the canonical sense of 'intellectual', I can quite understand it — very few women would claim to be 'intellectuals' in that sense. Yet right from the start, from *Monkey Grip* onwards, in both her fiction and non-fiction, the questions that have interested her are questions of how one lives — primarily as a woman, but not only as a woman. Helen asks broad questions that engage us all about how we live our daily lives — our ethics, our priorities and how we arrive at them, and how we incorporate them into our feelings, how we make sense of them in relation to our lovers, our children, even the meals we eat. She's always opened that area up in her fiction, but there's been no master narrative saying 'This is the answer'. It's been much looser than that, with a nuanced texture of character, situations and images which allow for a range of different answers. It's her images, stories, characters and narratives which require us to think about the issues.

In that way Helen could be said to be in an intellectual tradition. People like Virginia Woolf, Doris Lessing and Dorothy Richardson[14] all asked those kinds of questions — as did many others in the nineteenth century — but for women to ask these questions was not enough to earn the label of 'intellectual', although Virginia Woolf might be the exception. As she herself would have said, they didn't speak Greek — her shorthand for explaining why women were outside those canonical discourses termed 'intellectual'. Yet they've all profoundly influenced the way in which people conceive of their lives, and conceive of the kinds of issues and questions which need to be confronted.

I think that part of the problem with *The First Stone*, for example, arose out of a confusion of traditions: although readers had become used to a non-master narrative from Helen (an open text, one which took in feeling and dealt with it in a myriad of complex, crystalline ways), *The First Stone* was read as a master narrative, as a narrative which gave 'the answer'.

Now, this was quite a misreading of the book, in my view. Seeing it as simply 'journalism' or 'non-fiction' gave rise to a whole lot of expectations based on a different discourse around intellectuality. Given this clash between two ways of thinking about the intellectual, I'm not at all surprised that Helen demurs from the term, which is an alien, master-narrative one. In other words, I think she was writing in one tradition and being read in another, even though (or perhaps because) she was one of a number of writers — Elizabeth Jolley, Jessica Anderson and Thea Astley, for example — who had turned Australian writing around so that more open forms of writing had become respected and, indeed, loved.

It's also worth remembering in connection with *The First Stone* that Helen comes out of the seventies (as I do), and one of the axiomatic positions she shares with people formed in that period is an anarchist position — personal empowerment, suspicion of the State

---

14 Dorothy Richardson (1873–1957), now less well known than Woolf or Lessing, was a modernist novelist particularly noted for her sequence of stream-of-consciousness novels entitled *Pilgrimage* (1915–38). See also *Journey to Paradise: Short stories and autobiographical sketches of Dorothy Richardson* (Vintage, 1989).

and a deep-seated antagonism to any notion that personal life can be regulated. 'Not the Church and not the State' — you'll remember those old slogans we grew up with. Those attitudes are deeply embedded in her thinking and come out in *The First Stone*.

Yet she was addressing a world from which that particular discourse has largely disappeared. Nowadays it's all a matter of rights — whose rights, your rights versus my rights, his versus her rights — the whole public discourse now is rights-based. One of the things *The First Stone* was doing was battling with the new way of framing the personal in relation to the public. A clash was inevitable.

The
Historians

Henry Reynolds

John Hirst

Jill Julius Matthews

Greg Dening

‘An historian must interpret the past,

and, in terms of being a public intellectual,

it helps to be writing the past of your own society.

If you're writing the histories of distant societies

a long time ago, it's obviously less easy to

contribute directly to ongoing public debates.’

Henry Reynolds

O NE OF THE MOST FIERCELY CONTESTED AREAS *in Australian intellectual life is history — the teaching of history, the question of hidden histories, the theoretical debates about the retelling of histories, the epistemological problems of what can be known and what can't.*

The Tasmanian writer and historian Cassandra Pybus, for example, has lamented the virtual disappearance of history as a major high-school subject, claiming that 'history has been robbed of its stories[1], while Keith Windschuttle, in a book both lavishly praised and roundly condemned, has accused the cultural theorists of nothing short of the murder of history[2]. On the other hand, the Civics Education Group under the chairmanship of John Hirst has recently been set up at a Federal level to systematise the teaching of basic Australian history in Australian schools. And certain historians, if not the subject they teach, continue to play a prominent role in the country's intellectual debates — one need only think of the almost iconic status achieved by Professor Manning Clark, and the continuing ferocious battles over the question of his political judgment. Clearly more is at stake than the political probity of one respected historian[3].

All the same, historians seem less visible on the public intellectual stage than they once did. They're there, of course, shaping the way we think about ourselves, but they're no longer quite the storytellers to their tribe they once were — perhaps, as Cassandra Pybus has suggested, because so many of them have stopped telling stories, anxious about what they might be implying about 'the truth'. Consequently, the tribe doesn't seem so interested in gathering around them to hear what they have to say.

Modern thought has been circling suspiciously for decades around the question of truth: how knowable is it, can it ever be objectively communicated, and what power games might we be playing when we choose our words to describe what we think the truth is? These are

---

1 In the sixth program of the original Radio National series, 'Re-thinking Australia: Intellectuals and the public culture'.

2 *The Killing of History: How a discipline is being murdered by literary critics and social theorists* (Macleay Press, 1994; revised edition, Free Press, 1997).

3 Two of the clearest statements of the opposing views on Clark and his politics are given by Robert Manne and historian Humphrey McQueen, to be found in Manne's 'Christ and Lenin' in the *Australian's Review of Books*, October 1996, and 'Battle for history's high ground' in the *Weekend Australian*, 7–8 June 1997, and in McQueen's *Suspect History: Manning Clark and the future of Australia's past* (Wakefield Press, 1997). The first volley, however, had been fired by Peter Ryan in *Quadrant* in September 1993.

questions of no small consequence to historians as they take up their pens. They can make it difficult for some historians ever to get around to telling any stories at all.

Whatever theoretical position an individual historian adopts, however, few historians would deny that there is a difference between the writing of history and the writing of fiction. At some level the notion that history's stories are 'true', whatever the gaps in the record and however those gaps are filled in, remains in force.

For some historians, one way out of the dilemma about truth is to strive to establish some kind of moral truth as they sift through evidence from the past, rather than a more elusive objective truth. This has been particularly true of the rewriting of the history of settlement in Australia. Here the question of how Australians should now think or act seems to hover over almost all their deliberations, whatever their notions of truth — indeed, the historian's role as moralist has become almost paramount[4].

The most prominent historian in this field is doubtless Professor Henry Reynolds of James Cook University in Townsville, the author of a series of books on the impact of white settlement on the indigenous population[5], and one of the writers, together with Professor Marcia Langton, of the highly confronting ABC Television series 'Frontier'[6]. Henry Reynolds is certainly engaged in the project of sifting through documents to establish the real story of white settlement in Australia. In this sense, at least, he's an old historian rather than a new historian, and his determination to intervene in our history has changed the story of Australia, the very course of our history. The moral imperative to do something first made itself felt when Henry Reynolds moved to North Queensland many years ago.

---

4 Professor John Mulvaney exemplifies this view of the historian's moral role. In *Prehistory and Heritage: The writings of John Mulvaney* (Department of History, Australian National University, 1990) he argues vehemently in favour of the 'moral and ethical need for [historians] to take some public role', as in campaigns for the preservation of cultural heritage, as opposed to an interest in public history motivated by economic necessity. An excellent and detailed picture of Mulvaney's contribution both to the discipline of history and to public debate is to be found in *Prehistory to Politics: John Mulvaney, the humanities and the public intellectual*, edited by Tim Bonyhady and Tom Griffiths (Melbourne University Press, 1996).
5 These books include *The Other Side of the Frontier: Aboriginal resistance to the European invasion of Australia* (Penguin, 1990), *The Law of the Land* (Penguin, 1992), *Frontier: Aborigines, settlers and land* (Allen & Unwin, 1987) and *Aboriginal Sovereignty: Reflections on race, state and nation* (Allen & Unwin, 1997).
6 First broadcast in March 1997 and available on video.

Henry Reynolds

Almost on a daily basis I saw indigenous and settler Australians meeting in every possible way, from the inspiring to the horrifying. So I was always keenly aware that my historical research should interact with my present, day-to-day experience. There was never a time when I lacked the sense that what I was doing as an historian had profound relevance to the contemporary scene.

One step on from that was the writing of *The Other Side of the Frontier,* my first book of any consequence, which seems to have had a powerful impact on many people. What I was trying to do was to change two generations of forgetfulness. After ten years of research, shuttling back and forth between the European and Aboriginal sides, I wondered if I could write history from the Aboriginal point of view. Over the years small bits of evidence had been building up, and it seemed to me that I probably now had the material to write it. It's still in print and still read.

Subsequently, the area where I have had the most direct input into contemporary life and change — into politics — has been in the two court cases, Mabo and Wik. That's because in *The Law of the Land* I was able to present to an Australian audience a great deal of material about the law, which was little studied in Australia. (I actually had no legal training — I taught myself the law. I just sat down in the library of the High Court in Canberra for months and months reading. I read every case over and over again until I felt I understood native title and land law.)

In another more direct way, I suppose I had an important influence on the Mabo case, in the very early days, in that I was the person who explained to Eddie Mabo that he didn't own his land, which he had never realised. I also told him about the famous court cases of the 1820s and 1830s in the United States that had dealt with native title, and I can remember telling him I thought he had a real chance of mounting a case. So I felt very personally involved with the Mabo judgment — and probably even more directly so with the Wik case. That's because the basic historical foundation for the judgment came out of work that I'd done over about a five-year period.

The point is that I taught myself enough about the law to be able to write for lawyers — the lawyers realised that I knew what I was talking about. But I wrote about it in a different way, a new way in Australia, I think, as an historian with a political position. The way my work is impinging on the law has, I think, been as significant as either the recovery of the story of conflict and violence or the endeavour to make it possible for white Australians to begin to understand and empathise with Aboriginal Australia.

The question of how interventionist a public historian should be obviously has no single answer. However, for an historian such as yourself, as for any public intellectual, the extent to which you should be calling for action on a reconceptualisation of Australia presumably needs constant serious consideration.

I suppose I intervene politically in the sense that I get involved in day-to-day politics by speaking on the radio, appearing on television and writing articles for newspapers. Those interventions are often connected, quite obviously, with my historical work — in a sense they gain authority from my profession as an historian. All the same, I think I understand the difference between propaganda and history, partly because I have written some propaganda, so I know what it is. So, while my profession as an historian is clearly intensely political, I think, I also work within a discipline which has its own rules and traditions. It's essential, for example, for an historian to strive to be dispassionate, to be fair to all sides in a way I'm less inclined to be when I'm dealing with contemporary issues as more than just an historian.

How ideological can an historian afford to be? If someone is known to be a Marxist historian or Catholic historian — linked, in other words, to an established ideology — how might this affect our attitude to his or her work?

It's an important question. In the past I'd have seen myself as partly Marxist — I came out of the secular, Left-wing Marxist tradition. I've moved away from that, although that tradition has still given the basic shape to my understanding of how societies work and change. For example, I still think the material foundations of a society have to be assessed in order to understand that society's ideas, although not in the mechanical way in which Marxists used to think.

Yet you are trying to change society through ideas.

Well, you have to be realistic about the influence of your ideas. I'm aware of how slowly people's ideas change and of the limited impact that ideas alone can have, and especially the limited impact that changing language alone can have. Still, having said that, I've been closely involved with the two profoundly important court cases of Mabo and Wik, and in the area of the law, it's obviously possible to bring about dramatic change through ideas. So, although I might begin from a materialist point of view, I clearly wouldn't spend my time talking, writing and advocating unless I thought that without revolution change was still possible.

The evidence for public interest in history sometimes seems contradictory: on the one hand the subject is far less popular in our schools and universities than it once was, while on the other hand the public passion for stories about the past, for restoring and preserving buildings and artefacts from the past, seems to be growing.

It's a strange situation in a way. Historians and other academics feel that no one is listening to them and that it must have been much better in the past. I don't think that's the case. I think there's a passionate concern about the past in Australian society. Even if history is not flourishing in the schools, there's still a strong feeling that the past is important in its many, many forms — in terms not just of ideas, but of a heritage, of buildings, of our ancestors, our families. For instance, much of the debate about Australia's position in the world, as well as about Australia's relationship to its indigenous people, is carried on in historical terms. In fact, I suspect that it is in the nature of New World settler societies not to take the past for granted as much as older societies, in Europe and other parts of the world, tend to do. Settler societies have to be constantly thinking about where they've come from and where they're going. The idea that they're only interested in the future has always been a misconception, especially about Australia.

In fact, there's a deep anxiety about the past in Australia and I think it's growing. There's a malaise about the nation, about the blocks constituting society in many parts of the world — in North America, of course, but also in Europe. The end of the Cold War has allowed some of these issues to rise to the surface again. Australia began this century with the idea of the nation and the idea of the State fused together. It was seen as a British nation and the nation and the State fitted together. Policy was designed to make sure that continued, so people who weren't at the very least Northern European were kept out. But since the nineteenth century and throughout the twentieth century, there's been a growing consciousness that each State contained within it peoples with different traditions, languages and historical memories — different nations, in other words. (There are a few exceptions — Iceland, mainland Denmark, Portugal — where nation and State fit neatly together.) In Australia there's still confusion about nation and State: the two ideas were welded together at the beginning of this century and we haven't learnt to deal with them separately.

I think there are basically three nations within the Australian State: the Aboriginal nation, the Torres Strait Islander nation and the mainstream nation. Immigrants belong either to the mainstream nation or to their nation of origin — I don't think immigrant communities have the same claim on separate nationhood as do indigenous peoples who had Australia thrust upon them. In North America it's accepted that there are First Nations, and I think that's a useful way to understand the situation. There are now about 200 States in the world (there were only about 50 at the end of World War Two) and about 5000 nations, but, for the time being, I think there's a belief that small nations will have to find a way of accommodating themselves to their existing States, unless they can demonstrate to the international community that they are profoundly oppressed and able to secede. It's a global question, not just an Australian one[7].

---

7 Henry Reynolds discusses these questions in detail in *Aborginal Sovereignty*.

It's actually impossible to understand any of the significant issues faced by Australians today without an understanding of our history. It's hard to think of any issue at all that doesn't have a history which needs to be understood — obviously that's the case with Aboriginal affairs, but it's also the case with the constitution and even, I would suggest, economic policy. On that question, for example, despite their current dominance, economists largely come out of schools of economics offering virtually no economic history. So our economists actually know very little about the history, not only of their own discipline, but of economic policy in Australia.

But history is important in even more critical ways, I think. In my view Australian democracy is powerfully and deeply part of Australian society, but predominantly because it's rooted in the habits of people, and I'm not sure that will be enough to protect it in the future. Knowing so little about the origins and the history of Australian politics, we're in real danger. The study of history, I believe, should be central to the education of society. I've come more and more to feel that we can't take our future as a democratic society for granted, and I think it's essential we understand the European roots of democratic traditions and the history of those ideas in Australia. I think we'll need that understanding more and more as we come into contact with societies that don't share many of those assumptions.

❖

John Hirst is another very public historian working in a broad field, determining what is distinctive about Australia, what its defining characteristics are and where they come from. (If you want to be a public historian, you probably have to work to some extent in a broad field.) John Hirst is also chairman of the Federal Government's Civics Education Group, as well being Convenor of the Victorian Branch of the Australian Republican Movement[8].

As an historian (he is Reader in History at La Trobe University) John Hirst has no problem with the notion of establishing 'what really happened', and letting the public know what it was.

---

8 Hirst's book on the republic is *A Republican Manifesto* (OUP, 1994).

John Hirst

The historian's task, as I see it, is to understand Australian society, what sort of place this is, what its defining characteristics are, how it's come to be as it is. Sometimes people lose touch with that. Specialism has, in some ways, overwhelmed the discipline, and people forget what the larger project is. But it's in that larger project that I want to come to rest.

To carry out that task you'd have to believe that certain things about the past are discoverable as objective facts.

Yes, I do believe that what really happened can be established. Of course, it's an ideal to be approached, but I don't want to give up that ideal and enter the modern hall of mirrors, where so many historians find themselves today. That just seems to me a totally unproductive way to approach history. So many historians nowadays, as well as many others in the humanities generally, are concerned with questions of how we know anything, with language and how it's constructed, and I think you can become a prisoner of that way of thinking, you can become very inward looking, just circling around in your own uncertainties. In that way I am old-fashioned, and I still think of my job as historian much in the sense of establishing what really happened.

You are, all the same, deeply interested in language — in the way in which, by choosing one word rather than another, an historian can cast a particular and different light on both the present and the past. Indeed, you 'interrogate' certain words (as a cultural theorist might put it) in a completely contemporary way, with an eye out for whose interests or ideology a given interpretation might serve — words like 'tyranny', 'discovery', 'civilisation' and 'multiculturalism'.

One of my responses to the new theorists is to point out that historians have always been interested in language, that it is not true that we've been mere transcribers of the words used in the past. One way we trace cultural change is to be alert to the changes in the meanings of words, and when a new word appears, we ask who has created it and what uses it might be put to. I think we've always done that. To that extent I suppose I'm on side with modern theorists.

I like not only to argue about the uses certain words have been put to, but also to rescue certain words from misuse. Take 'multiculturalism', for example[9]. At first I was an opponent of 'multiculturalism', thinking it not a particularly useful word — I didn't think it was true to its own project. If you look at official statements about what multiculturalism is, for example, they generally include some statement about there being 'an overriding allegiance to Australia and its values'. Yet the word 'multiculturalism' itself doesn't reflect any of that — it only reflects diversity, the sort of diversity that will continue indefinitely. In fact, some multiculturalists speak as if it should be part of government policy to keep the Greeks Greek. What's actually happening on the ground, of course, is very different from that notion of multiculturalism. In reality, there's a lot of intermixing and intermarrying as well as a strong attachment amongst the various migrant groups to Australia. As far as I'm concerned, the problem is not what is happening, but the word that we've hit upon to describe it — 'multiculturalism'. It's a word that puts lots of peoples' backs up — it put my back up for a while, until I accepted the fact that most people now take 'multiculturalism' to mean something like 'tolerance for ethnic diversity', a sort of new name for the old Australian 'fair go'.

'Overlooking difference' is your particular way of putting it.

Overlooking difference, yes, not insisting on conformity, while not expecting difference to be paraded, either. Needless to say, many people find this habit of overlooking difference a distressing one, suspecting that Australians dislike openly discussing and confronting difficult issues, preferring to glide over and fudge them. My own view is that in this huge project we've undertaken since World War II, it's an attitude that has in fact served us well.

---

9 Hirst's views on multiculturalism are summarised in 'Australia's Absurd History: A critique on multiculturalism' (*Quadrant,* March 1991) and 'National Pride and Multiculturalism' (*Quadrant,* November 1994).

The sort of society you seem to be in favour of is one in which certain core values are taken to be accepted by everybody, and differences in interpretation or in belief or value systems are politely overlooked — so long as they don't cause violent social disruption.

I don't think I would want to live in quite as bland a society as that. In some ways I think there's a temptation to tread too warily as it is. As an intellectual I'm all for critical debate about key issues — on some issues I don't think we have enough debate at the moment: multiculturalism or the position of Aborigines in this society, for example.

Perhaps we're not impious enough for your taste. You yourself can be quite impious in the way you write on certain subjects — Aboriginal issues come to mind, and especially the question of how indigenous Australians lived before white settlement[10].

Yes, I think there's a sort of Romanticism around about traditional Aboriginal society. I don't think the claim that the Aborigines have against Australian society now has to rest at all on what traditional Aboriginal society was like before 1788. Yet some people, in order to press that claim, talk of them as Romantic savages. Textbooks have actually been edited in recent times, for example, to remove references to intertribal violence, initiation ceremonies and the practice of sorcery. Well, I think that's unnecessary.

On the other hand, of course, you don't want to be seen to be insulting present-day Aborigines by referring to certain traditional practices. There are real difficulties here. My view is that both the Aboriginal and European populations in Australia are very different from what they were in 1788. It's absurd and self-defeating to try to imagine Aborigines back into the situation in 1788 — it's impossible for them to be the people they were in 1788. I think we have a joint history and have to deal with each other as we find ourselves now.

---

10 See 'Who Discovered Australia?' (*Quadrant*, July/August 1990); also 'Australian History and European Civilisation' (*Quadrant*, May 1993).

You're also quite insistent on the need to acknowledge the British heritage shared by all Australians[11]. In fact, you say that Australia is unintelligible unless you do. You don't have to go right back to Charlemagne, perhaps, but you believe we should at least know something about our more recent roots in England and in Europe. Not all history departments would agree with you, I gather.

I think we probably went overboard in the sixties and seventies, when we decided that, since Australian history hadn't been taught enough in our schools and universities, we'd now teach Australian history and we'd teach it often. But we taught it in a sort of nationalist way, as if Australia were self-sufficient and Australian history had begun in 1788. I actually think the old-style history, which just tacked Australia onto the end of British history, in some ways made more sense than starting in 1788 and talking only about Australia. After all, how are we to characterise this place? It is an offshoot of European civilisation. Unless you understand those origins, you aren't really going to understand this place. I think there's a movement back now towards this older view — take, for example, Alan Atkinson's new book[12], at least half of which is about Britain in the eighteenth century, the popular culture of the time, the change to a more bureaucratic society and so on. That's the background you need to understand Australia. And, in fact, what we also need to pay more attention to is the construction of a British identity, which happened more clearly in Australia than anywhere else, with the English, Scots and Irish living amongst each other, rather than in their separate patches as they did back home. In other words, Britishness is invented in the colonies.

How interventionist should an historian be? Someone like the prehistorian John Mulvaney, who fought against the Franklin Dam, the reburial of Aboriginal remains and what we might call the Dawkins revolution, to name just a few of his public interventions, seems almost to be an exception at the end of the century.

---

11 Again, see 'Australian History and European Civilisation'.
12 *The Europeans in Australia: A history* (OUP, 1997).

Well, against that view, obviously not all historians can go public all the time. And, indeed, some would say that Australian historians have an amazingly high public profile — particularly people such as Henry Reynolds, Geoffrey Blainey, Manning Clark — and that it would be difficult to think of British historians who have that kind of influence in Britain.

You yourself are interventionist in the republican area, and that debate is a good example of how, to form a worthwhile opinion, you need to know something about the history of both the monarchist and republican models.

Yes. Part of the republican project is to educate the public about our institutions. We tend to think politics can look after itself, which can be dangerous. Yet we need to be able to imagine a polity where the citizens are committed to its institutions and know and understand them.

One of the historians you write about — one of the great figures in the writing of our history — is Manning Clark. Why is Manning Clark such a prominent figure in our cultural history and how influential is he today as an historian?

For historians of Australia, Manning Clark was a godsend, because I think he was the first person who wrote about the history of this country as if it were something of high significance. He was able to give it a grandeur and a significance it hadn't had before, and that was because of the breadth of his conception of Australian history — his interest in the coming of European civilisation to this ancient, crazy country.

He saw three strands of European civilisation taking root here: the Enlightenment, Catholicism and Protestantism, and his project was to explore what happened to them in this place. As a student I found that inspiring. For the first time it seemed possible to be an Australian historian and do something worthwhile. My disappointment with the project was that Manning Clark lost faith in it himself, so that at the end — not so clearly in his *History*[13], but more in his occasional writing — you found him saying that the British came to Australia and did three great evils: they were brutal to the convicts, they killed the Aborigines and they raped the environment — period. That, it seems, was the end of it, as if he really even doubted whether the word 'civilisation' was applicable to these people any more. He then preferred to speak only about British philistinism — and you can understand what he meant, of course: until quite recently Australia was a colonial, parochial place.

Yet even the colony of a great civilisation can carry most of that civilisation in some form. When Manning Clark went to Melbourne Grammar, the headquarters of the Melbourne bourgeoisie (or at least one of its stamping grounds), his headmaster introduced him to Dostoyevsky, and Mozart became his favourite composer. Yet, by the end of volume six of his *History*, he wrote as if the way forward for Australia were to turn its back on Europe. He began barracking for those who were looking for a highly distinctively Australian literature — this is in the 1930s — even for those who went as far as to promote tariffs on books from elsewhere in order to support Australian writers. Yet, for Manning Clark himself, nothing could be more significant than European civilisation and its works, so there seemed to be a disjunction between his life and his history. I think he finally allowed some of the faddishness of the last two decades to control him and lost that larger vision.

It's hard now to imagine, since history turned for him into a personal quest and great literature, but Manning Clark began at the social science end of the spectrum. At the beginning he produced a book of documents with introductions which were the thorough accounts of the Australian economy and its political history in all its nitty-gritty detail, the things he became increasingly cavalier and indifferent towards in his later work. He was happy to say, 'This is my personal view of Australian society — highly idiosyncratic, ignoring

---

13 Manning Clark's *A History of Australia* was published by Melbourne University Press in five volumes between 1962 and 1981. Clark also published *A Short History of Australia* (Heinemann, London, 1964). An abridged version of the *History* called *Manning Clark's History of Australia* was published by Melbourne University Press in 1993, abridged by Michael Cathcart.

the sorts of things you'd expect to find in a standard history book about agreed significant matters, but my personal view'.

✧

When we think of the household names in Australian history, men — and they were men then, such as Manning Clark, Geoffrey Blainey or the pre-historian John Mulvaney — it must strike us that these historians of an earlier generation all worked with overarching projects, uncovering facts and reinterpreting them, and that they all took their influence on society as a matter of course, part of the job description.

Nowadays, at least in the academy, being an historian can often mean something rather different. In the first place, your main concern as a new historian may well be to debate theories of knowledge or to analyse texts as illustrations of your theory of knowledge, rather than to establish what happened as opposed to what didn't — to look at how a particular explorer, for example, read the land and to draw meanings from his reading of the land, rather than to recount the story of his expedition. Another project that may interest the new historian is the uncovering of hidden histories — making public stories which have been suppressed, particularly women's stories and the stories of minorities and communities whose voices the wider public had largely ignored or discounted — and not necessarily for sinister reasons: some stories weren't told because they weren't considered grand or central enough to be worth telling — the history of surfboard riding, say, or hats, or shopping malls, things once thought too domestic or trivial to matter, things about which you usually can't tell a story in the sense you can about Genghis Khan or Richard III.

Jill Julius Matthews is Reader in History and Women's Studies at the Australian National University and, like many of the new historians, negotiates what is sometimes quite a difficult path between the two kinds of history[14].

---

14 Her published work includes *Good and Mad Women: The historical construction of femininity in twentieth-century Australia* (Allen & Unwin, 1984) and a contribution to *Feminist Histories*, edited by Bain Attwood and Joy Damousi (History Institute, Victoria, 1991). She also edited *Sex in Public: Australian sexual culture* (Allen & Unwin, 1997).

Jill Julius Matthews

History has changed shape over the past 20 or 30 years, since the development of the new social history in the late fifties and early sixties in Britain. Out of that grew feminist history, gay and lesbian history, cultural studies and so on. Basically these sorts of history work from the bottom rather than the top, breaking up the solidity of the historical subject matter as seen from the top. If you have a God's eye view, then you can take it all in, picking up the prominent bits. But if you're a social historian, you're down there among the bits and it doesn't look as unified as it once did. A social history of Australia, for example, could include almost anything — shopping, beach behaviour — but it wouldn't be what the British historian G. M. Trevelyan called 'history with the politics taken out' because there's been a reconceptualisation of power. We're not just interested in the power of political parties, or parliamentary or governmental power, but in power in everyday life, the power of relationships within the world. And a crucial dimension of this kind of analysis involves gender and race.

When I began my own historical work in the early seventies, I took on as my own project the history of the inarticulate — a rather pompous way of putting it, probably. Still, it remains very much what I'm concerned with, and it's a concern, I think, running right through the new history. The difference, I would suggest, is that in the seventies we talked about mute history, inarticulate history or hidden history, about making things visible and so on, but almost 30 years later we've now done a lot of that. Certain things no longer need to be confronted, the orthodoxy is not a powerful monolith any more, and the new social history (or whatever we're calling it) has had an enormous impact. People now are really just getting on with it, rather than having to lay claims to hidden or mute history. It's really only hidden or mute now from the perspective of the old orthodoxy. (Of course, some people say it's the new orthodoxy and it's being fought against by other contenders.)

The new historians are also using new tools. You have suggested that their analytical perspective is a juxtaposition of various approaches — Marxism, say, together with literary criticism, or it might be post-structuralism and psychoanalysis — in each individual case the mix will be different, although most of the elements would be thought of as coming to Australia from Europe, via the United States and other parts of the English-speaking world.[15] *I wonder why it is this particular set of tools which turned out to be so appropriate to the new history and whether, in fact, in some ways the tools determined what kind of history would now be written.*

There was a marvellous article published in the *American Sociological Journal* in the late seventies called 'How to Become a Dominant French Philosopher'. It was a deadly serious account of how in fact a series of French philosophers became dominant. It examined the intellectual and social structures, the relationships between France and America, in particular — as an analysis of the political economy of fame in the intellectual world it remains a highly salutary piece of reading for all of us.

I don't think that the tools of the French are totally dominant, however. In many ways what actually happens is that people working in a particular field develop their own strategies, their own subject matter, their own methods of working, and then later they acquire the imprimatur of theory or the French. For example, I've been teaching a history of Western sexuality recently. Now, the place of Foucault in that history is absolutely central, but there were a number of people working in the field well before Foucault wrote or published his *History of Sexuality* in 1978. When you invoke Foucault's name, though, people know where you're coming from intellectually, they know what track you're on, they can place you — Foucault works like a code word, if you like.

Or like the team flag.

Exactly, I think that's a very good analogy — as if to say 'that's the side I'm on'.

---

15 In 'Doing Theory or Using Theory: Australian feminist/women's history in the 1990s' (*Australian Historical Studies*, vol. 27, no. 106, April 1996).

Can this not, though, sometimes cut off dialogue with members of other teams who don't like your team?

I think anyone who adopts rabid fan mentality is impossible to talk to. But if you don't take it on quite so dogmatically, I don't think there's a problem. As far as I'm concerned, historians are odd creatures who work between empirical grubbing and high theory, alternating and moving around in that very broad field. By necessity, most of us become very eclectic. If you become too enamoured of any one theory or any one methodology, from my point of view, you cease to be a good historian. You become more concerned with the theory itself than with what the theory does.

And the result might be that you ended up basically talking to other people engaged with theoretical problems rather than to the public in the sense of a general audience.

I think that's the case, especially with some elements of our post-graduate education. For most work in the humanities and social sciences now, there is an imperative for PhD candidates to come to terms with theory. They look around and they try to find a theory and that often leads them to quite rigid ways of conceptualising their own work, partly because they're inexperienced and partly because they see particular forms of theory as being very exciting — both fashionable and useful, although the usefulness is not yet tested. These scholars, having emerged from their cocoon, either go down the path of theory and methodology or have to develop other ways of coping with the mass of historical data and with the conceptualisation of their historical subject.

Your phrase 'empirical grubbing' calls to mind the widespread public suspicion that historians today have a certain disdain for talking to us about what happened, being more interested in the interplay of memories and the comparison of interpretations, whereas people in general are actually very interested in knowing and talking about what happened.

What's needed is a balance between the two. You can't write now as if you were writing 'the true history' of something, but, on the other hand, if you worry about memory and the nature of sources too much, you never get down to looking at the content of memory, what it's the memory of. And I think the best history does both — theoretically sophisticated while respecting both accuracy and the empirical bases: the work of Janet McCalman[16], for example, or the work of the American historian Judith Walkowitz[17] on late nineteenth-century Britain.

Of course, the question of 'the public' is an interesting one. From the God's eye view there was only one public, whereas the new historians have made it very apparent there there is a multiplicity of publics. When we speak of public intellectuals, for example, we tend to mean individuals who operate in a specific and fairly elite arena, bounded by certain forms of media and subject matter, whereas the public is enormously broader than that and we actually have public intellectuals operating in a multiplicity of domains. Historians, for example, are constantly writing to, speaking with, drawing from and engaging with people in the community in an enormous variety of ways. There is a whole range of publics, and to set aside one arena as 'the public' is simply to go back to a formalised, elite and hierarchical model. It's not that people should not be listening to those figures who stick up out of the intellectual landscape in a very public way, and engaging with them mentally, it's just that an earlier generation's style of addressing the public is not reproducing itself now, and we must not ignore what is happening now — the smaller voices talking in smaller arenas — we mustn't get stuck looking for the wrong thing. You know, there's that story of the drunk who's looking for his key under a lampost, and when someone comes along and says, 'Where did you lose it?', he says, 'In the bushes over there'. 'Well, why are you looking for it here?', asks the newcomer. 'Because there's light

16 Her works include *Struggletown: Public and private life in Richmond 1900–1965* (Melbourne University Press, 1988) and *Journeyings: The biography of a middle-class generation 1920–1990* (Melbourne University Press, 1993).
17 Her works include *Prostitution and Victorian Society: Women, class and the State* (Cambridge University Press, 1980) and *City of Dreadful Delight: Narratives of sexual danger in late-Victorian London* (University of Chicago Press, 1992).

here.' In other words, we should be looking for the intellectuals of the bushes in the bushes.

We may be guilty, in your view, of confusing famous intellectuals with public intellectuals.

That could be a good way of putting it.

In the kind of discourse we hear from the new social historians, binary constructions often seem popular — oppression or exclusion, for example, seems often to be explained in binary terms: white against black, lesbian against straight, non-English-speaking background against the so-called Anglo. It's terribly easy to slip into binary oppositions, which can then arouse a kind of acrimony and resentment in members of either group — after all, few of us want to feel that our lives or identity or interests can so easily be categorised.

Well, Noam Chomsky would say it was because of the innate structure of the human brain. While I don't quite agree with that sort of biological essentialism, I do think that in the Western tradition over thousands of years, that binary form of logic has been the central mode of making sense of the world. But I think that we may be at the beginning of a process of being able to research, write and understand that doesn't rely on binary opposition to the same degree. The notion of difference that emerged both in the politics of feminism and gay liberation, in particular, although also in the intellectual work of many new historians and post-modernist scholars, for example, is a more benign variation, if you like, on binary oppositions. The notion of difference is less a 'contradiction' in the Marxist sense of that word, or even a 'non-antagonistic contradiction' in the Maoist sense, than a benign variation. It's now much more possible in a world in which multiculturalism matters, diversity is recognised and applauded, and there's no longer one single value of normative purity that one either has or falls away from.

✧

Greg Dening, for many years Professor of History at Melbourne University,
is the prize-winning author of such books as Mr Bligh's Bad Language[18]
and, more recently, Performances[19], *a collection of idiosyncratic, highly*
personal essays about the writing of history — Greg Dening's sort of
history. Like so many of our better-known public intellectuals, Greg
Dening in some ways straddles two orthodoxies, fossicking around in the
space between empiricism and theory (although he probably wouldn't put
it like that). While not denying a discoverable truth about the past — and
his field is the arrival of Europeans in the South Pacific — his pleasure
and skill lie in its re-presentation, not (and this is important) as a costume
drama, but as a way of getting us to understand today the meanings an
event must have had for those present at the time it happened — at Cook's
murder, for example, or the arrival of the French in the Marquesas. Each
retelling is a performance, and none will be the whole story.

Greg Dening

I think the historian is primarily a storyteller, but a reflective one, a
storyteller who wants to give the reader the same sort of authority
the storyteller has, the same right to tell the story. The storyteller as
historian seeks to persuade the reader that there are many stories
even in the one incident — that there's no one story. Above all, I
think, an academic historian seeks to tell a story which is a real-life
story, not the blinkered, narrow, falsified view of, say, the social
scientists, or whatever blinkered view is required of various scientific
attitudes towards events and behaviour. The historian wants to keep
them whole. The historian has to see that none of those is true, or all
of them are true, and the story has to come out showing that life is
whole, life is multiple, life has many meanings, and that that 'story'
is a very complicated story. I think above all the historian, or at least
the academic historian, has to tell a story that's complicated, but to
tell it in such a way that its complications, while seen, do not befog

---

18 (Cambridge University Press, 1992).
19 (Melbourne University Press, 1996).

the story or close it over. The historian is interested in showing how events make a human event. When you tell your story to a judge, you're blinkered to focus on the legal truth; when you tell your story to a gossip, you're blinkered to focus on nastiness. The historian can't be blinkered in this narrow way, and doesn't want his or her reader to be, either.

For example, one of the real issues in my life at present is how to tell the story of the encounter in Australia and in the Pacific between the intruding strangers and the indigenous people already there. It's one of the most terrible stories in our past, a story in one sense that still hasn't ended — it's a story I don't expect ever to see the end of. Will I see the monument that brings to an end the 209 years war going on at present? No, I won't. It might be a war that goes on for a thousand years. I look on my histories as the first tracings of what those monuments might be, of what it might mean to bring to a close that part of our past.

One of the most moving experiences in my life was going to the Vietnam Veterans' Memorial on the Washington Mall. In the midst of a place full of white, phallic, erect symbols, all saying macho things about heroism and reverence for the past, there's this slash in the ground. It's black, there's nothing but chaos on it, the names have none of that archaeology of knowledge we require for ordered understanding — no alphabetical order, no regiment or rank — none of that, it's the day they died. And you see the days they died accumulating until, at the end, the number of them is huge. And, as you look at the memorial, what do you see? You see your own face. Now, I want to write history in which the true chaos of life is understood and seen, but in such a way that people see their own faces in it. We can't get away from the fact that the past is in some way making us, and out of that something must happen.

What is it that lets people 'see their own face' in history?

I used to tell my students that within just a few weeks of their researches, they'd be the world experts on their topic. The trouble is that nobody else will want to know what's in their heads. What everyone will want to know of them is how what they're saying joins up with the conversation we're already having. It's joining the conversation that is the most important thing. People will note the facts and abstract from them — the facts have to be there as 'reality effects' (in Roland Barthes' phrase) — the sort of thing novelists put into their novels to make people feel as if it's all 'real'. Historians often do that, too, pouring in the facts to give a sense of reality. Liberated readers, however, actually know that these facts are irrelevant to the meaning to be abstracted from them. It's the ability to contextualise the facts that signals the true class of an historian, the ability to make the facts larger than themselves.

You also believe, I think, that no historian should underestimate the entertainment value (in the very best sense) of what he or she does.

I do like to entertain my readers, to close them off from ordinary, everyday experience, so they can concentrate on what's on my stage and be entertained by what they see there. Entertainment in that theatrical sense is important, I think, and one of the things we demand of theatre is that it not be theoretical, that it not say what it means. Theatre acts things out. We demand the right to leave the theatre as critics and one of the most important things an historian can do is to liberate the reader to be a critic.

If you demand of historians that they repeat the past, you must ask them to tell that past as it actually happened — that is, not with all our hind-sighted certainties about what actually happened, but all the ambiguities, all the possibilities contained in any action, all the inconsequentiality of the things people did. The historian has to be able to tell life in the past as if that past were in our present.

How did you come to adopt this view of history? It certainly wasn't the orthodox view at the time of your formation as an historian.

That's something one would always like to know. I suspect I had a very privileged experience. I was a Jesuit priest, and one of the things which formed my way of thinking was the spiritual exercises of

Ignatius Loyola. I treasure those experiences very deeply, I attribute to them what I have since called my ethnographic bent, my constant effort to describe what actually happened in the past. That comes out of those exercises in the sense that the exercises require meditation on scripture, meditation on events, say, in the life of Christ, and demand that you in fact dramatise them — create theatre in your mind about where it happened, how it happened, what the touches and smells of a certain scene were, and then to reflect on the significance of what you've created. I did that for an hour or two a day, every day of my life for 30 years. It seems to me that an experience like that necessarily forms my approach. As a priest I was a professor of my beliefs, and as an academic professor I gave witness to what I really thought about issues — not to what the books said, but to my personal relationship to the things I was talking about.

What drew you to the South Pacific as an area of study? The South Pacific was hardly an orthodox field, either.

No, it wasn't. I give credit for that to an old friend, John Mulvaney, who taught archaeology and initiated a Pacific course for us in the 1950s. One of the most extraordinary discoveries was that the encounter in the Pacific had been described in myriad texts — it would take a lifetime to read even the smallest part of those texts — but it seemed to me that what we still didn't have was a two-sided view of that encounter in the Pacific. What I wanted to write was a two-sided history, and the only way to see the other side was through the eyes of those who experienced the encounter at the time it happened. I soon realised I didn't have the necessary reading skills to cope with the material I had to acquaint myself with, so I went and did anthropology at Harvard — I didn't want to be an anthropologist, I simply wanted the reading skills that anthropology would give me. (In cross-cultural history it's not just a matter of translating the words people do say, it's also about translating what they don't say — the silences that result from not being able to see what they're actually seeing. I felt I needed special reading skills to cope with that.) My professor at that time, when I went to tell him that I was going to do anthropology, said to me, 'Dening, this is the end of your academic career'. It was going to America — to Harvard — that upset him as much as anything (I was expected to go to Balliol or somewhere like that), but he also thought that history was really mainly about the public school tie, you simply didn't do the history of native peoples.

When you look at your career, it's easy to wonder why your history isn't read or why people aren't interested in the sorts of things you are. In terms of what people expect from history, Australian history can be very parochial, and it's also very difficult to interest people in the victims of history, even within our own parochial history, to make them listen to the victims of Empire — it's just not fashionable.

Perhaps not with the mass market — it's eminently fashionable, surely, at the level of the intellectual market. This disjunction is itself a telling reflection of the strained relations between the intellectuals and the 'masses' and their tastes.

Donald Horne

‘ Public intellectuals, so called, are simply certain

highly signposted performers

within public intellectual life.

But for there to be a public intellectual life,

you need many others. There are all kinds

of people at universities, for example, who produce

all kinds of ideas in their research and scholarship,

who simply don't enter the public stage,

but others get hold of these ideas and use them

and amplify them. ’

Donald Horne

F ANY AUSTRALIAN WRITER AND THINKER *is a highly signposted performer on our cultural and intellectual stage, it's Donald Horne. And in 1961, when he became editor of the* Bulletin, *he himself changed an important signpost on the cultural landscape: he got rid of the 'Australia for the White Man' slogan from the* Bulletin *masthead. That was a neat, eye-catching example of the kind of radical reconceptualising of Australia that's made Donald Horne such a prominent social critic over the past few decades.*

Soon afterwards he published The Lucky Country, *one of the best examples in our history of a public intellectual at work, re-thinking our national myths, including our Britishness, immigration, and our relations with Asia, in front of a vast audience. Indeed, apart from Manning Clark's* A History of Australia, *it's hard to think of another text which has had quite the same impact on how Australians interpret who they've become and why. While other sacred texts come readily to mind, texts (including Australian films) which, over the past few decades, have helped us re-mythologise our mental and physical landscapes, it's difficult to imagine any list of culturally significant Australian books omitting* The Lucky Country.

Since The Lucky Country *came out in 1964, a couple of dozen books by Donald Horne have appeared in our bookshops. Since that time, apart from when he was editor of the* Bulletin, *then contributing editor to* Newsweek International, *and lecturing at the University of New South Wales in the early seventies, Horne has published at least one book each year: social critiques such as* The Time of Hope *or* The Coming Republic, *cultural critiques such as* The Great Museum *or* Ideas for a Nation, *autobiography* (The Education of Young Donald, Confessions of a New Boy *and* Portrait of an Optimist), *and even three works of fiction. Donald Horne's contribution to our culture of ideas has been almost overwhelming.*

At the core of that contribution, right from the beginning, has been the notion of reconceptualising Australia. It's worth remembering that when he first became a public figure it was difficult enough to conceptualise Australia, let alone reconceptualise it. In the Menzies era, as Donald Horne has written, 'there was a disdain for the very idea of native intellectual excellence'.[1] *Not to be mediocre was to be anti-British in some ways, a*

---

[1] *Time of Hope: Australia 1966–1972* (Angus & Robertson, 1980).

line to which the British tabloids quaintly cling to this day. In 30 years a lot has changed, here at least, if not on Fleet Street, and it was recon-ceptualising Australia, in particular in The Lucky Country, *that Donald Horne first spoke about.*

THE LUCKY COUNTRY was a successful reconceptualisation of Australia, but it wasn't intended in any way to be a prophecy — I don't believe in prophecies, I don't believe in predicting the future. But, as it happens, it turned out to be a quite astonishingly accurate prophecy. Perhaps that was because I was working from a stable base: the Cold War ensured that there were no surprises coming up in relations between nations, and the great post-War boom, with its low unemployment and low inflation, gave the appearance that basic economic problems had been solved. So I could question matters like the White Australia policy or the treatment of Aborigines in a stable context. Very few others seemed to be thinking deeply about these things. It seemed to me it was going to be very hard to maintain those sorts of policies because Australia was not like South Africa, which had a laager mentality — although not everyone seems to have quite realised this yet. In South Africa they pulled their wagons into a circle and, when the Zulus attacked, they just shot the buggers. The enormous Voortrekke monument up on a hill in Pretoria commemorated this sort of occurrence: the Boers set off on their trek, the Zulus attacked them and the Boers killed them all. Well, we may have 'shot a few buggers', but we don't celebrate it in our public culture, we don't have monuments of that kind to appeal to.

It also seemed to be pretty obvious to me that whatever people felt about it, it was going to be rather difficult for Australians to avoid the fact that they were geographically contiguous to Asian countries. It was also hard to see how we could avoid the questions raised by technological change, not to mention the possibility of Australia becoming a republic.

The Lucky Country came out in a very different intellectual climate from today's: there was a lack of intellectual infrastructure in the early 1960s (fewer tertiary institutions and libraries, for example, a rudimentary local publishing industry) and a lack of confidence about the significance of our intellectual culture. But things soon changed.

It would be wrong to imagine that in the 1950s and early 1960s there was no intellectual life in Australia — that would have been impossible, there's always an intellectual life. The point is that it wasn't very connected. In 1958 I started a fortnightly magazine called *Observer*[2], which I think used to sell about 8000 copies, and there was another fortnightly magazine called *Nation*[3], which sold about the same number. There were monthlies and quarterlies being published at the time which sold even fewer copies and represented quite a wide range of approaches — about a dozen of them altogether. They formed a kind of original 'yeast' out of which grew new approaches and attitudes, to be picked up subsequently by the *Australian*, which was started by Rupert Murdoch in 1964, the *Canberra Times* and the *Sydney Morning Herald* after their rejuvenation by John Pringle, by the *Age* in Melbourne under Graham Perkins, and by some of the ABC programs of the time. Issues which had previously been very little discussed were now discussed in public. *Observer*, for example, was, I think, the first publication in Australia to publish regular articles about people from non-English-speaking backgrounds as Australians, as part of the Australian population, assuming that that was OK.

The 1960s, of course, simply didn't exist as a decade. In fact I wrote two books about that period, the first being *The Lucky Country,* about the age of Menzies in which everything seemed motionless, and the second being *Time of Hope,* about the other half of the 1960s in which everything moved. Up until then I had seen myself as a liberal conservative, hating the Labor Party — in fact, I'd written an attack on what we would now describe as Labor Party sexism and racism in the middle of the 1940s. In the late sixties a lot of these things began to shift around, so that the 'liberal' part of my liberal conservatism was actually being shared by all sorts of other people — some, like Paddy McGuinness, were enthusiastic at first and

---

2 *Observer* was published from 1958 until 1962, when it was absorbed by the *Bulletin*.
3 *Nation* was published from 1958 until 1972, when it merged with the *Review* to become *Nation Review*.

then retreated. At that stage in the development of a civil society in Australia, there was an enormous uplift, in which people began to imagine themselves as belonging to different groups, and all kinds of new ideas were thrown up in one big go. So, by the end of the 1960s, practically everything that had been seen as a new thought earlier in the decade, was up and away. Not multiculturalism, that took more time.

The Vietnam War was, in some ways, a base for these changes — although the actual agitation about the Vietnam War had very little practical importance on Australian policy, in my opinion. The Australians withdrew from the Vietnam War because they were losing it, just as the Americans did. But the changes became associated with the protests — the Vietnam War became a transcendent issue to which many other issues were then attached. (The same thing happened in Australia in the middle of the last century, after the 1849 protest against the transportation of convicts. This protest was linked in people's minds with the great revolutions and protests of 1848 in Europe — a pretty minor reflection, but characteristically Australian. That then became a transcendent issue which linked up with other important questions: the possibility of a democratic voting system, self-government, land reform and so on.)

Now, I don't have a great belief in politicians as anything more than people who classify and express what's already in circulation in society, but in the late sixties John Gorton, the then Prime Minister[4], put Aboriginal issues and the arts on the agenda. Whitlam then, in the early seventies, conceptualised these issues in ways people could understand — and he did it better than he knew[5]. I don't think Whitlam's intention had been to become Prime Minister of Australia because he believed in feminism or the arts or Aboriginal causes. What Whitlam believed in was the need to reform the welfare policies of the 1950s, as well as in a general kind of modernisation of Australia — as Patrick White had said, until then we'd had these

---

4 John Gorton was prime minister from 1968 to 1971, followed briefly by Sir William McMahon before the Labor victory in 1972.
5 Gough Whitlam became prime minister in 1972. The reform program of his government included diplomatic recognition of China, the abolition of conscription, the withdrawal of Australian forces from Vietnam, the introduction of free tertiary education and a national health care system.

'rustic clowns' representing us. The 'It's Time' campaign came to mean, not only that it was time to improve the welfare system, but it was time for a whole range of other reforms as well — and for certain groups in society to be seen at last. As a result, Whitlam assumed an enormous gloss. But it's unfair, I think, to give much credit for all that to Whitlam, except to note that he acted decently. John Gorton is the somewhat neglected figure in all this. I remember years later seeing an interview with Gorton on television in which he said, 'I did a lot of good things', and the interviewer asked, 'What were they?' Gorton said, 'Oh I've forgotten'.

The intellectual climate now is very different, obviously, and the infrastructure — the public libraries, the universities and colleges, the arts funding — is vast by comparison. How would you characterise the intellectual climate in Australia now?

It's much more diffuse now, of course, which is quite a good thing — there's a variety of avenues for discussion now. The public intellectual life is not just a matter any more of discussing who you should vote for or influencing government policies, but, just as importantly, of how you talk about existence — the criticism of existence, that's the basis of all intellectual activity and we have more of that now. Interestingly enough, there seem to be fewer young people active in the discussions nowadays — older people often ask why there aren't more. (In the 1960s, by way of contrast, the young were pushing people like me out of the way, protesting about generational atrophy.) Why this is the case is hard to define — you certainly can't say they haven't had a chance. The economic background is very different today, of course — the idea of the career is collapsing, employment prospects are much grimmer, and it's possible that certain modern intellectual movements have had an effect as well — to my mind they're often critical in a rather superficial kind of way. (Personally, I find nothing new in post-modernist ideas, for example. They're ideas I've been familiar with for a long time.)

In fact, you quote Foucault quite a lot yourself.

Well, in criticising post-modernism I'm not necessarily criticising all post-modernist ideas. What I'm critical of is the ideas all being wrapped up into one bundle. Post-modernism was particularly effective in regard to art and architecture, but in regard to literature I just find it inadequate, and in other regards, such as the meaning of existence and so forth, it's two or three thousand years old. Of course, it gives people a flip ability to look coherent when they're not — many of them people who haven't actually even read the earlier literature. As to deconstructionist approaches, well, they've been well known for a long time as well — indeterminacy of meaning and so on, it's scarcely news. I'd grasped it by the age of seventeen, as I've described in *The Education of Young Donald.* Deconstruction has value, but so does the old idea of appreciation. By that I don't just mean a liking for certain metaphors or rhyming schemes, but looking at things from the point of view of what I would call an individual criticism of existence. I believe that we each of us build up, in varying ways, our own individual criticism of existence — it may even be fully inherited, but whatever it turns out to be, since each individual's experience is a little bit different, each criticism of existence will be a different working model. To deny oneself the possibility of using what's thought of as a great painting or a great book in a positive way to build up this criticism of existence, or the possibility of developing one's feelings about it, rather reduces the whole potential of being alive. You can stand in the presence of a great painting, aware of its resonance as something that has been interpreted in many, many different kinds of ways — in fact, standing in its presence becomes much better when you are aware of that — while at the same time getting something out of it of your own.

✧

Donald Horne's curriculum vitae is impressive, a demonstration of the very public aspect of his intellectual activity. Apart from being the author of some two dozen books, fiction and non-fiction, and the former editor of both the Bulletin *and* Quadrant, *he has been former chairman of the Australia Council, as well as of a number of other cultural organisations,*

Emeritus Professor at the University of New South Wales and the former chancellor of the University of Canberra. A thumbnail sketch such as this can, of course, give us little idea of how Donald Horne became such a public thinker. Perhaps only a biographer could do that in any detail, and presumably many different factors played their part. Timing was no doubt important. The Lucky Country, as we've seen, came out at a critical moment in our cultural history, just at the point when we were beginning to decolonise ourselves intellectually and set up an independent Australian intellectual infrastructure. In 1964, it's worth bearing in mind, Donald Horne could write with impunity that 'intellectuals do not exist in Australia as publicly influential people'[6].

Part of the reason Donald Horne himself became 'publicly influential' might lie in a characteristic of the public intellectual he gives a lot of weight to: the ability to articulate clearly, to give shape to inchoate ideas already agitating the public mind. Some thinkers, of course, see the public intellectual's role as much more adversarial, and, in particular, subversive of power. Certainly that's one way to signpost yourself vividly and become a leader rather than a mediator. But it's not the flamboyant leadership role that Donald Horne emphasises when he muses on what the term 'public intellectual' means to him.

A public intellectual is a public intellectual *performer* — they're public performers who are intellectuals, not just talk-show hosts. And, of course, they can be good, bad, indifferent, stupid or intelligent — the word 'intellectual', I think, can sometimes be qualified by such words as 'ignorant', 'learned', 'intelligent' or 'stupid'. In fact, just as you can have a learned, intelligent intellectual, you can have a learned, stupid intellectual, an unintellectual scholar and so forth.

What sort of factors decide who is going to end up in the spotlight and who isn't?

It's a matter of circumstance, of course, but it's also a matter of pushing in. The intellectual performer has to be able to seize the

---

6 *The Lucky Country* (Penguin, 1988 edition), p. 224.

opportunities on offer. (In some ways, for instance, I consider that I wasn't entitled to take part in most of the carnivals I played a part in — it wasn't altogether obvious that there was any room for me in them, but I tried it out.) An absolutely essential quality in a public performer is the ability to project in ways which will capture people's attention. That doesn't necessarily mean that the ideas have to be devalued, it just means an ability to capture the public's attention, appealing to something that's already there. I think the only way to be influential in this business is to conceptualise, to put into words for people something that's already floating around in their heads, something they've never formulated like that before. It's there in solution, in other words, and the public intellectual crystallises it.

'The deciding classes' is one of your phrases. What role do these 'deciding classes' have in determining who is to become a performer?

I worked up the idea of there being a kind of a directive or deciding class in order to make more sense in Australian terms of Gramsci's idea of a hegemony, the idea that certain general ideas, values and habits come to permeate a society, becoming its common sense. Yet they're often the views of only certain types of people. In a deciding class all these people with shared values sit behind desks making decisions, which are then carried out by other people sitting at computers, who may in fact be quite critical of the decisions. (Calling it a deciding class is much better than calling it a 'chattering class', which is really just a way of denigrating people you disagree with.) People in the deciding class live a more interesting life than those who are not — they feel they have a certain freedom both to act on their decisions and to think up new decisions and be critical — the deciding class will not be without its internal divisions, with one group critical of another.

✧

In view of his reservations about the uses of post-modernist theory — reservations not unusual amongst Australian intellectuals of his and even later generations — it's at first surprising to find Donald Horne adopting a position on social reality which is, at the very least, highly congruent with the ideas of widely read post-modernist thinkers. In other words, vital to Donald Horne's thinking is the idea that we live mentally within established discourses about reality. Those discourses could be scientific, religious, sexist, rationalist, socialist, racially determined, anti-colonialist, presumably even post-structuralist. Indeed, what we believe to be real, as a society, our dominant myths, may be more important to our experience and more important to change than reality itself, if reality can ever be identified. Perhaps this straddling of the generations should not be so surprising, because Donald Horne himself identifies the ability to cross ideological faultlines, as he puts it, as a key characteristic of the intellectual. One of the public intellectual's main tasks, in Horne's view, is to come to terms imaginatively with society's dominant, conflicting myths.

I'm simply not equipped to handle some of the central technical problems of philosophy — and I'm not alone in that, of course. All the same, I've been happy to work out my own perspectives on existence — to cast different lights on existence. If you're a nuclear physicist, reality is simply a space filled with electrical activity; if you're a sociologist you'll have a different perspective on reality, and so on. All these realities I see as hypotheses. And we do the best we can with them: in theory at least, we experiment with them to see to what extent they hold together, we amend them, adjust them, and reject them if we can find no reason to continue believing them to be true.

At the moment I think that the great hypothesis or myth dominating us is the idea of the economy — the idea of economic man. According to this view the economy seems to exist irrespective of people. The economic perspective is a useful one, naturally, but so are others: the social perspective, with its emphasis on structural relations, the cultural perspective with its emphasis on people's ideas, beliefs and habits, or the environmental perspective. Yet for our most prominent commentators and our politicians the measure of human existence seems to lie in some half a dozen economic indicators. There's an obsession nowadays with quantification where quantity isn't the point, the universities being a striking example of how 'performance indicators' are applied where they're not relevant. This kind of extreme, utilitarian, Benthamite approach[7] is getting the better not only of us (Australia always has to some extent been a Benthamite country), but of the English-speaking economies as a whole. It's understandable in terms of the great post-War boom: the unparalleled expansion and production, high employment combined with low inflation, the expectations which followed and which then collapsed starting around the end of the sixties and the beginning of the seventies. For the moment this has made people cling to a kind of economic fundamentalism. (The expression 'economic rationalism', by the way, is, I think, a rather silly one.) Economic fundamentalism hits the Left very badly, of course, because, apart from the traditional Left (which was always highly 'economic' in its perspectives), most socialists had long given up the idea of trying to enlarge the human potential, concentrating mainly on the functioning of the welfare state and on pensions.

The point is that there's been an enormous simplification of our existence. Take the idea of the consumer: a consumer is neither a producer nor, of course, a citizen. The word 'taxpayer', for example, is used a hundred times more often than 'citizen' — we're forever reading references to 'the taxpayers' money' in the newspapers, although it might be better described as 'public money'. We have a duty to the taxpayer, but we also have a duty to the citizen.

At least economic fundamentalism (to use your term) is now being subjected to public criticism, but there are other myths which seem to evoke no discussion at all — 'democracy', for example.

Democracy is a question which is very much on my mind — I discuss it at length in my most recent book, *The Avenue of the Fair Go*[8]. The characters in this book begin to question electoral democracy as the beginning and end of political life — it's only one part. In Australia,

7 Usually considered the founder of utilitarianism, and a strong influence on John Stuart Mill, the political theorist and jurist Jeremy Bentham (1748–1832) held that the greatest happiness of the greatest number should determine our judgment of both institutions and individual actions. His theories are expounded in his *Introduction to the Principles of Morals and Legislation* (1789).
8 (HarperCollins, 1997). Horne describes the book, in which a tour group is led through a theme park of Australian myths such as mateship, the bush legend, globalisation and participatory democracy, as 'a comedy of ideas, a comedy of manners'.

it seems to me, we've paid far too much attention to what is, in effect, little more than party political manoeuvres, party political opportunism — what's happening in cabinet, what Beazley said yesterday, that sort of thing. In Australia that's 'politics'. The liveliness of the civil society is dependent on much more than that. Important ideas don't begin with politicians — the dismantling of the White Australia policy, for example, began with a group of people meeting in Camberwell in 1958 and then publishing a pamphlet called *Immigration: Reform, Control or Colour Bars?* I'm hoping to shock people out of their parochialism and, by introducing them to Spinoza, John Stuart Mill, Bismarck, Walt Whitman and so on, to show that there's practically no aspect of our political concerns today which has not been conceptualised over the last two hundred years or so.

All sorts of ideas in our present democratic system need questioning: the notion of a 'mandate', for example. Someone pulled the idea out of a hat that a government has a 'mandate' to do anything in the policy it presented to the electorate before an election. In fact, a mandate is an instruction — a government would have a mandate if there'd been a plebescite, say, instructing it to kill everyone of a certain religion. But most people, when they vote for one party or the other, have got enough brains to know that they're voting for a government, not for a policy — there may be many things in the policy with which they disagree, they may not even know what the policy is — they just think that this lot's better than the other lot. Anyway, when the government comes in, it usually chucks most of its policy away.

The other idea someone pulled out of a hat is 'the mainstream'. Mainstreams are usually invented simply to reflect policies politicians think will win seats in marginal electorates, or to represent a minority view they'd like to impose on everyone. These are all pseudo-democratic ideas that can be extremely illiberal and deeply intolerant. (The German 'mainstream', for example, doubtless supported Hitler — which doesn't get you very far.)

On the subject of Australian democracy, many questions are simply left unasked. The role of the High Court is a good example. Discussion of the role of the High Court has largely consisted of conservative politicians suddenly bucketing it in a disgraceful and stupid manner — I say that because the High Court doesn't make laws, and any common law changes it does make can be legislated against by the government. Then there's the idea of the rule of law, which is basic to the whole liberal–democratic enterprise, not just a conservative doctrine. Where do you see any informed discussion of the rule of law? And the idea of liberty rates scarcely a mention — the whole of that political correctness panic was one example of the kinds of problems that liberty can still face, as is the idea that community standards mustn't be affronted by videos. These things need to be talked about in an informed way in the context of a discussion of liberty. The whole idea of tolerance, for example, has gone backwards, in my view. Tolerance is seen by those on the Left as a kind of universal love of mankind, something which has not yet been characteristic of human behaviour. The seventeenth-century political philosopher Spinoza made the point that harmony could be achieved only by recognising difference — it's tolerance and recognition of difference which is the basis of true harmony, in other words. There are times when I doubt that the present government understands the difference between social conformity (there's just one way of being Australian) and social cohesion (there are many ways of being Australian, with some shared basic values such as not killing people or forming queues).

The Hanson affair has been interesting — it's told us nothing about racism, of course, that we didn't already know, but it's told us something very interesting indeed about equality. The idea of equality as envy has not been sufficiently discussed. For example, does equality mean an equal right to get food from a soup kitchen? What does equality mean in terms of a right to a literary grant? Complete equality might mean that literary grants had to be abandoned altogether because of the demand. Equality in these senses doesn't work. Notions of equality certainly need more discussion in regard to Aborigines, yet it simply hasn't been argued out. Non-Aboriginal Australians do not have the same rights as the Aborigines because the Aborigines alone were in possession of Australia when the Europeans came here, were dispossessed, saw their societies largely destroyed and their cultures endangered — whether by accident or design is irrelevant. As a result, even more than war veterans or disaster victims, Aborigines deserve special privileges, not just equality.

The whole question of social justice is something which is falling to bits — neither the practicalities nor the principles are properly discussed. Then there's the question of national identity, which clearly means something if you're talking about the demographic nature of Australia or the nature of our Federal constitution, but means very little if discussion is limited to diggers or Bullocky Bills, as all too often happens. Maybe the only possible national identity for an Australian is a civic identity — being a citizen of Australia.

Which brings up the question of the difference between a State and a nation — one is a citizen of a State.

There's a fundamental difference, which is not always fully understood. The Torres Strait Islanders, for example, are a nation (or perhaps two nations — there are certainly two language groups), but the Torres Strait Islands are not a State. Iceland is one of the rare examples in the world of a people who form both a nation (with a long history, its own language and so on) and a State. Australia is a State in which there are many groups and peoples who might be regarded as nations, the Torres Strait Islanders being only the clearest example for territorial reasons. It's a view long accepted in the United States and Canada, by the way, where various Indian peoples are considered to be nations — nobody gets upset about it.

What I would hope to see one day (despite the fact that everything seems to be going in the opposite direction at the moment) is the recognition that the Commonwealth of Australia is a State, committing us as Australians to the rule of law, liberal–democratic procedures, principles of tolerance (perhaps even the principle of the 'fair go'), equality under the law, guardianship of the land we share and so on, while also being made up of a number of nations. Those characteristics of the State would be what we meant by 'Australian' — it wouldn't be a matter of ethnicity. (Of course, the word 'ethnic' is going through a bit of a crisis at the moment because, although it sounds nice when you're contemplating a bowl of spaghetti, it has less pleasant connotations in the light of the conflicts taking place in so many parts of the world today.)

I hesitate to make predictions, as I've said, although I must say my record, particularly in *The Lucky Country*, isn't too bad. All I can say is that this is what I hope for — it may not come true, but it's what I hope for. At my age, I don't suppose I'll ever know!

✦

Despite the growth in an intellectual infrastructure in Australia over the last 30 years (the tertiary sector in education, for example, the Australian publishing industry, the museum and art gallery network, subsidised arts) there's still a lingering mistrust of intellectual activity in Australia, unless it's demonstrably pragmatic. One of the many myths Donald Horne writes illuminatingly about is the myth of pragmatism. In our kind of society we tend, it seems, to value something called 'action' (or at least planning for it) above something called 'words'.

This attitude is connected with a fear or misunderstanding of imagination. (Actually, pragmatism itself is one kind of imaginative device.) In Australia's case, the special fear of the imagination came from the early colonial period, when we were expected to be imaginative in terms of refrigeration or metallurgy or making wool grow where it hadn't grown before, but we didn't have to be imaginative in manufacturing, banking or services, let alone in intellectual life. There was a remark in the *Edinburgh Review* in the 1820s to the effect that Americans had no business concerning themselves with 'great ideas' when 'we' were concerned with them. In Australia, there was something effete about being imaginative, and that attitude was still current in the 1960s when I wrote *The Lucky Country*. Much more important than the idea of 'the clever country' (a phrase Hawke thought up and then forgot about) is the idea of the imaginative country. It's important not just for our intellectual life, but for industry, marketing — in all sorts of areas.

We've been a derivative society, taking ideas from other countries, using and transforming them, but now it's time we did more thinking of our own. Imagination is actually an important part of any productive process. How wonderful it would be if, instead of talking about economic indicators all the time, we talked about ways of making our society more imaginative and productive.

Queasiness about the imagination may also be connected with the dominance of the public culture by men. You have suggested that it's men who are usually the hero figures in our cultural myths, and men, in particular, who interpret the news to us[9].

Historically that's been the case in Australia. It depends on the nature of the society. Of course, there's nothing in the function itself which demands it. It's been easier for men to gatecrash these particular fields than for women, although the situation is changing. In the quality media, for example, women are much more prominent than they once were in carrying out this function, and particularly in drawing attention to alternative ways of thinking. The whole concept of public intellectual life as made up of the 'hard' topics — politics and economics, principally — is being gradually broken down, especially in academic life and in the social history and domestic areas, and women have played an important role in doing that.

Over and above those considerations, I do think we continue to have an English-speaking distrust of the word 'intellectual'. Journalists in particular use the word 'academic' in a derogatory way ('that's purely academic', they say), while academics, of course, use the word 'journalist' in a similarly derogatory way ('that's pure journalism'). Then both academics and journalists get together and use 'intellectual' in a derogatory sense.

Yet it's where the academy and journalism cross that something really useful happens, surely.

I think that's right. As far as the universities are concerned, there are difficulties at the moment with all this measuring of performance —

---

9 In *The Public Culture: The triumph of industrialism* (Pluto Press, 1986).

you only get a quarter of a point if you write an article for a quality newspaper, but 2 points if you publish a refereed article in the *Icelandic Journal of Nature Studies* which is read by absolutely nobody.

So the number of spaces where intellectuals can actually function publicly in Australia would seem to be quite limited.

Well, there are magazines like *Quadrant* — lots of people don't like it because they see it as Right-wing, but I think it plays an important intellectual role. In some ways, I'd say *Quadrant* is the best performer simply because of the quality of its English. Still, I always look at *Arena* on the Left and a number of other magazines which I'd call intellectual rather than academic or journalistic. Radio National, too, I think can be seen as an intellectual force in Australia. And we mustn't forget the movie industry — it's been of enormous reconceptualising significance, I think, much greater than television. The idea of Australia as a diverse, infinitely interesting society has come through most strongly in our movies. And that, to me, is 'intellectual' — it doesn't have to be in *Meanjin* or some refereed journal to be intellectual. And there are undoubtedly intellectual performers in what I called 'the quality media'. There are spaces.

Do think tanks have a part to play?

They haven't developed as strongly here as they have in the United States, and they tend to be right-wing, even extreme right-wing institutions. What I'd like to see would be the development of Left-wing think tanks.

Do you think anyone in the government would be listening? And do you think that the Labor Party and the Liberal Party are roughly equal in the amount of attention that they pay to intellectual activity?

I think that the present Liberal Government, particularly at its core, centring on John Howard and the Cabinet, is specifically concerned with not letting any ideas in — partly through preference and partly because they're thinking, 'Look what it did to Keating'. In the case of Howard (and one hopes this will change) you have a person of very determined belief, I think, that no further ideas are necessary. Now, to be fair to him, he's not a lunatic, and as events proceed, he may be challenged, but there's such a high degree of political opportunism in the cabinet that it's hard to be optimistic — polls come in each week telling them, as Howard once put it, what theory 'the mob' are believing this week. I think it's quite possible that you'd have had more discussion of ideas in a Menzies cabinet than in John Howard's. As far as I can work out, when ideas are brought up in cabinet, some of the real toughs usually manage to stamp on them — they don't want change at the moment, whereas the Gorton and even Fraser cabinets understood that things were changing.

The point is that we don't look to politicians for intellectual activity. They can get behind things if they wish, they're our last resort.

Keating, to my mind, was a rather bizarre figure: imagining he was born to be prime minister, he went about picking up these odds and ends of ideas, some of which were quite okay, but there's a lot more to politics than that and he forgot the other bits. One of the things I couldn't ever understand about Keating was that, despite carrying on about nationalism and so forth, he didn't want a national museum. He liked the idea of art galleries and museums — silver teapots and so on — I don't know if he ever went into them, but he liked the idea. But not of a *national* museum.

I really despair sometimes, you know, about the possibility of Australians implementing a really good museums policy, one that covers the National Museum to be opened in the year 2001 to celebrate the centenary of the Australian State[10]. Increasingly, as we know, we live in a world of things being like other things, where we no longer see the actual things themselves. My hope is that Australians could go to the National Museum and be presented with objects which are interesting in themselves — not just blow-ups and

10 The National Museum of Australia is planned to open in Canberra in 2001. While a Visitors' Centre and a growing collection have existed for some years, the building is still to be constructed. The National Museum will focus on Aboriginal and Torres Strait Islander art and history; Australia's national history and migration; and people and the environment since settlement.

audio and electronic models and so on, but the objects themselves. I'd like to see a museum which didn't just instruct you in the old-fashioned way in taxonomies — those are insects, this is the French school of painting and so forth — but which could be a place where you could argue about existence. Three things would be vital: examples of the characteristics of the physical environment (the hardest thing to do in a museum); physical manifestations of Aboriginal culture, including the present-day culture; and the diversity of Australian social experience. The museum would be a discussion place.

There's a wonderful museum (one of my favourite museums in Australia) called the Pioneer Women's Hut, in Tumbarumba, a town nestling beside the Snowy Mountains in Southern New South Wales — the location of our Mount Olympus in some ways, according to certain types of Australian mythology. The Pioneer Women's Hut was started by some women who wanted to show that there were not only men involved in pioneering, but women as well. And they got clothes pegs together, doilies and butterbox furniture, all that kind of stuff, things they collected themselves, and it fulfils one of the most important roles of museums: it helps you define yourself and interest yourself in your own life by looking at objects. There'll never be a great museum movement in Australia unless we move in that direction.

Marcia Langton

6 A man with a Scottish accent I can't even understand

can go on television and talk about [Aboriginal] matters,

but Aboriginal women can't,

the perception of who can appear on television or

in the media being based on all sorts of

cultural, ethnic, sexual and ideational factors

which simply eliminate certain people

from public life. 9

F EW ABORIGINAL INTELLECTUALS *have the public profile of Marcia Langton. Frequently called on by the media to comment on Aboriginal issues, she has made an unparalleled contribution, with her insistence on creative solutions to our problems, to changing the way Australians think about everything from land rights to copyright on Aboriginal design. Marcia Langton has also been an active member, over some twenty years, of numerous organisations, both grass-roots and governmental, dedicated to radically changing the lives of Aboriginal Australians for the better: from the Aboriginal Medical Service in Redfern, Sydney, to Black Theatre, the Australian Institute for Aboriginal and Torres Strait Islander Studies, the Central Land Council and the Royal Commission into Aboriginal Deaths in Custody, of which she was Head of the Aboriginal Issues Unit. In 1993 she was awarded the Order of Australia for her contribution to anthropology and advocacy of Aboriginal rights.*

But her participation in public life doesn't stop there. At present she occupies the Ranger Chair of Aboriginal and Torres Strait Islander Studies at the Northern Territory University and has lectured in anthropology at Macquarie University in Sydney. And over many years, both in Australia and overseas, she has pursued an interest in theatre and the arts, acting in revues, film and television.

Her work on the Reconciliation Council[1] has made her very aware of the different meanings this seemingly simple word — reconciliation — can have for Australians. While on the face of it reconciliation has connotations of healing old rifts and acknowledging the rights and dignity of old adversaries, in the Australian context reconciliation all too often seems to mean an acknowledgment on the part of Aboriginal Australians that they lost the war. The rest of the population is being asked to reconcile itself to very little. It's a stance that members of the Reconciliation Council, including Marcia Langton, are very aware of and, as she says, horrified by.

---

1 The Council for Aboriginal Reconciliation was established in 1992 with the aim of overseeing the process of reconciliation between indigenous Australians and the wider non-indigenous Australian community.

THE PROPOSITION OF RECONCILIATION is what is in the Act[2]. In order to avoid the emotions roused by the term 'treaty', the Reconciliation Council has a period of time in which to find out whether or not the people of Australia believe reconciliation could be achieved by a 'document or documents of reconciliation'. The notion of reconciliation was devised during the period of the Hawke Government from a number of sources: Robert Tickner, obviously, who was the Minister for Aboriginal Affairs, the views of Aboriginal people consulted during the course of the Royal Commission into Aboriginal Deaths in Custody, and the concerns of the Aboriginal leadership, particularly Patrick Dodson, who was the Commissioner into underlying issues in Western Australia in the Royal Commission[3]. Once we'd completed our consultations in the Royal Commission — I worked for the Royal Commission in the Northern Territory — it became clear that in rural and remote Australia, outside the cities, there's a detumescence of the frontier taking place, a suppressed anger and rage amongst the white population. It's non-specific in a way — they themselves don't understand and can't identify the reasons for their rage against Aboriginal people — but it's expressed in a number of forms: one of them, for instance, is the subtle, but nevertheless tangible, forms of apartheid existing in all rural and remote-area townships, the cultural regime of Them and Us.

One of the most significant expressions of this suppressed post-frontier rage in the white population is the way in which the police habitually lock up Aboriginal people. When I was working at Groote Eylandt in the Northern Territory on the Royal Commission, the Aboriginal imprisonment rate was the highest in the world, with nearly 3000 per 100,000 in prison. Of course, on Groote Eylandt we're talking about a tiny sample, but Berrimah prison, for example, just outside Darwin is packed floor to ceiling with Aboriginal prisoners, Aboriginal bodies are piled up to the rafters, while there are very few white prisoners. It's like that in all the remote-area prisons.

Until the Royal Commission, white Australia had very little sense

---

2 The *Council for Aboriginal Reconciliation Act 1991*.
3 Patrick Dodson was in 1989 appointed as a member of the Royal Commission into Aboriginal Deaths in Custody. He is former Chairperson of the Council for Aboriginal Reconciliation and was Director of the Kimberley Land Council.

of what it was doing to Aboriginal people, but now it can be described in terms of facts and figures. In my opinion, what reconciliation ought to be about is getting Anglo-Irish immigrants, especially those who've been here for a number of generations, the real post-frontier white Australians, to understand their own take on Australia, to examine the particular limitations they've placed on themselves through fear of and paranoia about the yellow hordes or Aboriginal people. (You might have noticed the high fences and savage dogs people keep in these towns — out of fear of Aboriginal people.)

Another instance: during elections here in the Territory, the message is always trotted out that 'Aborigines are getting too much'. It's trotted out by the provincial politicians, whether Country–Liberal Party (CLP) or Labor, although the CLP put it much more crudely. The northern suburbs of Darwin vote CLP basically in order to keep Aboriginal people out of town, although if you say that to them, they say that's ridiculous. Last year on the radio I made the point that out of a sense of decency somebody ought to warn those visitors to Australia for the Olympics in 2000 with brown skin and slightly flared nostrils that they should be very careful because they're as likely as not to be locked up and have the bejesus belted out of them by the coppers. Well, all these letters to Murdoch's local rag, the *Northern Territory News*, started coming in, demanding I be strung up and drawn and quartered for saying this. They hate to be told it, they don't like facing this about themselves, but it's the fact. They demand, in their turn, that we face the fact that we're getting too much, although the evidence points in the opposite direction towards extreme disadvantage and inequity. People speak of 'downward envy' and 'compassion fatigue' and so on, but basically it's a defence against facing the deeply embedded, deeply disguised white-supremacist foundations of white Australian culture.

As a result of the Pauline Hanson[4] phenomenon these feelings of rage and resentment are no longer quite as buried as they were a couple of

---

4 Langton's views on Pauline Hanson are expressed in her chapter, 'Pauline as the thin edge of the wedge', in Phillip Adams' anthology *The Retreat from Tolerance: Snapshots of Australian society* (ABC Books, 1997).

years ago. Isn't there at least some advantage in having all the cards on the table?

Yes, I think there is. It's important for intellectuals in particular, and I mean all kinds of intellectuals, including journalists — everyone who contributes to public life through images or words — to understand that there's a national hysteria about the Aboriginal question. Now, although nobody likes these kinds of comparisons to be made, there's a tone to the expression of this hysteria, a feeling to it, which you found in the Holocaust. The Holocaust was on a completely different scale and I'm not making a direct comparison, but there are similarities in the hysteria. And it's important to remember that it's over a tiny minority, a quarter of a million people, possibly one and a half per cent of the population.

So, I think it's important that people experiencing not road rage but Aboriginal rage get it off their chests and out in the open, that the supression of emotions be publicly acknowledged. That's better for everybody. It's through the suppression of rage, after all, that the Ku Klux Klan, the League of Rights and anti-Semitism work. Once it's out in the open we can deal with it. To that extent it's a healthy development, in my view. However, the assertion that these views have been suppressed needs to be put in context. John Howard's proposition that for thirteen years the country has been ruled by a politically correct elite, seeking to convey a black armband view of history, which paints the entirety of Australian history as something to be ashamed of, stopping the ordinary man and woman, the battler, the mainstream, from having their views heard — this proposition is, in my view, utterly ridiculous. It's also poisonous and a deliberate strategy for silencing the critique. To make such an assertion you have to take seriously the proposition that the ordinary man and woman's point of view has been suppressed. Now, that is clearly a nonsense.

At the same time, I don't want to go over the top about our tradition of democracy and free speech. There are, as we know on the other side of this debate, many subtle forms of silencing people: the unbelievably low standards of the newspapers, for example, the low standards of journalism and the low standards of public debate.

Then there's the question of who is allowed to appear as a spokesperson on television: you never see a traditional Aboriginal person on television arguing a case. When I've asked, for instance, that certain Aboriginal women appear on television instead of me, they won't have it, claiming these women don't have 'the right look' or aren't articulate enough. So a man with a Scottish accent I can't even understand can go on television and talk about these matters, but Aboriginal women can't, the perception of who can appear on television or in the media being based on all sorts of cultural, ethnic, sexual and ideational factors which simply eliminate certain people from public life.

So, this proposition of Howard's, or (shall we say) the Liberal Party spin doctors, about political correctness and the silencing of the ordinary man and woman is really saying that what was assumed to be normal, the centre and source of life in this country — that is, white Anglo-Australian cultures — has become so heavily contested that there's a danger that the powers that be will have to start examining some of their own concepts, peeling back the layers. And this they refuse to do. That's what it's really all about. That's why there are these fantasies about yellow hordes and an Australian president who is a half-Korean, half-Chinese lesbian[5].

How much debate is there within the Aboriginal community about immigration politics? What interest does the Aboriginal community have in the further immigration of non-Aboriginal people?

Since the levels of education amongst Aboriginal people are even worse than amongst Pauline Hanson's people, you naturally have exactly the same kind of debate going on there as in Australia as a whole. To be frank, there are some Aboriginal people who have adopted the white-Australian racist position on immigration, which is itself a remnant of the 'great chain of being' theory, with the British at the top, Aborigines at the bottom, and the Chinese and Japanese somewhere in the middle, after the Slavs. All the same, it can be much easier for Aboriginal people to do business with people

---

5 Pauline Hanson, *Pauline Hanson — The Truth: On Asian immigration, the Aboriginal question, the gun debate and the future of Australia*, (limited edition) published by P. Hanson, Ipswich, Qld.

who haven't come here with the old frontier mind-set — the Chinese, Europeans, people who come from somewhere else — than with white Australian companies. We've had no problems doing business over the last fifteen or twenty years under the Land Rights Act[6]— negotiations on mining and tourism, for instance — with companies who are prepared to do business with us without all the insulting nonsense about 'mobile sacred sites' of the kind the Hugh Morgan[7] faction in the mining industry puts about. Likewise, strong links have been developed with the indigenous peoples throughout Southeast Asia, especially in Malaysia, Indonesia and Taiwan — Aboriginal people are curious and excited to learn about these peoples. Your ordinary Aboriginal yobbo, though, can think about Asians in pretty much the same way as your local white redneck.

Since you mention sacred sites, why do you think non-Aboriginal Australians hold Aboriginal religion in such low esteem? There seems to be widespread scepticism about the very possibility of Aborigines having developed a sophisticated metaphysical system.

If you go back to the pre-frontier times, there was a debate about whether or not Aborigines were actually human beings, whether or not they had souls, and whether or not they ought to be saved. Christians in Australia were split on the question then, and that debate is still going on in Australia, although in a much more subtle way — usually in terms of the highest pinnacle of civilisation being British and the lowest point being Aboriginal. When Aboriginal people were finally severely routed, and the remnants incarcerated in settlements and reserves, the project of assimilation sought to turn Aboriginal people into white Australians, since the belief then was that there was nothing worthwhile in Aboriginal life. And that project is barely behind us. Here in the Territory it ended in 1972, and it wasn't until 1973 that the administrators of the settlements were

---

6 The *Aboriginal Land Rights (Northern Territory) Act 1976* was passed by the Fraser Government and proclaimed on Australia Day 1977. The Act recognised Aboriginal Land Rights in the Northern Territory and made provision for a land trust to hold title to Aboriginal land, including freehold title to former reserves.
7 Hugh Morgan is the CEO of Western Mining Corporation.

finally shipped out. Amongst white people the strong assumption remains, however, that Aborigines must really want to be like 'us', 'they'd be so much happier'. When I was at university, I remember, a woman in my class once said to me, 'Marcia, you're so beautiful you could pass yourself off as white if you wanted to, I don't understand why you don't'. Behind a remark such as that is a huge set of assumptions, such as how I could love my mother or grandmother, given that they could not have been 'beautiful'. This woman had no idea at all how insulted I was — she thought she was being nice to me.

Now, these attitudes have influenced perceptions of Aboriginal belief systems. It's very difficult to talk about Aboriginal religion and the philosophical apprehension of the world it provides. The anthropologists who documented these systems from the 1840s onwards have never, with very few exceptions, allowed their precious scholarly considerations to become matters of public debate. They're off having some obscure debate about Aboriginal identity and the fictionality or construction of identity, while Aboriginal leaders are trying to do something about the stolen children. So the belief systems are not something the Australian public is aware of, it has almost no understanding of them.

Now, instead of the anthropologists doing it as they might have done, we have a group of New Ageists doing it, causing enormous amounts of damage in their wake. There are various writings on Aboriginal religion such as Marlo Morgan's *Mutant Messenger Down Under*[8], the Didgeridoo Festival in Europe, and the ferals invading our communities, with some Aboriginal gurus amongst them. It's a nice scam. So, by and large, Aboriginal religion is perceived to be a set of primitive superstitions by most white Australians. There are very few Australians who understand that here is a perfectly viable religious system which is alive and well today, and indeed is the inspiration for the wonderful Aboriginal art which so excites European and American markets and which many Australians have stashed away in their garage as trinkets and souvenirs.

---

8 (HarperCollins, 1994). First self-published in the United States in the early 1990s as a factual account of the author's experiences, it was internationally published by HarperCollins as fiction. A group of Aboriginal people in Western Australia campaigned to stop publication in Australia.

Together with dance and music, in somewhat Westernised forms, it's the art that is perhaps most valued by non-Aborginal Australians and thought of as highly sophisticated. But that interest also brings problems with it, presumably.

Yes. Very few Australians would be aware when they're watching a dance performance (as, for example, at the opening of the Aboriginal Art Awards here in Darwin) that what they're being offered is like a prelude to a great performance. It's not the performance itself, it's not the whole orchestra and it's not Covent Garden. These excised stanzas, as it were, are taken from very long song cycles, whole cere- monial repertoires, which, when performed as part of Aboriginal life, involve numbers of groups of people preparing for weeks. Performances such as these might go on for quite some time, and they're perceived to have effects such as healing people's grief; setting the balance right between the human species, the non-human species and the ancestors; accepting a stance of contrition from people who are seen to have done the wrong thing; ensuring that all of the non- human species are able to reproduce and so on. This sort of thing is rarely understood.

What about the visual arts and the problem of the integration of non- Aboriginal techniques into Aboriginal art, and also, in the other direc- tion, the use of Aboriginal motifs and techniques in non-Aboriginal art?

There have been some quite crude appropriations of Aboriginal designs for various purposes, and there have been some cases of litigation as a result. Prominent early cases of appropriation include David Malangi's painting on the old one-dollar note, used without his knowledge, and a drawing of an Aboriginal boy with a morning star pole sculpted by Terry Yumbulul — a highly sacred object — improperly used on the Bicentenary-issue ten-dollar note with a holo- gram, again without permission. And there have been similar appro- priations of designs, on T-shirts, breadspreads, umbrella stands and more recently carpets. The carpets case has been called the Mabo of intellectual copyright and cultural copyright in Australia because it was the first case in which there was a decision by the court rather than an out-of-court settlement. The ruling was that the Aboriginal person who painted those designs has the authority and the rights under Australian copyright law, and that the appropriation of those designs is a breach of their intellectual copyright. We haven't yet reached the stage where copyright law in this country recognises cultural property — that the Aboriginal group from which the design emanates as a clan-design owns that design — so that the law might be extended to cover the ownership of the design under Aboriginal law and not merely under Australian law, in the same way that Aboriginal land tenure systems are recognised in the High Court's Mabo decision concerning native title.

What about less specific cases of cultural borrowing?

Sometimes it's appalling and sometimes it's brilliant. Cultural influence and diffusion can't be avoided. It's how cultures work — what a hybrid culture is. Sometimes there's official agreement to cultural diffusion, as in the case of Australia's Olympic Games emblem (the circle of dots, depicted in the logo in rainbow colours, being a very ancient Aboriginal symbol), and sometimes it occurs without official agreement. Many Australians who might hate Aborigines would not realise that the designs on their crockery or their bedspreads were in fact inspired by Aboriginal art, because they're seen as just part of Australian life. Since the thirties, forties and fifties, when the work of Margaret Preston[9], the Jindyworobak movement[10], and various graphic designers of the period became popular, and the first tourism posters

---

9 Margaret Preston's (1875–1963) evolving painting style led her in the 1940s and 1950s to declare there should be a 'national art' for Australia based on Aboriginal artforms. During this period she was highly influenced by Aboriginal art, reducing the range of her palette and simplifying her line to produce works such as 'Aboriginal Landscape' (1941) and 'Flying Over Shoalhaven River' (1942). 10 The Jindyworobak movement was established by Rex Ingamells in Adelaide in the 1930s. An expression of Australian nationalism, its aim was to free Australian art from 'alien influences'. While a largely literary grouping — at times such authors as Max Harris, Geoffrey Dutton, Judith Wright and Gwen Harwood were associated with it — there was an attempt to link with other art-forms, particularly from Aboriginal culture. This attempted connection was criticised, but Ingamells was convinced that Australian artists could learn from the close association of Aboriginal traditions and culture with the environment. Jindyworobak (the name chosen because it was 'aboriginal' and 'symbolic') was ultimately too narrowly focused and was overwhelmed by the onset of World War II.

designed by Gert Sellheim appeared together with his 1947 Qantas Flying Kangaroo, and became so much part of Australian life, it hasn't occurred to anyone that the inspiration for these designs was Aboriginal.

✧

One of the defining features of a public intellectual in Western societies is their ability to speak out on a range of public issues, usually moving outwards from some core of expertise. One problem for Aboriginal public figures in a position to assume this role is that no one seems much interested in their opinions on any subject except Aboriginal issues. Marcia Langton, for example, has extensive experience in the areas of film and theatre, but invitations to speak or write on these areas are non-existent.

I'm never invited to contribute to white Australian public life, except to comment on Aboriginal matters. I am not invited, say, to write a film or theatre review or to comment on any piece of work that is not produced by an Aboriginal person, unless it touches on Aboriginal life. But to say something about *Priscilla, Queen of the Desert,* for example . . . no.

Let alone adoption or Buddhism. Does it bother you?

Yes, it does. For me it's another aspect of the way the Australian version of apartheid works. It wouldn't occur to the ordinary white person that I might have a contribution to make to Australian culture in general. To get away from it I go overseas — Asia, America, Africa, London — to affirm my humanity, my membership of the human species, since white Australians are, by and large, incapable of treating me as an ordinary human being. At the private level, of course, I have friends who treat me as I would like — I insist on it — but in public life it's not the case. Nobody wants to hear my views on anything except Aboriginal issues. For that matter, I wonder if they want to hear the views of other non-White Australians — Vietnamese women, for example, or Chinese or Arabic women.

Except on immigration or multiculturalism.

What do they think about the big questions, though, what do they think about taxation, environmental laws, urban planning or public architecture? This is what I'd like to hear.

You've never been asked about public architecture in Darwin?

No, and I've certainly got some some views.

I wonder how people like you or Noel Pearson are regarded by 'ordinary' Aborigines. Do you ever get the feeling some of them might feel you've become an elite, or too personally prominent, or that you talk too much? Or is the feeling mostly one of pride?

I think there are lots of young people who've had a few educational opportunities who look forward to hearing what I have to say and reading what I write. They come up to me and say, 'You're a real role model, keep it up', to which I say, 'Look, that's very nice, but it's your job too'. It's good to know there's an audience out there, however small, and I'm getting through to it, it enjoys what I'm saying and finds it relevant. At the same time there are quite a few Aboriginal people who criticise me in what I think are ridiculous and crude terms. For instance, some Aboriginal men have said I don't have any right to speak in public at all because I'm a woman and under Aboriginal law women aren't allowed to do that. Well, I know a fair bit about Aboriginal law, and that's absolutely not the case. The strict gender segregation is very limited in its application, and in Australian public life I'm encouraged by the ordinary man and woman, under Aboriginal law, to say what needs to be said. That's because I have been given a voice and am acceptable to the media. And there are some Aboriginal people who say that my views on Aboriginal life are stated merely so that I can get myself a job, and that I'm patronised by the Australian intellectual elite. This is nonsense — I do what I do in the same way anyone else does who is employed by a university and seeks to maintain the tradition of critique Edward Said argues for in public intellectuals.

Some white intellectuals accuse me of the same thing. Their analysis is that people like myself were favoured by Keating's government and given prestige and influence in order to secure our co-operation. I reject that sort of ignorant analysis, whether it comes from white intellectuals or Aboriginal people who think I'm on a nice scam, like some of the Aboriginal gurus in the New Age movement. There's been no particular advantage for me in stating my position on various issues — for example, on native title — whether under the Keating or the Howard governments. Apart from finding myself constantly censured in public and encountering the opprobrium of a conservative Australian public in the workplace, in the shopping centres and elsewhere, I'm experiencing the difficulties many academics are facing at the moment. The sort of thing I do is considered an extra-curricular activity, it's not considered appropriate to be an academic and a public intellectual — in fact, it's not tolerated by the powers that be, who, following the hard Thatcherite line of economic rationalism, insist that the staff now have to make money for the university. The age of the public intellectual is coming to an end in Australia.

◆

What does self-determination mean to you? And what is the connection between self-determination and sovereignty?

Self-determination is a very simple and at the same time very difficult concept. According to the Universal Declaration of Human Rights[11] all peoples have the right to determine their own status. This was seen as particularly important in the immediate post-War years because of the displaced peoples and minority groups, and because of what had happened to the Jews. It's a very clear statement of group rights, not just individual rights, which are the traditional concern of small-l liberals, underpinning the position of the Liberal Party of

---

11 On 10 December 1948 in the General Assembly of the United Nations, 48 countries voted the Universal Declaration of Human Rights into existence, the result of three years' work of the UN's Commission for Human Rights. When the Declaration was made in 1948, it said, in part, that the 'recognition of the inherent dignity and of the equal and inalienable rights of all members of the human family is the foundation of freedom, justice and peace in the world'.

Australia and liberal American republicanism. Well, there are group rights as well, there have always been, and they're recognised in the developing international legal system.

So self-determination was one of those group rights that emerged in that post-Second World War period in order to have a philosophical basis for conflict resolution. It afforded minority groups the possibility of determining their own futures within the newly emerging post-colonial nation-states. Of course, the challenge of the twenty-first century is to solve the intensifying conflicts between minority groups (which are increasingly being called 'ethnic' groups). In the 1920s the Iroquois people went to the League of Nations to argue for their rights as a domestic nation within the American nation. They had always had the Federal Treaties and they didn't want them dispensed with, thereby eliminating the Indian jurisdiction in America. So the debate in Australia about self-determination really takes off from that domestic sovereignty position of the American Indians. Now you have the emergence of many indigenous groups around the world seeking self-determination, some of whom face particularly severe problems, such as the Guatemalan Indians, who were being wiped out by helicopter gunships — for indigenous peoples such as the Guatemalan Indians the right to self-determination is obviously a crucial issue. It's less obviously so to Australians who've had the old-fashioned liberal idea about human rights being equivalent to individual rights pummelled into them by the Menzies regime. The concept of group rights is weak and unelaborated in Australia.

So what self-determination for Aboriginal peoples involves is very simply an international legal basis for moving on from the assimilation period and working out through a cooperative method, through conflict resolution, through negotiation how Australia's indigenous people are going to fit into the modern nation-state — what rights we have have as a group and so on. I'm not at all convinced by the argument for Aboriginal sovereignty. Sovereignty is a concept emerging out of the development of European nation-states. The concept of self-determination, however, permits parallel government systems, parallel legal systems of the kind we hope will emerge in Palestine between Palestinians and the Israelis. The only hope for an end to the idiocy of the conflict in Australia, the race-based conflict, is an acceptance of parallelism, where Aboriginal government systems or institutions work alongside general Australian government systems. In that situation you'd have Aboriginal councils working alongside provincial governments and local governments, with many of the powers of those governments even being delegated to local Aboriginal governments.

✧

The historian Henry Reynolds considers that the tradition of an Aboriginal intellectual elite is probably much older than we think.

Henry Reynolds

I think it's a misunderstanding of the situation to say that an elite has only recently emerged. I think the first political intellectual of the modern sort was Walter George Arthur[12] in Tasmania. He was active in the 1830s and 1840s and had, I think, all the characteristics of contemporary Aboriginal people: he was Christian, he both spoke and wrote English, he had given up his tribal identity for a pan-Tasmanian identity — talking about Tasmanians as his people, almost like a nineteenth-century European patriot, in totally different ways from his father. Tasmania was at that time still a deeply divided society of tribes who couldn't understand each other's languages, were sworn enemies and so on.

One of the major influences very early in the piece was the use of English, which, as it became widespread, was a means of common

---

12 Captured at the age of ten during the guerilla war between the Tasmanian settlers and the Tasmanian Aborigines, Walter George Arthur was notable for his valiant attempts to conform to European behaviour. Taught to read and write at the Orphan School in Hobart Town, he then worked as a stockman and drover at Port Phillip, but was eventually sent to Flinders Islands where the remnants of the Tasmanian Aborigines dispossessed of their land had been exiled. Their harsh treatment at the hands of various superintendents, particularly Dr Jeanneret, eventually led Walter George Arthur and others of the group to petition not only the lieutenant-governor in Hobart, but, in 1846, Queen Victoria, to remind the queen that the commitments the crown had made in verbal peace negotiations with Tasmania's Aborigines in 1832 had been broken. George died in 1861 at just 41 years of age at Oyster Cove where the group had been dismally resettled.

communication which hadn't existed before. Equally, at an early period you had young people who learnt how to deal with Europeans, acquiring skills they could use in the European workforce, learning to speak English and understand the whitefella and his society. They may not have had much power within their own society, but in a way they came to play an important role because they could live in both worlds.

What's happened in recent times is the setting up of institutions of all sorts — by governments, but also by community organisations — and this has meant that people from all over Australia have met, establishing networks of influential people right across the country who know one another, deal with the mainstream society, are increasingly well-educated and, indeed, in a sense may be seeing something like a pan-Aboriginality emerge.

Now, some of them come from societies which do not have powerful tribal traditions still surviving, while others come from some of the most traditional parts of Australia — the Yunupingus[13], for example, or Noel Pearson and some of the people at Hopevale[14], who are really extraordinary in their capacity to live in two worlds socially, culturally and intellectually — they are extraordinary people. But I don't think the fact that they are now able to impact so importantly on the mainstream society is a new development — they're perhaps better at it than anyone was in the past, but even Walter George Arthur was able to petition Queen Victoria, which led to the British Government deciding that this was a major issue and, if the humanitarian lobby got hold of it, they'd cause a lot of trouble in the House of Commons, so something should be done about it. As I say, I think we'll find a tradition there which is waiting for its historian: a tradition of people who, while remaining in their own societies, were able to cope quite well and impact on the mainstream society.

---

13 Galarrwuy Yunupingu is the senior member of the Gumatj people, who since 1983 has been Chairperson of the Northern Lands Council. Also a member of the Council for Aboriginal Reconciliation, Galarrwuy Yunupingu was Australian of the Year in 1978. His brother Mandawuy was also Australian of the Year, but in 1992. The leader of the very successful band Yothu Yindi, he has been involved in reviewing education for Aboriginal and Torres Islander people.

14 A mission originally set up in Far North Queensland in 1885. After a difficult history, the community became the first in Queensland to receive land under the Deed of Grant in Trust, at Hopevale's centenary in 1986.

Surely there was a shift during the Keating years?

Yes, there's no doubt that the setting up of ATSIC in 1990 was an extremely important development. Through this initiative of the government establishing an institution which came in over the top of all those existing community organisations — largely Aboriginal-run legal, medical and media services which had been incorporated, and therefore received government funds — large numbers of Aborigines and Torres Strait Islanders were recruited into the bureaucracy, so in that sense a national political class was created which had not existed before. At the same time, with the High Court's Mabo judgment, there had to be negotiations at the highest level, so a group which was partly self-selected and partly chosen by government negotiated with the prime minister, senior ministers and senior bureaucrats — that was certainly a new development, no doubt about it. So people like Marcia Langton and Noel Pearson have now had that extremely important experience of negotiating with government, almost in the Canadian sense of talking nation to nation. De facto I think that's what happened in Australia. So, in brief, I think this tradition goes back a long way, although it wasn't conceptualised that way at the time.

Telling the Truth

Barry Jones

Margaret Wertheim

Raimond Gaita

❝ Since the seventeenth century in the West,
we've looked to science to tell us
what the fundamental nature of reality is. ❞

Margaret Wertheim

❝ To paraphrase Simone Weil, if you want to know
how bright a torch is, you don't shine it into
your eyes and look at the bulb, you
flash it around to see what it lights up. ❞

Raimond Gaita

J UST A FEW CENTURIES AGO *in the West, the study of 'what is really there' — truth, in a word — was more or less encompassed by what was called religion. Philosophers, theologians, physicists and others, all worked more or less within the very broad church of the Christian Church. Knowledge of the truth was its business, even if they differed in their paths to it.*

At the end of the millennium, however, things look rather different, with science, philosophy and religion tending to operate in different spheres. Fashionable scientists refer to God, of course, and philosophy can scarcely ignore either the physical sciences or religious argument any more than religious thinkers can philosophise without reference to the other two disciplines, but they tend to present themselves as very different kinds of discourse about what is really there, with different rules and different ideas about how to behave, given what is there.

And just to complicate matters, there's a widespread belief in many intellectual circles in the West today that no one can ever know what is really there anyway. The idea of seeing truth face to face is, to them, a nonsense, at least in theory. Or perhaps only in theory.

In the conversations that follow, I talk with three Australians who speak and write about these questions, three thinkers who do, in fact, cross boundaries between disciplines in their pursuit of knowledge of what's really there. The first, Barry Jones, being both 'politically and scientifically literate', as he puts it, has worked tirelessly to make science an important part of our lives. He was the first minister for science ever appointed by an Australian government, and he's been involved in numerous projects over the years to make the opinion of scientists count in shaping Australia.

Although we live in an age of scientific achievement, the names of few scientists working in Australia come immediately to mind when we think of who our most prominent public intellectuals — Peter Singer[1], perhaps, Gus Nossal[2], Paul Davies — a few do, but not as many as we

1 Philosopher, bioethicist and outspoken campaigner for animal rights and the environment, Singer is author of such books as the award-winning *Rethinking Life and Death: The collapse of our traditional ethics* (Text Publishing, 1994) and *How Are We to Live: Ethics in an age of self-interest* (Text Publishing, 1993).

2 Sir Gustav Nossal is an internationally recognised immunologist and science administrator, who, for 30 years (until 1996), was the Director of the Walter and Eliza Hall Institute for Medical Research in Melbourne. He is Professor Emeritus of the University of Melbourne and Deputy Chair of the Council for Aboriginal Reconciliation.

might have expected. How successful are our scientists at popularising scientific concepts?

Barry Jones

I once gave John Howard a copy of *War and Peace* after extracting a promise from him that he'd actually read it. He said, 'Why are you so keen for me to read it?', and I said, 'If you become prime minister, it will make you a better prime minister'. On the evidence I'm not absolutely sure that he's read it.

At one level there's a high degree of public interest in science, as measured by the coverage in the media and the high ratings of ABC programs such as 'The Science Show' and 'Quantum', and in terms of scientific literacy, Australia does as well as Great Britain and rather better than the United States. From that point of view we're not doing too badly. On another level, when you think of the number of people who are recognisable as spokespersons for science, there are very few. People like Adrienne Clark[3], Paul Davies[4] and Gus Nossal come to mind, of course, but Gus Nossal in particular has a political mind-set, he understands how you have to alter the message to pitch it to a particular audience.

There's an explanation for this: this is an age of super-specialisation in science. As a result, a lot of people climbing up the ladder want to concentrate on their subset of interests in a particular discipline. They feel there's nothing whatever to be gained by moving into broader issues. Now, this is partly a generational thing. In earlier generations scientists weighed in on very broad issues indeed (Albert Einstein being easily the best known, but it was true of a lot of his contemporaries as well). They talked about war and peace and life and death

---

3 From 1991 to 1996, Adrienne Clark was the Chair of the Commonwealth Scientific and Industrial Research Organisation (CSIRO), the first woman to hold this position. She holds a Personal Chair in the School of Botany at Melbourne University, is Director of the Plant Cell Biology Research Centre, and also Lieutenant-Governor of Victoria.

4 Paul Davies is a world-renowned physicist based in Adelaide. The winner of the Templeton Prize for Progress in Religion, he is Visiting Professor at Imperial College London. Among his books are the Eureka Prize-winning *The Mind of God* (Penguin, 1992), *Are We Alone?* (Penguin, 1995) and *The Fifth Element* (Viking, 1998).

and the meaning of life — a very broad kind of agenda. And it wasn't held against them that they were talking outside their own particular discipline. Now you'll find that particle physicists think it utterly disreputable to be talking in public about anything other than the subject of particle physics. You can see it in the cases of people like Stephen Hawking[5] or the late Carl Sagan[6]: the fact that they were public figures was really held against them. Stephen J. Gould[7] is in exactly the same position: he's dumped on, sometimes publicly, but mostly privately, by colleagues complaining that he's not concentrating on his own discipline.

And science and mathematics are really foreign languages. When you talk in a foreign language such as algebra, you may as well be talking in German. So people say, 'Look, without a translator, I don't understand it'.

But there must be translators there somewhere. In any case, it seems to me that there are public issues, such as euthanasia, immigration and race — all issues high on the public agenda — on which science must have vital things to say, from an almost neutral position.

I'd like to think that was actually so, but let me give you an illustration of how difficult it is to bring people together on common ground. When I was chairing the Committee on Population[8], we asked the

5 A theoretical physicist and mathematician, Stephen Hawking holds the Lucasian Chair of Mathematics at Cambridge once held by Newton. His research helped confirm the Big Bang but his main area of research has been into black holes. He is the author of the runaway success *A Brief History of Time* (Bantam, 1988).

6 Carl Sagan (1924–96) was Professor of Astronomy and Space Sciences at Cornell University. His long-term fascination was with the origin of life on Earth and the possibility of life elsewhere in the universe, and he was an adviser to the National Academy of Science and to NASA. Many of his books have been reissued including *Cosmos* (Little, Brown & Co., 1996), based on his television series of the same name (1977), *Pale Blue Dot*, (Hodder Headline, 1996) and *Billions and Billions* (Hodder Headline, 1997). His novel, *Contact* (Little, Brown and Co., 1997) was made into a 1997 feature film.

7 Professor of Geology and Zoology at Harvard, Gould is primarily a palaeontologist and evolutionary biologist who has developed a modified version of Darwin's theory of evolution. A successful populariser of science, among his award-winning books are *Ever Since Darwin* (Penguin, 1987), *The Panda's Thumb* (Penguin, 1987) and *Wonderful Life* (Penguin, 1991).

8 In 1994 the Standing Committee on Long-Term Strategies held an inquiry chaired by Labor Minister Barry Jones into Australia's population-carrying capacity. Most submissions argued for population stability or a reduction in population growth. The report into the inquiry was published in 1994.

committee members, all reputable scientists, to suggest an optimum population number for Australia. Their answers were dramatically different: for example, Professor John Caldwell, probably Australia's leading demographer, with immense international experience and a better knowledge of the field than anyone I can think of, said he'd be quite comfortable with a population of between 50 and 60 million; Professor Jonathan Stone, the Challis Professor of Botany at Sydney University, speaking as the representative of the Australian Academy of Science, had come to the conclusion, after working closely with other scientists, that 23 million was the optimum figure; and Tim Flannery[9], highly regarded in his own expert field and also a very gifted writer, considered there was extreme danger unless Australia cut its population back to around 8 million.

Now, you might say that surely somebody ought to be able to take a neutral stand on the scientific evidence. But it's really a matter of interpretation. Here you have three people, Caldwell, Stone and Flannery, interpreting the data base in radically different ways on the basis of philosophical and even political assumptions about the way in which people live.

Yet, in the present Hanson controversy, the voices of scientists aren't actually being heard at all — at least, they're not published in the Age *or the* Sydney Morning Herald *with any prominence.*

Well, since you've mentioned the 'H' word, let me say that the common element running through the whole Hanson phenomenon is not an anti-Aboriginal or anti-migrant thread, but anti-elitism. It's the argument that the political is being unduly influenced by elites. The reaction of a lot of people in the community to experts from the Australian Academy of Science assuring them that they don't need to worry about immigration levels is to say, 'Thank you, we'd like to make our own minds up on that. We don't want somebody coming

9 Tim Flannery is the principal research scientist at the Australian Museum in Sydney. He is internationally recognised for his contribution to the fields of palaeontology, mammology and conservation. Among his books are *The Future Eaters* (Reed, 1994) and *Throwim Way Leg* (Text Publishing, 1998).

along clothed with the authority of the Academy telling us to shut up and listen because they know best.' This phenomenon, I think, partly comes from the fact that academics have quite often been used as sources of information which governments then use or misuse as they see fit. The academy has also not really been prepared to take part in the cut and thrust of public debate. Many people in the scientific community are very reluctant to join any active debate at all. So you've had an eerie silence from the intellectual community. I'd have thought that on the population question we might have had some robust debate in which a whole lot of demographers and other experts took part, but it didn't happen.

Would you agree that in some sense science is a kind of truth narrative? Its conclusions certainly need interpretation if they're to be applied to the real world — to politics, ecology, education and so forth. But don't scientists themselves see their job as investigating or shining a light on a truth of some kind? And how free do you feel as an individual to move out into more speculative, philosophical, perhaps even religious dimensions in your own thinking?

Well, not being a card-carrying scientist, I don't regard myself as being absolutely bound by what the scientific community says. I mean, I understand what the scientific community is saying, but then scientists don't all, in fact, speak with the one voice, they have a variety of approaches. There's no party line.

Still, you would presumably more or less accept evolution, for example, as a truth.

Yes, but not necessarily the whole truth. The fact that I believe in Darwinian theory doesn't mean, for example, that I accept the concept of eugenics. The great debate that went on in the beginning of the twentieth century, and in some cases no doubt still survives — indeed, I would say it's a fundamental element in the stolen generation report — was about accepting the whole idea of selective breeding. The logic follows inexorably that to breed a higher level of people we ought to make sure that mutations don't survive. This is to take a scientific line and say, 'This is my concept of truth, and I'm going to push this concept of truth at whatever cost, no matter how much pain it causes'.

There's a very controversial new biography of Thomas Jefferson[10] which argues that Jefferson was so carried away by the principles of the Enlightenment, so excited by the principles of absolute reason and scientific certainty, that, in order to confirm these principles, he believed it might be necessary to bump a lot of people off. Well, I'd have to say I dissent respectfully from the view of Jefferson. What I'm conscious of is that while science certainly appears to be a truth narrative a lot of science is really counter-intuitive in its nature. I mean for example, commonsense and observation shows us very clearly that the earth is flat and that the sun moves round the earth. Then the scientist comes along in his white coat and tells us we've got it wrong — it's the other way around. And if you say, 'Well explain it to me', the scientist may well say, 'It's a bit difficult to explain, I'm afraid, and I haven't got the time. I've got more important things to do. Just accept it on faith.' And, in fact, we do accept it on faith, even though it's counter-intuitive. With the exception of people such as Stephen Hawking, Carl Sagan and Paul Davies, scientists are not good at advancing persuasive arguments the public can grasp.

What is it about the writing of the people you mentioned that makes it so persuasive and accessible?

They start from the premise not of what they know, but what they believe people in general know and understand. For example, in a recent book of essays[11] Stephen J. Gould, writing about theories of probability, starts off in the context of baseball, talking about calculating baseball scores and the odds of a home run. So people realise they're talking about statistical probability all the time.

---

10 Max Lerner, *Thomas Jefferson: America's philosopher-king* (Transaction, 1996).
11 *Dinosaur in a Haystack: Reflections on natural history* (Crown, 1997).

By the sound of it, the Australian scientific community could do with more good, lucid communicators. And Margaret Wertheim has an idea or two about how to fix that.

✦

Margaret Wertheim is an Australian science writer who now lives in California. With a background in physics and mathematics, she very effectively communicates her insights into science and technology, and how those particular knowledge industries work and are shaped through magazine articles, television and radio. However, it's her recent book, intriguingly entitled Pythagorus' Trousers: God, Physics and the Gender Wars[12], *which has turned her into something of an international celebrity — a public intellectual with a public in a dozen countries. Briefly,* Pythagorus' Trousers *is about how physics in particular, in Wertheim's view, has grown out of the concept of God as a divine mathematical creator, but has never quite broken free of its institutional origins in Christianity. And those affinities have had their consequences.*

Margaret Wertheim

As knowledge systems, physics and religion both try to articulate the cosmology within which humans live. They both ask, 'What is the world around us and how does it operate?' Sociologically they have a common factor: it is through religion that people articulated what is fundamentally real and what isn't — that's been its classic role. But since the seventeenth century in the West, we've looked to science to tell us what the fundamental nature of reality is. Science, and in particular physics, has taken over that role in the official arenas of our culture. We live in an interesting age in the sense that the official epistemological line comes from science (and I mean what's taught in schools, what you'll hear on the ABC and see in encyclopaedias and the more serious newspapers). Beyond those official organs, of course,

---

12 (Fourth Estate, 1997).

there's a sea of people out there who believe in psychic channelling, astral travelling, reincarnation and so on, so the official line doesn't reflect the beliefs of the whole of society — perhaps even the majority of society. So, while science might be the official epistemology, we have to ask firstly how much of the scientific world picture people understand, and secondly how much of it they accept.

What happened in the seventeenth century to make some people believe that the scientific approach was more valid in the search for truth?

Partly what happened in the seventeenth century is that there were all kinds of practical questions people now wanted to address, because this was the age of navigation. The European countries were sending fleets out to the New World, they needed tools such as navigational aids (requiring mathematics among other things) and they needed better ships. In other words, there was a desire for technological enhancement in all sorts of areas, and the old Aristotelian science was unable to answer the questions that arose.

So, there was a feeling in the early seventeenth century that a new science was needed, both for practical reasons and I think also for quasi-religious reasons. The feeling that the old Aristotelian system was flawed and couldn't answer these sorts of practical questions fed into developing new methodologies and new ways of seeing nature — a secular knowledge — and I think that because of the religious wars of the sixteenth century many people, particularly humanists, were looking for a form of knowledge that was not so allied to dogmatic religious belief, which had led to so many bloody wars.

And this secular knowledge, the scientific approach, produced results (was 'practical', as you put it) in a way in which other kinds of knowledge did not.

There was a desire for new technological knowledge, certainly, and science helped discover it, and the work of artisans also helped — the metal-workers, the wood-workers. But, although it's true that the scientific revolution was in part inspired by the desire to create new technologies, the actual knowledge that science, and in particular physics, produced, didn't in fact lead to a great deal of new working technologies at the time. There was a belief that it could and eventually would, but in fact it was really not until the nineteenth century that physics actually produced much in the way of practical technologies.

So, one of the questions that has to be asked is: why did science get going despite the fact that it actually didn't produce much for quite some time? In *Pythagoras' Trousers* I put forward the view that one of the major reasons is that there was a new conception of truth: that the ultimate truth was mathematical because God had in some sense created a world according to mathematical relationships. Therefore, when we find those mathematical relationships, we are reading the mind of God.

And this truth was now knowable as opposed to religious truth.

Well, one of the things about this truth that was different from religious truth is that it was testable, it was empirically testable. You could do experiments, measuring how gases behaved or how water behaved in pipes (hydrodynamics), or taking measurements of the exact positions of the stars to see how closely they matched your equations. Mathematics was a form of truth that could be demonstrated concretely, and this appealed to people. One of the major issues in the seventeenth century for the founders of modern science, particularly Galileo, was the question of what constituted proof, of how we demonstrated that certain things are true.

In Pythagoras' Trousers *you hint that in the twentieth century, as opposed to the nineteenth when indeed there was some conflict between science and religion, the two disciplines can be seen to be talking about similar sorts of things again. But wouldn't it be true to say that by religion you mean something rather different from orthodox Christianity or Islam. I mean, we don't really find Stephen Hawking or Paul Davies discussing the Trinity, let's say. They're interested in something which, to my ear, sounds much more Eastern.*

Yes, that's precisely the point I'm making in my book. When these physicists write about the mind of God, what do they mean? They don't mean anything like the God the Christian praying in church means: it's not the God of the Trinity, it's not the God of salvation, it's not a God of love, it's not a personal God in any sense.

So the question has to be asked: what, then, is the physicist's God? And the way that I explain it is this: traditionally the Christian deity had two functions — He was God the Creator, the force that created the world, but also, and primarily, God the Redeemer, the great force of love that would ultimately redeem mankind from sin. Now, up until the seventeenth century, Christianity's discussion of God had been primarily focused on God the Redeemer — that was His main function. There was some discussion of God the Creator, but it wasn't a primary function. But in the seventeenth century a major shift took place, whereby the discourse refocused much more on God the Creator than the Redeemer. And since God had created the world according to mathematics, when we discover these mathematical relationships we are reading His mind. Yet, even when people like Kepler[13] and Newton talked in these terms, they were always aware that God the Creator was actually secondary to God the Redeemer.

In the late twentieth century, the God of people like Stephen Hawking is purely God the Creator: His only action was to create the world 15 billion years ago, bringing the supposedly transcendent equation into manifestation, and He's done nothing since and will do nothing again. So He's not really a God, except for the mathematician.

And for redemption we look to the economists and the ecologists.

That's a nice way of putting it. Some people, of course, seek redemption in new forms of religion — I think this is one of the reasons we have so many new forms of religion, particularly in America where I

---

13 Johannes Kepler (1571–1630) was a German astronomer and court mathematician to the Holy Roman Emperor, Rudolph II. His three laws accurately describing the elliptical revolutions of the planets around the sun were the result of calculations based on Tycho Brahe's observations and were physically explained by Isaac Newton with his laws of motion and gravitation. A highly readable fictionalised account of Kepler's life and thought can be found in John Banville's *Kepler* (Secker & Warburg, 1981), now a Minerva paperback.

live. People need a God who offers love and redemption, and physics can't say anything about that kind of God, so they look elsewhere, in all kinds of places. Even if people don't turn to religion, they seek solace in things like 'spiritual' books, such as *The Celestine Prophecies*[14], which has been a huge hit everywhere.

Turning to the public face of science: as in the Church, we seem to expect the high priests of science — those who mediate between humanity and truth — to be men. (From women we may expect grace, but not mediation with truth.)

I think that's exactly right. I believe that one of the reasons that physics is the branch of science in which women participate the least is precisely because it is the science that has by far the longest and deepest entwinement with religion. In fact, physics really emerged from a religious tradition with Pythagoreanism two and a half thousand years ago, and has been a quasi-religious activity ever since. So the fact that you have all these physicists talking about the mind of God is not something new, it's a part of this very long tradition. There's a very real sense in which physicists are the high priests of science, and it's no coincidence that women are largely absent from that science. The unconscious cultural resistance to having women as the high priests of science reflects the belief in our society that it's men who carry authority.

In reviewing *Pythagoras' Trousers*, some people were quite willing to accept that there was a religiosity in physics in the past, but physicists in particular became very upset at the implication that there is religiosity in the field today. Yet it's not me who's writing books about God and physics, it's the physicists themselves. And in our culture, both from the Judaeo-Christian and the Greek heritage, we have a very strong tradition that priests are men.

Physicists sometimes seem to have a strange, ninteenth-century view of what religion is.

---

14 (Transworld, 1995).

It's true that one of the problems in this area is that many physicists have no idea what religion is. Why do we accept the rantings of Stephen Hawking, who has no theological training, on the subject of God? It's an interesting question. If plumbers or carpenters started rabbiting on about the mind of God, would anyone pay any attention to them? I seriously doubt it. So why is it that we accept that physicists have the authority to talk about God despite having absolutely no training in the subject?

What would the effect be, do you think, if there were more women representing science to the public?

One of the huge differences it would make is that they would serve as role models for young girls, encouraging young girls to see that science is potentially a womanly activity. They would feel less alienated by it and might therefore be more encouraged to study it at school and then go on to university. Studies around the world show that girls drop out of science in puberty, basically at the time they start being interested in the opposite sex. Again, studies show that, almost universally, boys and girls both believe that having a maths–science brain is profoundly unsexy and unfeminine in a girl. One way to help overcome this would be to have more female public faces in science — and not just in documentary programs, but in fiction as well. In 'Star Trek' or 'Dr Who', the maths–science brain is usually a man, perhaps with a woman assistant. Why can't we have a Dr Who who's a woman?

Are you also suggesting also that the projects women might undertake would be different? That the way they talk to the public might be different?

I have no doubt that they would talk differently. Whenever I've seen women scientists talk to the public, it's been very different from the way men talk. For instance, a couple of years ago I went to an astrophysics conference where there were some 50 papers, three from women. It was amusing to see how many of the men shuffled up to the podium, shabbily dressed, doing an Einstein, to give rambling speeches — it was almost as if they were proud to be lost in the higher things of science, beyond concerns about their appearance or giving a coherent paper. All three of the women, smartly dressed and crisply presented, gave papers which were paragons of clarity — you could actually understand what they were saying. I've never heard a woman physicist speak publicly who wasn't well prepared and coherent. I'd also say that, in my experience, they almost universally raise issues of both social and personal concern, they're interested in questions of how their science fits into society at large, what its human and social implications are. Of course, there are men who think this way too, and women physicists who don't give a damn. But it's my observation that, on the whole, more women in science think seriously about those issues than men do.

And so might be less interested in spending billions of dollars on finding out if there's life on Mars, say, and more interested in spending billions of dollars on producing more nutritious food more efficiently.

Well, that's a tricky area. I'm not saying there's anything innate about women that makes them caring and sharing or makes men selfish bastards, who just want to get on with their science no matter what the cost.

Can you be quite sure about that, by the way? Can you be quite sure there's nothing that genetically determines this?

I can't be sure, but then no one can be quite sure. I certainly believe it, though. I don't believe that men and women are intellectually determined differently by genetics. It's an act of faith on my part, but then the other position's an act of faith, too. The real issue here is that women and men are socialised differently. So, when women come into fields like law or making television programs, they change the field. Why should it be any different in the case of science? Take the issue of cost: science costs a lot of money and we have to ask what society is getting for its money. When you're suggesting spending, say, ten billion dollars or more on building a super-conductor or super-collider to look for particles nobody has ever heard of, very real questions have to be asked: what is the point of the project and is public money being well spent? Now, it's my observation that women tend to ask these questions more often. And part of the reason for this, I think, is that women are raised to think about such things, raised with the idea that they'll probably have children who will inherit a world. So, it's not that I think women couldn't be totally disregarding — I'm sure there are some women scientists who just think, 'Oh, bugger it, I want to go to Mars' — but on the whole I think that because of the way women are socialised in all fields they are more likely to ask those questions about the point and value of a project and less likely just to say, 'Look, the public ought to give us ten billion dollars'. I think one of the reasons there aren't more women in a field like particle physics is because fewer women than men actually see it as a valuable and socially useful activity.

Of course, if you'd asked about the project to build Chartres Cathedral — if it was a useful and valuable social activity — one answer might have been that, no, it was a waste of resources and that the money could have been better spent on sinking more wells. And, although the search for life on Mars is not a physical cathedral, it is a sort of mental cathedral, an infinitely complex, beautiful thing in terms of knowledge, just as Chartres was in terms of stone and glass.

Yes, I quite agree. In my view, for instance, the so-called Theory of Everything, the desire to have a theory that would unify relativity and quantum mechanics, is a tremendously beautiful thing, worth realising just for the sheer beauty of the knowledge. All the same, there's a very real question of how much money society should spend on such projects. (Some people at the time may have thought the building of the cathedral was socially irresponsible.) If the main by-product of the science is going to be the beauty of truth, then it becomes an aesthetic project and then you have to ask, 'OK, well, at a time when we're slashing funding for the arts right, left and centre, and artists and theatre and opera companies are being asked to get by on the smell of an oily rag, how can we justify giving physicists billions of dollars to give us beautiful knowledge?'

✦

Philosophy just won't go away. On the one hand, anyone who seeks wisdom is a philosopher in some sense: Marx, Kant, Paul Davies, Jesus, perhaps even Shirley MacLaine or your Uncle Harry are all philosophers, all putting forward versions of reality and how to know it. You shouldn't need a special discipline to keep reasoned argument about economics or bioethics or the nature of the self bubbling along.

On the other hand, philosophy in the Western tradition of great thinkers thinking about the great questions in the light of what earlier thinkers in the tradition have said — Socrates, Aquinas, Kant, Hegel, Heidegger and so on (everyone will have their own list) — is suddenly fashionable again, with literally millions of non-specialist readers in Western countries.

It's Jostein Gaarder's introduction to philosophy in Sophie's World[15] *that has been the number one best-seller worldwide, not Patricia Cornwell's novels, or Stephen King's, or even Hawking's* A Brief History of Time. Sophie's World *is a Norwegian schoolteacher's musings on the old questions (who am I? why am I here? why is there something and not nothing and can it be known? and so on) that seems to have struck the loudest chord with the world's readers in recent years.*

As Professor Raimond Gaita[16] of the Institute of Advanced Research at the Australian Catholic University in Melbourne, might suggest, part of the reason for this enduring interest in philosophy in these rudderless times might be that the great questions — and the great answers — are still pertinent today. There's been no closure.

---

15 A 'novel about the history of philosophy', first published in 1991 in Norwegian, in 1995 in English, and now in a Phoenix paperback edition. His second best-seller, *The Solitaire Mystery,* is published by Phoenix House (1996).

16 Raimond Gaita's essays and articles appear regularly in a number of Australian magazines and newspapers, including *Quadrant, Arena* and *Eureka Street.* His autobiographical *Romulus, My Father* (about growing up with his father in country Victoria) was published by Text Publishing in 1998.

Raimond Gaita

I actually have some concerns about the academic subject I'm associated with — moral philosophy. To the annoyance of my colleagues, I've sometimes pointed out that you could be foolish, shallow and wicked yet deserving of a distinguished chair in moral philosophy. Students, too, can be really quite shallow, yet deserving nonetheless of first class honours, because they have learnt to use the analytical tools while remaining tone deaf to sensitive and serious ways of describing moral problems. So, in what I write, I often try not so much to argue a point as to characterise what our sense is of what is at issue. On euthanasia, for example, I've not so much tried to argue that it's right or wrong, but to offer a richer, more complex sense of what is at issue for people who might characterise their position as one that holds life is sacred.

When I was a student, I worked for a time in Mont Park psychiatric hospital in Melbourne. It was really terrible, an old Victorian building surrounded by a big iron fence with one sparse tree, as I remember, and no grass — it looked a bit like the elephant enclosure at the zoo. The patients, some of whom had been there for over 30 years, were often treated really quite brutally. When I saw *One Flew Over the Cuckoo's Nest* I really thought that it wasn't for the most part an exaggeration. There were two or three psychiatrists there who protested against the indignities, insisting that these people were human beings too and our equals. As a young man I admired them enormously for that. They were often ridiculed with a ferocity that was astonishing, not only by the nurses but also by other doctors.

Then one day a nun came to the ward — I don't know if it was important that she was a nun, but as it happened she was a nun. And everything about her, the way she spoke to the patients, the way her body, as it were, inflected in relation to them, showed up the psychiatrists as being, despite themselves, condescending. It was in her manner of speech and in the way her body entered into a relation with these patients that one saw a compassion without a trace of condescension. And I found that utterly astonishing, not so much for what it showed me about her — that she was a fine woman and so on — as astonishing that it could be true, that people who had irretrievably lost everything we thought made life worth living, could still be precious in some way. (This was in the sixties when there was a cult of the beautiful people, self-realisation and all the rest of it.) I don't know how to describe it: if you were religious you'd simply say that she had shown that they too were sacred; if you were not religious, you'd hunt around for inadequate expressions... I sometimes say she showed that they too were infinitely precious, but that sounds a bit precious itself.

It's really quite astonishing how much the mainstream philosophical tradition has been uninterested in the characterisation, so to speak, of individual worth, in whose light our moral concepts acquire the sense they do. In this regard, the example I gave is interesting for a number of reasons, I think: it sounds quite irrational — Aristotle would have thought it quite absurd to think that people who have lost everything should be the proper objects of our non-condescending pity; and it gives me a sense of mystery, but not of the kind a superior intelligence could penetrate. (That's one idea of mystery: that things are mysterious to us because of our limited powers of understanding, while to creatures from other planets, say, or to God, they're not mysterious.)

Some things are, I think, essentially mysterious, and I think death is mysterious in that way. It's natural to be bewildered at the disappearance of a human personality, people find it somehow unbelievable that someone has died, but it's not as if they're asking for supernatural answers as to why that person has died or what happens after. Or sometimes in the presence of great evil people have a sense of mystery. I once saw a French woman on television remembering a German officer who every day took children off to the death camps. She asked herself how he could have done it. But it wasn't as if she expected an answer — as if the sociologists and philosophers had failed to provide one and now she expected a supernatural one. It wasn't a question that expected an answer.

Does academic philosophy still ask the grand questions of the 'who am I?', 'why am I here?', 'does God exist?' kind? Or does it tend to parcel itself up nowadays much more into ethics, sociology, questions of social justice, aesthetics and so on?

I think the answer is that it does both. I don't think there are many philosophers who would think that there are many big philosophical questions that have really been settled. And so philosophy must be one of the very few discursive disciplines in which you can go back 2000 years and engage with Socrates or the pre-Socratics and still feel that you're learning from them, that you yourself still don't know what you would say about this. Of course, there are always times in philosophy where someone thinks they've solved all the problems of philosophy, and post-graduate students are especially excited by the thought that now this problem has been solved. But ten years later the inadequacies and difficulties show up again.

Is there a fashion at the moment?

Well, philosophy has to be divided into the analytical tradition mostly practised in England, America and Australia, and the continental tradition. In both camps there are fashions. In the continental tradition there's a fashionable scepticism about truth and objectivity, but that's not the case in the analytical tradition at all, for the most part. There is scepticism, there has always been scepticism about whether moral or aesthetic judgments, for example, are true or false, but never a scepticism that invited nihilism. Sceptics have always wanted to say, 'Well, of course, a moral judgment may not be true or false, strictly speaking, but that is no reason for us not to make them as passionately as we ever did'. In the continental tradition there's always been a sort of toying with nihilism — it's a kind of posturing, I think. The reason I say that is that I have never — and I say this without exception, after teaching for God knows how many years — come across anybody who has seriously been prepared to profess nihilism when presented with certain kinds of examples.

You mean examples like the Holocaust?

They don't have to be as dramatic as that. You can say to a student about certain clear examples of evil, 'Now, look, I know what the arguments are and what the difficulties are, but for the moment, I'm asking you, as Socrates asked his interlocuters, not to tell me what someone else might say, or what someone has said, but to tell me honestly, in your own name: will you say that you don't know whether this is wrong?' And it never happens.

The interesting question, of course, is why. The first response is to think that we've been so culturally indoctrinated to think in terms of right and wrong that it's impossible for us even to contemplate questioning it. That can soon be shown to be wrong. What we're left with is the need to take a fresh look at all the pressures to be sceptical and why they arise. And unless that happens, I don't think the discussion can be serious, and you'll find yourself having to go through endless postures, where people are pretending radical scepticism when you know very well it's just talk (as we say). I don't know anyone in the mainstream tradition, either, including Nietzsche, who has seriously professed, in their own name, a radical scepticism of a kind that invites nihilism.

I don't think the post-modernists are any different in this respect. What they have done is take very seriously what follows when we accept that we are thinking necessarily 'in the midst of things'. (And on the whole I don't think the analytical tradition has done that. Although it's strong on abstract conceptions of truth, I think it has neglected the many ways in which we speak of truth and the different things that truth may amount to.)

This post-modern position connects with aspects of science. I remember when Konrad Lorenz[17] wrote about animals, he was often accused of being sentimental in his descriptions of what they were capable of. In such a case you can imagine a research scientist saying, 'Now, this old man has written all this stuff claiming that geese can do this and that, and very likely it's all the product of his sentimentality

---

17 Konrad Lorenz (1903–89), Austrian zoologist, the founder of ethology, and joint winner of the Nobel Prize for Physiology or Medicine in 1973. Lorenz applied to the human species his ideas on animal behaviour, such as aggressive and warlike characteristics which he considered innate, although modified by the physical and social environment.

— his prose gives him away. But I'm not really interested in whether what he says is sentimental. All I'm interested in is whether his claims are true or false.' Here the idea of being sentimental is treated as a kind of bad influence on his thinking, much like a hangover. And I think that makes perfect sense. What's interesting about the Sermon on the Mount, for example, is not whether it's sentimental or not, but whether it's true or not. But consider a different case with animals. Supposing somebody says, 'Look, I think it's right and fitting as an expression of what animals can mean to us that when your dog dies you build a tomb and each year light a candle in its memory'. Now, if somebody then says, 'Look, I think that's sentimental', sentimentality is being seen as the way in which the thought (building the tomb and lighting the candles) is false. It's not an external thing, like having a hangover that addles your brain, it's seen as the way the thought is false.

What I'm trying to get at here is that in some discussions about the nature of life and living, form and content are utterly inseparable — you can't idealise thinking as is done in the first example. In the first example we might think, 'If only we could get rid of encumbrances such as sentimentality and become pure thinkers, no longer vulnerable to the emotions (and headaches and tiredness) that addle our brains!'. But it makes no sense, I think, to try to think about life and death with that sort of model in mind, where one would try to think as a pure thinker only contingently vulnerable to sentimentality. In that regard I agree with the post-modernists.

The useful concepts are those that tell us whether we're thinking well or badly, not just concepts such as true and false, but also concepts like sentimental or jaded or banal, concepts which rely on our embeddedness in a particular form of life. If we try to imagine ourselves thinking from an Archimedean point, or, as an American philosopher, Tom Nagle[18], has put it, 'thinking as from no point of view at all' — or God's eye view — then we lose our subject matter.

---

18 Yugoslav-born Professor of Philosophy and Law at New York University with a special interest in ethics, philosophy of mind and ancient philosophy. His books include *Moral Questions* (1978), *The View from Nowhere* (OUP, 1989), *What Does It All Mean?* (OUP, 1987) and *The Last Word* (OUP, 1996).

*What is the relationship between philosophy and the exact sciences —
biology, astronomy, genetics and so on?*

Analytical philosophy is now working very much hand in hand with
the sciences, especially the cognitive sciences. A lot of the current
philosophers of mind are working closely with clinical psychologists
— people like Daniel Dennett[19] for example — in fact, more now
than in the history of the subject.

What brought about this shift?

In the 1950s there was a form of philosophy in the analytical world
called linguistic philosophy, which many philosophers came to consider trivialised the subject[20]. In reaction against linguistic philosophy,
there was a movement towards applied philosophy (in medical ethics
and so on) and in more mainstream areas there was also a recovery
of the sense of metaphysics — the 'big questions' in philosophy, the
nature of substance and so forth. There has actually been a revival of
interest in the philosophy of religion, in the God who is discovered
through metaphysical speculation. Now, these developments led in
turn to the thought, which certain forms of linguistic philosophy
had expelled, that there can be real discoveries in philosophy, that
philosophy can advance human knowledge and not just clarify the
muddles we've got into, and that it can do this in friendship with the
sciences. In the case of analytical philosophy, the sciences with which
it is in closest friendship revolve around the study of the mind.

Why do human beings seemingly have a basic need for a concept of truth?

---

19 Director of the Center for Cognitive Studies and distinguished Arts and Science Professor at
Tufts University, author of *Brainstorms: Philosophical essays on mind and psychology* (1978), *The
Mind's I: Fantasies and reflections on self and soul*, with Douglas Hofstadter (Basic Books, 1981) and
Consciousness Explained (Little, Brown & Co., 1991).
20 The term 'linguistic philosophy' was applied to the form of analytic philosophy which
flourished in Britain and the United States between 1945 and 1960 in rejection of positivism. Its
leading exponents were Ludwig Wittgenstein, J. L. Austin and Gilbert Ryle. Linguistic philosophers
tended to see philosophy's purpose as the clarification of obscurities and conceptual confusions
through the analysis of the language employed in discussing philosophical problems. Knowledge for
linguistic philosophers was not necessarily based on empirically verifiable facts.

I think it's connected with the need human beings have for meaning. This comes out especially clearly when human beings are suffering or when they're deeply aware of their mortality. Most people in these circumstances say they've reassessed things, they've come to see what they think is important as opposed to what isn't important, and so on. And that kind of reassessment involves some conception, surely, of whether they're right to reassess it one way rather than another. There's been a deep inclination in philosophy ever since Socrates to think that this need for truth is somehow grounded in the very nature of our humanity, rather than just being something that some people have as opposed to others.

I think there's some reason for thinking that. The reason emerges if we reflect on something basic about the inner life — 'the life of the soul', if you like, although not in the sense of some metaphysical substance, but in the sense people use it when they say things like 'This is soul-destroying work' or 'Suffering lacerates the soul'. You don't have to speculate metaphysically to think that the word 'soul' there has an important function words like 'psyche' and 'personality' can't fulfil.

There are two important things about the life of the soul: the first is that the states that compose it are largely shaped by a response to certain big, defining facts of the human condition, awareness that we're vulnerable, that we could lose everything we care for at any moment, that we're mortal, that we're sexual beings and that sexuality, whatever morals we surround it with, is something that goes deep in our lives.

The second thing — and this is where it touches on truth — is that the inner life is composed of states requiring us to distinguish between their real and their counterfeit forms. This is something that Plato noticed first, and Aristotle made something of as well, but it's been almost completely neglected. For example, we distinguish between real love on the one hand and infatuation and the many more subtle forms of false love; we distinguish between real grief and sentimental self-indulgence; we distinguish between sober remorse and self-indulgent forms of guilt; and so on. It's a need we seem to have under pain of superficiality. It's hard to imagine anybody who is in love being completely indifferent to whether it's really love or something more superficial, even though we can certainly imagine lots of people believing you'll ruin things if you think too much about them, considering that to be a kind of navel-gazing.

Now, this distinction between the reality of the inner state, whether it be grief, love, whatever, and false appearances, requires us — under pain of superficiality — to think about the question of whether something is real or an appearance, to try to see things as they are. This applies from the sciences right across to the area we're speaking of now. The distinction, in other words, requires a concept of truth. It allows me to say, 'Look, I don't think that's grief, it's just sentimentality'.

Thought about these things is inescapably 'in the midst of things'. We could imagine rational beings from another planet who shared none of our forms of life, but still had intelligence, had the concept of truth and falsehood, of a good and bad inference in logic and so on. And we could imagine that they might understand as well as we do the facts about the death of our species, the biological facts that tell us why the species die. But they couldn't think about the meaning of our mortality in the way that someone does when faced by it — to do that you have to live our form of life, share our way of living with creatures who are mortal and think about mortality in a human way (whether they're being sentimental about it or facing things as they are). That's why I draw the conclusion that there's something deeply right in the Socratic idea that the unexamined life isn't worthy of a human being.

I agree with Iris Murdoch when she says that we have to do justice both to Socrates on the one hand and to the virtuous peasant on the other. And if you emphasise, as I do, the need for lucidity about our inner life, under pain of superficiality, you capture something of what Socrates was saying. But, of course, the lucidity doesn't have to be that self-conscious, philosophical questioning that intellectuals go in for. It can be delivered in all sorts of ways by a fine culture, and be done relatively unselfconsciously.

The trouble is that if you're unlucky enough not to have such a fine culture, then reflection is forced upon you much more than it is in cultures where lucidity comes relatively easily to the unreflective participants in that culture. I don't think that's so for us — that is, for Westerners living in our very fragmented, highly controversial sort of culture. For us it's very hard to be lucid without actually thinking, and that's unfortunate, but it just happens to be the case.

Phillip Adams

'I do not regard myself as an intellectual –

I don't like the word, I think it's a silly word.

It sounds to me like the neuronal counterpart of a gymnast,

it's a word I find really embarrassing.

But yes, I like to think that I'm a thinker,

a hunter-gatherer of ideas and information.

And the thing that's driven me from day one has been

the stupefying realisation that

life is both short and essentially tragic

and that we exist for just a nanosecond in

great

oceans of

darkness.'

WHO ELSE BUT PHILLIP ADAMS *could this be? In fact, despite his typically Australian discomfort with the word 'intellectual', Phillip Adams, as he hunts and gathers ideas, does with panache exactly what public intellectuals are most valued for doing and all too rarely in their sedateness actually do. Day after day, year after year, in books, newspaper colums and on the radio, in speeches and at conferences, Phillip Adams rages at his fellow Australians, argues with them, makes them laugh, entertains them and infuriates them, indulging in what is almost an orgy of communication.*

Paradoxically, he does this from a position approaching solitary confinement. There is something of the dilettante about Phillip Adams in the very best sense: motivated by an informed, but not necessarily professional, passion for certain ideas and causes, he makes forays out into the world to engage with them publicly.

He's a philosophical omnivore, with an amazingly broad notion of the public culture — and a vast public.

To be a dilettante of the Phillip Adams kind does not imply any lack of commitment to ideas, of high seriousness when called for, or of specialised knowledge. Any listener to 'Late Night Live' on Radio National or regular reader of his Saturday columns in the Australian *will have a strong sense of Phillip Adams' obsession with justice and injustice, for example — society's, the government's, even God's (or at least the injustice of the absence of God), as well as of his gritted-teeth conviction that tolerance is a vital ingredient in a just society. He's a man who believes that this nation is in big trouble. For all that, he's no pessimist — in fact, the old pessimist/optimist dichotomy doesn't quite apply to Phillip Adams — and he likes to quote Pablo Casals, who said on his eightieth birthday: 'The situation is hopeless. We must take the next step.'*

The gritted-teeth nature of his tolerance is worth mentioning because the vehemence of his belief in it can sometimes give his words an almost intolerant ring — or so I suggested when we began speaking about his skills as a public negotiator between varying bodies of opinion and belief — another role of the public intellectual Phillip Adams fulfils with great flair.

OKAY, I'LL ACCEPT THAT, but I would argue that within all of us there's a demon of authoritarianism fighting liberalism to some degree. There was a time when as a young man I was briefly ensconced in the Communist Party where I wouldn't have hesitated to be proscriptive about human behaviour. I got out of the Party pretty quickly when communism began falling apart in the fifties and sixties. (It didn't really fall apart at the time of the Berlin Wall or Gorbachev, by the way, it really fell apart with Khrushchev's denunciations of Stalin, with the Soviet invasion of Hungary and the tanks rolling into Prague.) So, leaving an authoritarian structure behind, over the years I became more and more liberal — more and more libertarian. But you're right, there are times when one's instinct is to come out and crush the horrible manifestations of bigotry we see around us in society with something pretty tough.

In due course, though, when those questions arise, I always end up taking the libertarian position. For instance, I was one of the relatively few on the liberal left to oppose the racial vilification legislation[1]. There was, it seemed to me, a consensus that legislation of this kind was a good idea. I thought then, and still think, that it was a bad idea. I'd rather bigots identify themselves, stand up and be counted, so we can see who they are and contemplate how we might deal with them than have them intimidated and not allowed to speak out. In fact, I think to some extent — just to some extent — that the Hanson phenomenon is the product of a period of stultification, when people felt they were not being allowed to say what they thought (about racism and the other bigotries that assail us).

This doesn't mean that I accept the argument that John Howard runs that political correctness stopped people talking. People were always free to talk on the Alan Jones program[2], for example, or to state their feelings with a spraycan on a freeway wall.

Yet they may have felt that their opinions were having no impact or power.

---

1 Racial Hatred Bill 1994. The bill was passed in Federal Parliament in August 1995 after the Senate had removed the criminal sanctions the then Labor government had wanted to make central.
2 Alan Jones is the talk-back host of 2UE's breakfast show in Sydney. Adams' views on Jones and 'shock-jocks' in general are detailed in *Talkback*, coauthored with Lee Burton (Allen & Unwin, 1997).

Well, that seems to be the case. But let's remember the last election: there we all were, wandering around in an Australia which we felt had come to terms with multiculturalism, which was quite proud of Mabo and which was moving steadily, albeit perhaps a little reluctantly, towards reconciliation. And the day after the election we woke up in an Australia we didn't recognise. Nobody predicted that — nobody. The Liberal polls didn't predict it, the private polling didn't pick it up, no one anticipated the Hanson phenomenon — and she's not the only manifestation of racism and bigotry. Everyone expected Labor to lose, yes, but no one expected the vehemence, the sheer vindictiveness in the outcome. And the swing happened not only in Hanson's seat — that's simply the best-known example. It was almost as extreme in a number of other seats, particularly in those seats with a large number of Aboriginal constituents.

Now when I examine that phenomenon, I have to acknowledge that I understand the feelings of bigotry in the community because they exist in me as well and I have to deal with them. They're demons you inherit, they come with your mother's milk. Now, my father was a Congregational minister. (I think he's dead. I haven't seen him or heard from him in over 30 years.) When I was a child, he taught me anti-Semitism. He was a part of a belief system that had the Jews as killers of Christ. Now, it wasn't something that he banged the kitchen table about, but it was there, it was a subtext, and a certain amount of it was encoded in me.

Did he not mention that Jesus was a Jew?

I think a lot of Christians find that very embarrassing — it's a great shock to many Christians to think of Jesus as Jewish. Hollywood is given to showing him as blue-eyed and blond. So, when I learnt about the Holocaust, when I discovered the greatest atrocity of our century had occurred because of this conflict between Christian and Jew, I did my best to suppress it in my mind. I must have been pretty good at it, because my daughter, who's a psychiatrist in New York, has converted to Judaism. Now, one of the reasons she converted, I think, is that she was brought up in a house where the Jewish contribution

— the secular Jewish contribution, admittedly — to the great wealth of human creativity and intellect was celebrated.

Yet that antagonism is still there. When I go down to Double Bay to have a coffee, which I do every day in Sydney, I see aspects of Jewishness that affront me: I see the conspicuous vulgarity of some of the Jews of Sydney — which you don't see, say, in Acland Street in Melbourne, where there's a different sort of Jewry. I admit to this and, because I admit to it, I can deal with it.

I can remember, too, the first time I ever saw Aborigines. They were blowing gumleaves on Princes Bridge in Melbourne, and my father told me to avert my eyes. At that time as an Australian kid, I was taught to think of Aborigines as less than human. Now, I have dealt with this as best I can, yet, when I visit an Aboriginal outstation in the middle of nowhere, I see what Hanson sees: I see children who are being in effect neglected, I see the signs of glue-sniffing, I see rubbish everywhere. I would be a total liar if I didn't say that I am not affronted by that, despite my deep friendship with many of the great Aboriginal activists in Australia, despite the fact that I've been involved in campaigns on Aboriginal issues for the last twenty years — something from Princes Bridge is still in me. And if anyone tells me they're free of bigotry on any level, I simply don't believe it. I think what we do is suppress, repress, those beliefs, overlaying them with a more sophisticated and developed view.

'Bigotry' is a word that's often used in a religious context. I imagine there are many Christians in Australia who feel that your attitude to Christianity is less than balanced — you do kick Christianity very hard very often. In fact, in the light of the vehemence of your views, it seems at times that you may well have some sort of deep-seated anxiety about Christianity, that you're not really quite as happily atheistic as you claim to be. It's noticeable, for example, in your dialogues with Paul Davies[3] how often you refer to the fact that you are an atheist.

---

3 See *The Big Questions: Paul Davies in conversation with Phillip Adams* (Penguin, 1996) and *More Big Questions* (ABC Books, 1998). These conversations were based on two six-part television series shown on SBS.

That's simply because Paul's principal claim to fame is not that he's a very good scientific populariser, but that he extrapolates from his scientific investigations the strong possibility of a God. That, in my opinion, is the reason Paul Davies is so famous and so susceptible to appropriation by various Christian theologians and New Agers, although his God, of course, has absolutely nothing to do with theirs. It's natural for these questions to come up when you're sitting in the desert doing a television series with Davies.

Paul Davies did say to you that God certainly wasn't a certainty.

Well, Paul was being a bit clever there. He wins the Templeton Prize[4], a million dollars, for postulating a God. Under pressure, though, he admits, as any rational person must, that he can't prove it, any more than I can prove there isn't one.

This religious side to Davies' thinking seems to annoy you a little bit.

It doesn't really. I have to say that I've never believed in God — it's not that I've lost a belief in God. There was never a moment in my life when I could believe in God. And my attitude to religion is a bit more catholic than that: I regard all religions as basically fairly silly. I understand the yearnings of religious belief and the fears that drive religious inquiry, but I disagree with the conclusions. If I come into the fray on Christianity, it's because I very often feel provoked by Christians. I mean, what is Christianity? Christianity is the religion that endorsed apartheid; Christians are the people who dress up in white sheets and burn crosses on African-American lawns; Christianity justified many aspects of the Holocaust. Then there's the good sort of Christianity — the worker-priests and so on. In the end I don't think Christianity means anything. So, when I attack Christianity, it's usually

---

4 The Templeton Prize for Progress in Religion (£700,000) has been awarded annually since 1972 to 'a living person of any religious tradition or movement' for 'pioneering breakthroughs in religious knowledge', either in the year prior to the award or over an entire career. Paul Davies won the award in 1995. Previous winners include the Chief Rabbi of Great Britain, Lord Jakobovits, Stanley L. Jaki (Benedictine monk and professor of astrophysics), the geneticist Charles Birch, Aleksandr Solzhenitsyn, and the founder of the Taize Community in France, Brother Roger.

on social and political grounds. I'm equally disappointed in, say, Jewish fundamentalism and the ravages of Hindu fundamentalism, any sort of fundamentalism, I get angry. But my anger isn't focused on Christianity, not for a second. It's just that I live in a Christian society and there aren't many Hindus around with whom I can have an argument. My reservations about religion also apply to Islam, and I get just as many letters from angry members of the Islamic faith as I do from Christians.

Finally, you see, I don't think it's that important. I know this must sound strange coming from someone who writes about it as often as I do, but frequently, when I'm replying to an angry letter from a Christian, I say, 'Look, don't let a little thing like God come between us', and I say that because on most issues I would agree with most Christians: I think it's a good idea to love thy neighbour, I think it's probably not a bad idea to avoid stealing or coveting thy neighbour's BMW. I mean, most of the Ten Commandments strike me as being fairly intelligent.

At the ethical level.

At the ethical level, yes.

At the metaphysical level, obviously, you would part company.

And yet do I? You see, one of the things that annoys me about people of religious faith is that they have a special language, special words such as 'spiritual' and 'mystical', and they seem to claim copyright on them, as if someone like me couldn't have a spiritual experience. Now, I may have difficulty with the word, I may feel it's a bit too loaded, but I have to tell you that when I'm standing in the desert gazing up at the Milky Way my feeling of the numinous is at least as great as theirs, I suspect. And for me, mystical experiences are not uncommon. They come to me through a different paradigm, but I still have them.

✦

Something about Phillip Adams' furious, high-octane engagement with the world and its problems has to do with his awareness of mortality.

I've been driven by a heightened awareness of mortality since I was four years old. It's been the most significant factor in my thinking life ... The thing that's driven me from day one has been the stupefying realisation that life is both short and essentially tragic, and that we exist for just a nanosecond in great oceans of darkness. Now, many people manage to avoid facing this certainty, but I have felt it within me, with absolute conviction, from the time I became truly conscious. I don't believe that this is unusual.

I was isolated as a child, you see. I didn't live with my parents, I was in the care of my grandparents, and I slept in a little galvanised-iron sort of outhouse, a sleep-out — I wasn't even in the house, I was in the sleep-out. And I think I've been in the sleep-out ever since. I'm never really in the house. For instance, I work for the ABC, but I go in at 10 o'clock at night when the building is empty. I've written count-less millions of words for Australian newspapers over 40 years, but I never go to newspaper offices. I'm always sort of apart. So here I am, apart in my sleep-out, trying to come to terms with the idea of infinity and eternity, realising in my tiny little cosmological way that God was a redundancy, an unnecessary idea.

I am not so much afraid of death as I am exhilarated by life's brevity — I wish that other people recognised that life was as brief and as precious as it is. Most people squander it, treating it as if it came every day with the milk or the newspaper, as if there were an infinity of days. You and I both know that's not true. My favourite metaphor is Captain Hook's crocodile, walking behind me with the clock ticking in its tummy. Remembering that image intensifies my experience of life, ensuring that I don't waste too much of it. There's a tired old homily they used to write in greetings cards:

> *My candle burns at both ends;*
> *It will not last the night;*
> *But, ah, my foes, and, oh, my friends —*
> *It gives a lovely light.*

I use death as an aphrodisiac for living.

You must have had friends who contemplated ending their lives. What did you say to them?

I've had a few friends who, on considering their lives, made a reasonable choice to commit suicide. One was the educationalist and pundit Henry Schonheimer. Henry decided that for various reasons his life was for all practical purposes over — he wasn't terminally ill, he just decided that he'd done his dash. I didn't try to talk him out of it, nor did I encourage him — I thought it was a reasonable decision. And I've known other people who, like Henry, have chosen to terminate their lives. It's not something I can imagine doing myself — I might have played with the idea, during 'dark nights of the soul' but because of my feeling of life's preciousness I think I'd always choose to stay alive, even if I found myself in extremely unpleasant circumstances.

I've always been in favour of voluntary euthanasia. I've always thought that suicide, whether physician-assisted or not, is one of the very few rights that human beings have. It's partly the libertarian in me, I suppose. I'd never seek to talk anyone out of suicide if they'd come to that decision after mature reflection. In the case of a teenager, of course, I'd do my best to talk him or her out of it, to try to make them realise that what they were going through now would not last for the rest of their lives. But if, at the end of a productive, creative or exhilarating life, some says, 'well, enough's enough', that's their business.

So it's not so much that death makes you feel life is meaningless?

Well, life *is* meaningless, as far as I'm concerned, absolutely meaningless. I live in a universe without an author, and where there isn't going to be a moral at the end. To me it's not a parable, it's an extraordinary, miraculous event — but it *is* meaningless, so you try to seek out subjective meanings to get you through it from womb to tomb. That was what propelled me when I was young from staring bleakly into the great abyss of time and space into Left-wing politics — living in a world without an author and without a destiny. That's a fairly terrifying position to be in. Yet as a child I was surrounded by people who claimed to be quite tranquil and happy because they lived in a world where there was a sequence of events mapped out for them. There was a book, a textbook you lived by, and there were places you went to on Sunday which gave you moral instruction. Now, I didn't belong in that world, so in my early teens I tried to find a world where there was some other sort of meaning I could live by. And I found it one day in the Kew Municipal Library, when a very charming librarian who knew I'd exhausted all the Mary Grant Bruce, Richmal Crompton and Biggles books, took me up a step from the kid's library into the grown-up library and handed me *The Grapes of Wrath* by John Steinbeck. At the age of thirteen this was it for me. Here was a book, here was a new testament which gave me a sense of outrage at social injustice. It was that book which propelled me three years later to join the Communist Party (under special dispensation — I was allowed to join when I was only sixteen). And although the Communist Party phase didn't last very long (I was a member of a largish group of people such as Stephen Murray-Smith and Ian Turner who were either expelled or resigned), it gave me a lifelong commitment to political issues and to activism. (If I reject the term 'intellectual', I'd accept 'activist'.)

That sort of commitment is needed at the moment, I think. As we sit here, I'm in a state of rage about what's going on in this new country I've discovered I live in, this new Australia I didn't know existed — or rather thought had died. The Australia I thought was gone is now back with bells on, and as I look at the reactions to the Wik judgment, as I listen to the venom and bile being churned out on talkback radio programs, as I read the columnists in the tabloids, as I contemplate the possibility of a double dissolution to be fought on racial issues, I'm almost *exhilarated* by anger.

All that was always there, surely. It had never really gone away.

I was convinced it had — I think many of us were. I know that Keating was as astonished by the nature of the defeat as by its magnitude. Let me tell you a little parable: a couple of years ago I was appointed to the COAG[5] Committee on the Centenary of Federation. It was our job to wander around the country to work out how we should celebrate the centenary of Federation. It was a very broad church, this committee, because there were people on it who'd been appointed by the Conservative governments but, at the end of it, after conversations in every major regional city with every organisation you can imagine, from the RSL and the CWA to the Boy Scouts, it was still quite easy for us to sign off on a report which took the following truths to be self-evident: that Australians were intensely proud of what they regarded as the triumph of tolerance in this country, that they were absolutely at home with the concept of reconciliation, and that they were committed to, or at least acquiescing in, the notion of a republic — not necessarily viewing the republic or reconciliation with enthusiasm, but thinking that the time had come. We found nobody in our trips around Australia, in all the hearings that we had, who spoke out in a prejudiced or bigoted way on these issues.

Those were also the sorts of findings that market researchers like Brian Sweeney were getting. Nobody knew that under the surface it was all just waiting to explode, like the war in the Balkans, where everyone was just waiting for the appropriate moment after the death of Tito, or the raging religious fundamentalism and anti-Semitism now boiling up in the ruins of the Soviet Union. We didn't know it was there.

I don't believe for a second that John Howard knew it was there. He always suspected there was resentment about Asian immigration, but I don't think he realised that it was just ready to blow. It's like anthrax, in a way: the spores lie on the ground, and they can lie there indefinitely, but under the right circumstances, with the right temperature — Bing! Off it goes! And suddenly we're back to being not simply as bigoted as we were in the days of the White Australia policy, and in the days before we counted Aborigines in the census, but in a way more bigoted. As Faith Bandler[6] said to me the other night, 'At least there wasn't organised bigotry then'. And now there is.

---

5 Council for Australian Governments, Federal States and Territories.
6 Dr Faith Bandler AM was a leading light in the ten-year 'Referendum Campaign' that led to the historic 1967 referendum which gave indigenous Australians full citizenship. An active worker for Aboriginal housing and education, she is a founding member of the Women's Electoral Lobby and the Australian Republican Movement.

Isn't it all too easy to concentrate wrong and evil in the character of one woman, to ridicule her, to criticise the way she speaks English, her social origins?

Absolutely, and there was bigotry in the response to Pauline Hanson, there was chauvinism because she was a woman, there was this ludicrous nonsense about the fish and chip shop ... had the fish-and-chip shop belonged to Chifley or Curtin, it would now be a sacred shrine venerated by the Labor Party, like the grotto at Lourdes. This sort of thing isn't on. In fact, I don't believe that Pauline Hanson is finally all that important.

There was a wonderful documentary on the ABC a few months ago which demonstrates that lightning doesn't go down, it goes up. Just before a great flash of lightning, apparently, you get these little filaments all over the ground, waving up at the sky from blades of grass, fenceposts, lamp-posts and trees, saying 'Choose me, choose me'. Finally, this great power in the sky chooses one of these little waving filaments and you get this great bolt of lightning. To me that's what happened with Hanson — the lightning bolt chose that filament. In some ways I'm glad it happened — the catharsis has to be dealt with or else we have no hope as a nation. I don't want to sound apocalyptic, but even if the politicians don't talk about it, everyone knows this nation is up for grabs in the next century. It's by no means a foregone conclusion that this nation will survive. A nation of eighteen million people geographically located where we are can't expect to nourish racist attitudes towards the rest of the world and survive.

The trouble with the way the debate has been conducted, though, is that it's made it virtually impossible for the time being to question immigration policy at all. If you raise any questions at all about the ideal population size for this continent or even hint at the tension between cultural diversity and cohesion, you're in danger of being branded a racist. Great caution has to be exercised in public in expressing any opinion on Aboriginal issues. It's difficult now, as a result of the Hanson debate, to say part-way things, to say 'on the one hand this, but on the other hand that'.

How difficult is it really? I must admit that when a couple of quasi-environmental groups began emerging in the 1980s talking about restrictions on immigration based on environmental considerations, I was willing to listen to them. Then I saw them being infiltrated by white Australians in green camouflage — there was an attempt by people with a racial agenda to take over these organisations. It was Barry Jones who alerted me to the problem, actually, and a little later Peter Garrett began to find this infiltration a significant problem. I now think it's fear of the Yellow Peril which underlies most of the arguments against further immigration. It takes a different form nowadays, of course. In the old days it was based on a conviction that Asians were less than human — you just have to read Hansard to see how prevalent this view was. Now white people around the world have to face the fact that their moment in history is in majestic decline, and that the Asians they once regarded as little more than faceless, numberless coolies are now in the economic and political ascendancy. Could it be that China is about to resume her historic place as a dominant culture in the world? So, while the anxieties and hatreds are different now, at heart there is still a dread that our tiny number of Anglos is about to be overwhelmed. It's very hard to have a debate about immigration in a country where there are so many myths and terrors.

Your awareness of the two sides of the argument should make you a very good negotiator — which is what a public intellectual should be, even if you disclaim the title.

I looked at the faces of people screaming at Hanson, for example in Newcastle, and I saw there the face of the bigot. I don't think they're that much better than the people on the other side screaming in support of Hanson. (This is *not* to pick up — God forbid — on John Howard's attack on demonstrations against the woman: he was more critical of the demonstrators than he was of Hanson herself.) The point is that when people are so desperately polarised, when you get two groups yelling slogans at each other, discourse becomes impossible.

I've always been a pluralist. Now, one of my problems is that the longer I live, the more complicated, the more multi-layered issues appear, and the more difficulty I have in pulling out a simple synthesis. It gets to the point where I find almost every view I hear at least to some degree plausible, almost every argument to some degree persuasive and seductive. Now, this doesn't mean I'm an imbecile, it simply means that that's how complicated reality is. You've got to layer paradigms one on top of the other before you've got any hope of seeing how things really are.

So I suspect chanters of slogans, just as I suspect theorisers. And in a sense, by the way, I'm as uneasy about literary theory as I am about overly simple political theory. I don't find them useful. It's important, I think, to admit to complexity, to admit to difficulties, to admit to shades of grey. Now, having said that, I will still go to the barricades over Wik, because I believe it's taken us 200 years to get this on the table, and I believe it to be a moral judgment of immense force. The great tragedy of this nation, surely, lies in its treatment of its indigenous people, and until we deal with that tragedy honourably we haven't got a hope of creating a nation worth living in. I think the White Australia policy internally and externally was at least as significant and horrible a proposition as apartheid. And so I want to see this fought out. If it comes to a double dissolution, I'll be out there campaigning, crusading and waving banners with the best of them. But I hope it doesn't come to that, I hope we can head this off at the pass.

If there is a double dissolution over the Wik issue, I think the Prime Minister will win, by the way. I asked Faith Bandler whether she thought the 1967 referendum on changes to the Constitution in regard to Aborigines[7] would be passed if it were held now, and I agree with her that it would be, but by a much reduced majority. In other words, we've gone backwards in some way since then. And we've got to sort this out,

Apart from the issues of reconciliation, multiculturalism and immigration (issues, broadly speaking, concerned with race), what in your opinion are

---

7 The second of the two referendum questions was approved by an overwhelming majority of Australia's population. It allowed the Constitution to be altered enabling the Commonwealth to legislate on Aboriginal issues (until 1967 the province of the states only) and to include Aboriginal people in the national census.

*the other big issues our intellectuals and public thinkers, including our
thinking journalists, should be concerned with?*

There are many other attacks on tolerance, not all of which are motivated by questions of race. I'm amused, for example, when intellectuals
assure me that the Age of Ideology has passed — I don't see much
evidence of it. I see the old ideological arguments on censorship
resurfacing, for example, and I hear exactly the same tired arguments
being trotted out in the nineties as were trotted out in the sixties. I'm
just waiting, too, for people to start agitating for capital punishment
again in Australia — I promise you, it's only a matter of months until
they do. And it worries me, for example, that not enough of our intellectuals are fighting the great threat of global Americanisation by
osmosis. Globalism itself is not a threat — I'd love to live in a global world
where we hybridised cultures, genuinely picking and choosing from
amongst various cultures. It troubles me that we're overwhelmingly
dominated by one culture, the American, and that's what I mean by
'Americanisation by osmosis'. And there are lots of other issues which
should concern us: from problems in the film and television industries
to drug policy, law and order policy, and the incarceration of children
on 'three strikes and you're in' legislation.

I see America as calling too many of our shots. I was fascinated to
hear the film critic Adrian Martin on this program actually celebrating
the triumph of American popular culture. (He was being coquettish
and naughty, I'm sure, but it's a line I've often heard from people who
spend their lives going to films.) Adrian actually celebrates the triumph
of American popular culture throughout the world, he thinks
American popular culture is terrific, as do many other people. But I
don't think he goes out in the streets, I don't think he averts his eye
from the cinema screen often enough to see how this dominance of
American popular culture is playing out in social policy and in the
political realm. Now, that's something I wish there were more social
engagement with. Not that we can do a damn thing about it — I think
the battle is lost.

I've spent most of my adult life fighting for an Australian film
industry, and we now have one. It's pretty much what I had in mind

in the sixties: a small industry, making boutique films for grown-ups. But overwhelmingly, we are losing the fight against the Americanisation of Australian culture. But I like losing battles — I just wish some of our intellectuals were more concerned about it. Most of them regard the whole question as passé, but I don't think it is, because a lot of the virtues of Australian life, which coexist with our bigotry, have come from a pluralist, laconic, ironic attitude to reality which I think is often missing in American culture.

Another thing in which people who define themselves as intellectuals are spectacularly uninterested is the realm of science, and science is, I believe, the realm of greatest intellectual achievement in our century. Scientists are not invited to the intellectuals' dining table. If anything, they're viewed with hostility. The attack on science from left and right is very powerful, yet if I want to be exhilarated by ideas, I turn to my old pal Martin Gardner[8], a theist, a sceptic, but a great writer on science. What I'm interested in (in intellectual terms) is artificial intelligence, for example, and trying to work out what the hell quantum mechanics and the latest ideas in cosmology are all about. I'm much more interested in those areas than I am, say, in gender politics. Yet very rarely have I heard people discussing science as a form of intellectual excellence or intellectual pursuit. Why is this? Why are scientists not invited to the intellectual table?

Take Richard Feynman[9], for example. Richard would have regarded most of the intellectual pretensions and prognostications of the social scientists of today as totally inept, of a very low order of truth, whereas the great discoveries chalked up on blackboards at Harvard and Cambridge he would see as rock-solid, or at least as building blocks we can safely rely on. It's the old two-cultures argument: they don't come to the table, nor are they invited. I would like to live in a world where, more often than not, we did invite participation in philosophical

---

8 Gardner is a prolific author of books for a wide audience on mathematics, especially mathematical puzzles and mysteries, as well as on relativity, bogus science and related topics. His latest works are *The Night is Large: Collected essays, 1938–1995* (Penguin, 1996) and *The Last Recreations: Hydras, eggs and other mathematical mystifications* (Copernicus, 1997).
9 Richard Feynman (1918–88), US theoretical physicist who worked on the first atomic bomb at Los Alamos; winner of the Nobel Prize for Physics 1965. James Gleick's biography of Feynman, *Genius: The life and science of Richard Feynman* (1993) is published by Vintage.

discussions by people who have spent their lives in cosmology, say, or quantum mechanics.

After all, the public obviously wants it — in best-seller terms Stephen Hawking seems to have sold almost as many copies of *A Brief History of Time* as the Bible. People may have had difficulty reading it, but its popularity shows that there's a great interest in these areas, which the conventional intellectual, the university-based, humanities-based intellectual just isn't interested in. Not that I claim to understand thinkers like Hawking — I struggle through book after book, essay after essay, but most of our so-called intellectuals don't appear to do even that.

One of the other problems, of course, is that what the scientists are discovering is counter-intuitive. It goes against any concept of logic that most of us would be familiar with. You're asked to come to terms with things which are simply madder and odder than anything in *Alice in Wonderland*, things to do with our notions of time and space, the macro and micro. We live in an increasingly astonishing universe.

You asked me about my attitude to God and death. Interestingly enough, that's a question very rarely asked of public intellectuals. If I had my 'druthers', I would begin every chat I have with almost any-body on any issue by asking them what their cosmology is, what their theology is. I might listen to Meaghan Morris with immense pleasure, but what I'd like to know is: does Meaghan believe in God, does Meaghan believe in a life after death? I would like to put the same question to Donald Horne, for example, and to all the others you've spoken with in this series, because I think it's an immensely important question. Yet it's not brought to the table, we're almost embarrassed by it. We're very frank about gender, but we still have great difficulty, it seems to me, in discussing what are, finally, the most personal truths — life, death and meaning — truths about our role in this great cosmos.

I did notice that issues of gender and sexuality were not amongst the burning issues you mentioned.

No, I've never been particularly interested in them, to be honest. All the same, I have always been interested, for example, in homosexual law reform, partly because I knew so many people who were gay — my oldest and dearest friend Brian Robinson, who founded the Swinburne Film School, was gay — I've missed him every day since his death a couple of years ago — so I knew people who were being caught by *agents provocateurs* in the bogs around Melbourne, who were being murdered by rough trade, whose entire professional lives were constantly imperilled — if they were outed in those days, it was more than just a social embarrassment, it was the end of a career. So at the time of the Wolfenden Inquiry[10] in England, I decided it was time we did something about it here. I tried to get the Left, and in particular the Fabian Society, to do something about it. So there was that moment of great interest in homosexual law reform, but now that the love that dare not speak its name is as culturally triumphant, as powerful and influential as it is...

'In the ascendancy' is, I think, a phrase you've used somewhere...

Well, I think that's a fair comment. It's certainly gone from gay people living a life of political and social terror to gay people being intensely fashionable and, in many spheres, culturally dominant. Now, that's fine, but it's not a culture I'm particularly interested in. I find that as boring as triumphant heterosexuality. If anything, I find triumphalism in the gay culture rather like the macho behaviour associated with rugby or football. It's just not something that interests me.

You're an autodidact. It's unusual for someone with your kind of public profile and your intellectual range to be an autodidact — you left school, after all, at fifteen.

Actually, I think there are quite a lot of us about. Paul Keating is another one — Paul's completely self-educated. Still, despite any advantages,

---

10 A study published in 1957 by the Committee on Homosexual Offences and Prostitution in Great Britain, and chaired by Lord Wolfenden. It recommended removing from the domain of law homosexual acts between consenting adults, and legislation was introduced accordingly in 1967 under the Sexual Offences Act.

just as it's said of someone who represents himself in court that he has a fool for a lawyer, autodidacts could be said to have had fools for teachers. There are great limits on what this way of gleaning information can provide.

In my case there's another problem: I'm not only self-educated — and I've done it almost entirely through reading or just knocking about — but I'm also interested in just about everything. It's a problem because it means you're constantly darting about, you're a dilettante, you ricochet from subject to subject, from issue to issue. You finish up knowing a little about a lot, as opposed to a lot about a little, as the kosher intellectual tends to do. To paraphrase a secessionist senator from Western Australia[11]: I'm the lowest form of colour on the intellectual spectrum. As I said earlier, I'm just a hunter-gatherer.

The good thing about that is not being constrained by the rules of some faculty, by the limits of some reading list or the need to publish. You make connections. So people like me hunt and gather, and then cross-reference, amassing huge amounts of sometimes quite nonsensical information from all over the place. However, in bringing it all together, you can often communicate with ordinary people in a way that a 100-megatonne intellectual cannot. Take Gareth Evans, for example. Gareth is one of those rare creatures: an intellectual in politics. Now, Gareth is incapable of communication, absolutely incapable. You can interview Gareth, as I have done, for two hours at a stretch, and at the end of the interview, he'll say, 'How did I go?' And I say, 'Well, Gareth, you came out with a million sentences, each of them perfectly grammatical, and not once did you say "um" or "ah", and no one understood a word you were saying'. I feel much the same way about some of the intellectuals Radio National allows a lot of air time to: they are erudite, they are astonishing, they are, in fact, gymnasts of the neurones, but at the end of it, I'm none the wiser — I've got no idea what they were talking about.

So there's a role for people like me, I think: to gather together what we see as the essence of what is to be communicated and to try to

---

11 The Liberal Senator Ross Lightfoot has recanted from his formerly held position that Aborigines in their native state are 'the bottom colour of the civilisation spectrum'.

make it intelligible. And I think that's an honourable course of action. We'll never shake the world, we don't claim a piece of turf for ourselves, but we can in fact communicate over a long period of time with a lot of people, standing as gatekeepers to areas of interest for them.

I'm just wondering about what motivates a young autodidact such as you were, consciously or unconsciously: is he perhaps trying to prove something to his father? Is he trying to say, 'Look, OK, you've treated me badly, I'm sleeping in the sleep-out, but I'm going to make it'?

Oh, there's certainly some of that. It wasn't the sleep-out that was my problem, though, it was moving in some years later with my mother and her second husband, who was a psychopath. I was living in a bedroom I was terrified to leave, because life was very dangerous for me with this loony outside the door. What I did is in a sense a metaphor for my life: I covered the walls, all of them, and the ceiling as well, with pictures I cut out of magazines and journals. A few months ago I found them again in a box, with all the Sellotape still stuck to them (it was Durex then), and I pulled them out and looked at them. It was an astonishing, very catholic array of images from various times and places — they had nothing in common with each other. Through cutting out those images and sticking them on the walls I created a room in which I felt comparatively safe — in fact, a universe I could occupy. And, to stay sane and help myself cope with the dangers in my life, I also started to read and write constantly — it was therapy for me. And over 40 years later, it still is.

I wonder, given your enthusiasm for Egyptology, if any of the images were of pyramids or pharaohs?

Quite a few of them were from the ancient world, yes. And the reason is that, living (as I did) in an Australia where nothing was old, apart from the landscape (the oldest buildings where I lived dated from the 1940s), we didn't know anything about 60,000 years of Aboriginal habitation, the attraction of ancient Egypt was a very important part of my fantasy life.

These days, of course, I live surrounded in my house by the real thing, with Egyptian mummy cases and artefacts galore. But, you know, my attitude to them has changed. There was a time when I was on top of them, as it were, when one's youth and vitality and vibrance made it possible to be perfectly at home with the ancient, to feel in some way that one was going to outlive it. As I get older, I find (shock! horror!) that the pyramids are winning, and that the artefacts I thought I owned I just have on short-term loan — they're going to last a lot longer than I am! So I'm no longer collecting artifacts from the ancient world. They've won, I'm losing.

Is this, though, what you might call an area of expertise within your dilettantism?

No, it isn't. I don't read hieroglyphs, and although I've read oodles of books on Egypt and wander around it with deep pleasure, I'm not a scholar. I don't pretend to be a scholar on any issue. I mean, I worked in the film industry for 30 years, but my interest in film has never been a consuming passion, so I can't regurgitate the names of the grips and best boys on 500 feature films the way, say, David Stratton can on SBS.

I feel immensely fortunate. Every day, like His Holiness the Pope, Australian intellectuals should kiss the tarmac in gratitude for being allowed to play the role they do. It's an immensely privileged one. And just as artists are to be envied because they can turn the pain of their lives into art, I'm lucky because I've been able to turn a lot of the pain I've experienced (particularly in my psychologically abused childhood) into a process of communication.

And it's two-way communication. I get an unbelievable amount of mail, and all my life I've answered that mail — that's where the quarantine breaks down a bit: I have a relationship with the people who write to me, although it's admittedly at a remove, I avoid direct contact.

There's an intriguing contradiction here: on the one hand you stand at the centre of so many fields — you're on Radio National four times a week, in the Australian *every Saturday, your books are best-sellers, you serve on key committees whose decisions have a measurable impact on our lives... while on the other hand you live so resolutely apart.*

Yes, I still take shelter in my sleep-out — refuse invitations, live half the time on a farm, have virtually no social life and so on. As far as the committees are concerned, I've actually resigned from them all in view of the current political climate — for their own protection.

If you had, let's say, half a dozen intimate friendships, I wonder if they might in some way discharge the tension with which you invest ideas at the moment.

I don't know. I've never had half a dozen intimate friendships at one time, although I've had a series of intimate friendships over many years. My problem is excessive busy-ness: because I am so concerned about mortality, about life rushing past, I've never really allowed myself the time to commit to personal relationships. I've been too busy acquiring, accumulating and trying to recycle or pass on ideas. If I'm lucky, I've got 7000 days left to live. Years and years ago I worked out that the average life expectancy for an Australian male was around 600,000 hours. For the first 100,000 you're too young to know what's going on, and for the last 100,000 you're ga-ga, for another 200,000 you're asleep, and for 50,000 or so you're sitting on the loo, dragging the dustbin down to the front gate or wiping the dishes. I mean, there's not an awful lot of time left, and I've chosen to spend that time writing, reading and thinking, rather than having social relationships. Now, I'm not advocating it, I don't think it's a particularly sensible or healthy course of action, but it's what I've done, and it's what I now do habitually.

You seem to discount the loo, the taking out of the dustbin and sleeping as somehow not real time.

Do you have a Zen Buddhist experience sitting on the loo? I try to read on the loo, in planes, in the back of taxis, so the time isn't wasted. I wish I could read while I was asleep.

Conclusion

Andrew Riemer

Tony Staley

Drusilla Modjeska

Judith Brett

Suzanne Kiernan

Peter Beilharz

Wendy Bacon

❛ **The public intellectual... is capable of** broad, analytical thought, **even theoretical thought, above and beyond a particular discipline or expertise...** **For a public intellectual to function there must be a** genuine urban culture **that provides a** matrix of talk. **That talk can be banal, or opinionated, even offensively opinionated, but out of it emerge people who raise the** chatter **into a** discussion of ideas of society. ❜

Andrew Riemer

I N THINKING THROUGH *what makes a thinker a public intellectual, and what kind of society is most likely to raise mere chatter into intellectual discourse, the contributors to this series, despite the diversity of their backgrounds, have found themselves agreeing to a surprising extent on the public intellectual's basic attributes. They have emphasised in particular a commitment to the public good, a commitment implying a responsibility to negotiate conflict between individual rights and the good of society; a maverick independence from institutions and their interests; a capacity to move well beyond a core area of expertise; and an ability to speak as if 'the public' were society as a whole. Underlying these assumptions about what a public intellectual is are some deeply ingrained notions of a rather old-fashioned concept: citizenship and its responsibilities.*

In a similar way, underlying many of the anxieties expressed by the contributors about the problems the Australian public intellectual culture faces (the lack of national forums, the fragmentation of the public for intellectual discussion, the dearth of independent intellectuals, the cor-poratisation of the academy, even the spread of excluding, specialised languages and the gender imbalance in the culture) is an apprehension that at the end of the twentieth century ideas of citizenship and an Australian polity are under threat. Increasingly, Australians have the sense that they are less equal citizens of a coherent polity than clients of competing profit-making organisations (the State of Victoria, Western Mining, the Packer empire, something called 'the Federal Government' and so on). In this environment maverick thinkers committed to the public good have little opportunity to play a part.

On many questions, naturally enough, there has been disagreement. However, the general tenor of the remarks of many of the other partici-pants is captured quite nicely in the comments of Andrew Riemer. Hungarian-born, a lecturer for some 30 years in the English Department at Sydney University (he left feeling he was 'out of sympathy' with the 'new university'), a scholar who recovered and edited sixteenth- and seventeenth-century texts, Andrew Riemer is now a freelance literary commentator whose books include the three volumes of memoirs, Inside, Outside *[1992],* The Habsburg Cafe *[1993],* America With Subtitles *[1995], as well as* The Demidenko Debate *[1996] and* Sandstone Gothic *[1998].*

Andrew Riemer

The public intellectual, I suppose, is capable of broad, analytical thought, even theoretical thought, above and beyond a particular discipline or expertise. The circumstances do not exist in this country — or at least in Sydney, where I live — for such an individual to emerge. Now, of course there are self-styled intellectuals, and people publicised as intellectuals, but their claims to the title are usually dubious.

For a public intellectual to function there must be a genuine urban culture that provides a matrix of talk. That talk can be banal, or opinionated, even offensively opinionated, but out of it emerge people who raise the chatter into a discussion of ideas of society. In the back of my mind is the kind of chatter you got in places like the Café Hawelka in Vienna or the chatter you could hear in French cafés in the sixties — it's not there so much now. A public intellectual can raise that undisciplined chatter into a discourse, often about politics — I think it's difficult to detach the concept of a public intellectual from the discussion of politics.

But what sort of influence can café chatter have on society at large? How can it affect how politicians behave, for example?

What happened in France, at least in the golden days, was that the public intellectuals picked up the concerns of the talk and transformed them into ideas. Of course, they enjoyed great respect — not always benign respect, but respect nonetheless. One of the extraordinary things about French society still is that politicans do listen to intellectuals, perhaps not very closely, but they do listen. I don't think we could say that of any government in this country.

There's another kind of public intellectual that arises in repressive, dangerous societies. It's a noble tradition and in the course of this century it arose, of course, in Central and Eastern Europe, first under Nazism, but more particularly under Soviet totalitarianism in the satellite states. These intellectuals expressed in a focused way the fears, resentments and the sense many people had that life held other possibilities apart from the grim present. This kind of intellectual begins to merge with a more unusual figure: the prophet or religious reformer. Solzhenitsyn might be one such figure, although he's so eccentric that I have my doubts. The figure I think of immediately is the Hungarian novelist and thinker György Konrád[1] who managed to survive in that system, but also to make the people in power in Hungary listen to other voices. He made dissent respectable and gave it substance. It took a long time, but ultimately they had to listen.

As a footnote to that, I might say that when I was in Budapest quite recently people suggested that public intellectuals no longer existed there, because in that mercantile, money-oriented society, with no ideas or ideals, just prejudices and desires, that focusing role of the public intellectual, which is almost an heroic role, is no longer available to anyone.

It sounds as if you share Edward Said's view that public intellectuals have a duty to give some kind of voice to the voiceless in society.

They work out of the inarticulate or unarticulated, I think — longings, fears, even thoughts in society. I don't think they're just megaphones, though — they transform those things because of their large view and awareness of history. To be a public intellectual you have to have a very strong awareness of history, although not necessarily of culture. I think you can be an uncultured public intellectual.

Can you be an intellectual at large, then, or must you always be a Hungarian or Brazilian or Australian intellectual?

Well, to turn it around the other way, was Simeon Stylites[2] an intellectual? While I'm sure he was a very thoughtful chap, sitting there on his column in the wilderness, I don't think he was an intellectual, let

---

1 One of Hungary's most noted intellectuals and dissidents in the post-1956 period. At one time President of PEN International, Konrád is known for modern fictional techniques at variance with official socialist realist policies. He has several books in English translation, including *The City Builder* (1977), *The Intellectuals on the Road to Class Power* (1979), *Antipolitics* (Harcourt Brace, 1984) and *A Feast in the Garden* (Faber & Faber, 1992).

2 St Simeon Stylites was an early fifth-century Syrian ascetic who lived on platforms on top of stone pillars, preaching to the pilgrims below. He stayed on top of the final pillar for 30 years.

alone a public intellectual. That always depends on having a relationship, no matter how troubled or tenuous, with a particular society. You can be meditative without such a relationship, but you can't (in my understanding of the term) be an intellectual. There has to be a dynamic between the intellectual and the public.

Earlier you mentioned 'broad, analytical thought'. Now, 'broad' implies 'non-specialist'. Does this mean that a scholar is not suited to being an intellectual? Our institutions, of course, encourage specialisation and scholarship.

I spent the greater part of my working life as a scholar. The role of the scholar, I think, is to collect, interpret and disseminate information and knowledge. I think I was in the business of knowledge. In order to do this kind of work, you need to have a certain amount of detachment from the knowledge you're accumulating and sifting through, you have to have a certain indifference to it. To be an intellectual you have to have passions, commitments and beliefs. I think it's possible to be both a scholar and an intellectual, but those two sides to your life have to be kept somewhat apart. You see, I became obsessed with Shakespeare in my early twenties — the resonances, the qualities of the verse (rather than the intellectual qualities of the plays) — and this created my English-speaking self. As a university teacher I saw it as my duty to transmit some of those feelings and that excitement, and to look at the aesthetic, cultural, literary and social phenomenon that we call the canon of Shakespeare's plays and what they may have represented in late sixteenth- and early seventeenth-century society. The intellectual's role might be to say what the relevance or use of these plays is to late twentieth-century Australia. By training and inclination I stopped short of doing that.

As he is probably all too aware, Andrew Riemer is picturing a society dotted with public intellectuals which some might say has had its day. The matrix of informed talk, and the dynamic relationship growing out of it between public thinkers and society at large, exists in a far more complicated form nowadays than it did in the heyday of the Café

Hawelka and the Deux Magots. Ideas do their work in cyberspace, in cinema auditoriums, at myriad international conferences, on advertising hoardings, in hundreds of thousands of books pouring out of tens of thousands of publishing houses.

Despite this transformation of the matrix, however, if you want to reshape society, to have an intellectual impact on large numbers of your fellow citizens, you might find the old structures still remarkably effective and resilient.

❖

To test the common view expressed by Andrew Riemer, that the lines of communication between public intellectuals and politicians are mostly 'down', I asked the Federal President of the Liberal Party, Tony Staley, how he thought things stood between politicians and intellectuals.

Tony Staley

There are those who say that politicians and intellectuals are at war. I think that's nonsense. It needs to be understood that the work of the politician is not the work of an intellectual, although the best people in politics combine ideas with action[3]. Politicians trade in ideas in action. Politics is about principles as well as practice, and people who think it's just about numbers aren't going to last — they're not going to drive governments over the long haul.

What public intellectuals say, and the intellectual life of a country, will sometimes have a significant impact on politics. It won't always be admitted, of course, but their ideas help inform the atmosphere. When intellectuals talk, they're by no means just talking in a complete political vacuum.

---

3 This distinction between 'intellectual activity' (thinking and talking about ideas) and 'action' is, of course, a common one, particularly amongst politicians. Both Neville Wran and Bob Carr have made similar distinction in public statements about the politician's role, claiming that what people want from their politicians is 'action', not just 'words'.

Where should intellectuals be talking if they want to be heard by politicans? Must they talk on the ABC and SBS and in the pages of the Australian *and the* Sydney Morning Herald *in order to be heard?*

No question. If they want to have any impact, that's where they must go. And those who can bear it ought to talk to the politicians themselves from time to time.

How do they meet them? By inviting them to their festivals and seminars?

Yes. If you have ideas you want to get across to politicians, you some-times have to make an approach. Politicians aren't as fearsome — or fearful — or as stupid as people think. People are appalled sometimes when I tell them that by and large politicians are as intelligent and decent as they are themselves.

You make it sound so easy, but I don't quite believe that, if I write a letter to the Prime Minister saying 'Look, I'd like to talk to you about green-house emissions', he'll ever even see the letter.

No, it's not possible for him to read many letters personally. Still, let me say that, when I was minister for communications (the minister looking after the arts for the prime minister), I at least skimmed every letter that came in — and there were thousands in that year — and while there were form replies, I personally signed the replies, unless the letters were part of one of those write-in campaigns. And many of my colleagues in government did the same thing. Not the Prime Minister, of course. Nevertheless, there are lots of other people you can talk to in order to influence the Prime Minister and the political system. One of the mistakes people make is to assume that nothing can ever be done.

Is it possible for politicians to keep abreast of what comes out in the Australian, Quadrant, *the* New York Times, *the* Guardian Weekly *and so on?*

No, not all of them and not regularly. It's true that politicians don't read a lot, except, perhaps, when they're travelling — the pile of correspondence, briefing papers and so on is simply too high. Still, it's surprising how knowledgable they can be: when I sit talking with colleagues, I find they're often more across things than I'd have expected. Still, the fact is that once you're active in politics there's little time for cultural pursuits apart from the odd opening night.

However, belief in ideas must be continually encouraged — belief in the value of thinking and pure research. Although we've had to get better as a country at commercialising the output of our universities, at commercialising research and developing it, we must never lose sight of the importance of ideas and pure research for their own sake. Yes, these things matter in commercial terms, but they also matter in terms of what life is all about.

Many Australians probably suspect that politicians are out of touch with the real world. Sequestered in their palaces on the hill, surrounded by press secretaries, driven about by chauffeurs, they're out of touch with our real lives.

Most politicians might reply that they go to the footy, after all, but when people put this point to me during my time as a full-time politician, I used to say: 'I keep in touch with the real world by reading poetry. Poetry keeps me in touch with a world it's so easy to fall out of touch with. That's for me the real world.'

✧

Not quite the reality check we might have expected! And we might not have expected it because poetry belongs to a domain of feeling, emotion and sensitivity to language which is usually seen as the converse of the domain of reasoned, masculine action in the 'real world'. Thought and action, words and action, feelings and reason — these are familiar dichotomies in our perceptions of how thoughtful people react to the world around them. At this point in our history, a public role in the discussion of social issues or societal transformation clearly belongs on the action/reason side of the fence. This has gender implications, as Drusilla Modjeska points out, in terms of who is most readily thought of as a public intellectual.

Drusilla Modjeska

There's an assumption that intellectuals are male, evoking a long Western tradition of intellectual thought based on a history of philosophy and rationality. So the question of why there are so few women public intellectuals is akin to the question of why there have never been great women musicians and artists: the question is set up in such a way that the activity of an intellectual precludes women. This image occurs to me: Odysseus, tied to the mast with bees' wax in his ears to get past the call of the siren. The vulnerable and scared in him, his feeling side, have to be tied to the mast. It may be a feminist caricature, but it's what happens in the case of the canonical, masculine intellectual — he has to get past the call of feeling, to do so is heroic. I'm not totally against that notion — without it we'd be much the poorer — but it leaves a lot out. Vulnerability and feeling have to be let back into the way we think about ourselves.

At a seminar at the ANU a few years ago on the independent scholar I made a plea for allowing a space in intellectual discourse for the non-rational, so thought could be fully felt and feeling could be fully thought, bringing both poles into play. This was interpreted by several men in the audience as the non-rational querying the rational, and they argued that, if we give up the rational, we give up law, we give up logos, and we're back into the anarchy of primeval feeling. My point was that the non-rational is not the irrational and that the non-rational and rational can be made to work together. Coincidentally, I've just been re-reading Virginia Woolf's *To the Lighthouse*. There's a large section of the novel set during a meal. Mrs Ramsay's mind is drifting off into dreamland, worrying about everyone's connections around the table — that's one pole, and if the world were left to Mrs Ramsay it would be a flaccid, hopeless place. But at the other pole you have Mr Ramsay and the horrible Mr Tansley ('women can't write, women can't paint') and if we left the world to their highly sterile, high intellectual, dissertation-based view, there'd be no marriages, no meals, no joy. *To the Lighthouse* is an argument for the two coming together, which was always the position that Dorothy Green[4], one of the unsung intellectuals in this country, one of the most important women intellectuals of her generation, always took. In thinking about how I work in the world, I realise it's been axiomatic to me that I should bring those two poles together, the thinking and the feeling, and if we reopen the question of the intellectual from that angle, then we might find we can put a different construction on it.

A different construction could also be put on 'the public'. Women are a powerful but unrecognised public. We know, for example, that the readers of novels are largely women, but they are not considered 'the public' in terms of who is in receipt of intellectual material. Women are not equally present. This is another example of the masculine habit of universalising its own position: men who are interested in the sorts of thinking men do think that this is what 'the public' is interested in. The public is a canonical reflection of themselves. In fact, the public is much more than that, and it's a highly sophisticated public because women have to have double vision, understanding both the masculine tradition and the one that speaks to and for us, both the master narrative and the feminine — vulnerable, non-rational and other forms of speech which are not the master narrative.

✧

Earlier in this series of discussions, the historian Jill Julius Matthews also spoke forcefully in favour of broadening our view of what 'the public' was, proposing that we move away from hierarchical models, with public intellectuals 'sticking up out of the landscape' of society like towering eminences, towards something more horizontal — a patchwork of interconnected publics, perhaps, with which the intellectual might engage,

---

4 Dorothy Green (1915–91), essayist, critic and poet, with a strong commitment to contemporary issues. She published widely on Australian writers such as Martin Boyd, Patrick White, C. J. Brennan and Christina Stead, and her substantial work is her critical biography of Henry Handel Richardson, *Ulysses Bound* (1973).

listening to the 'range of smaller voices' coming from tnose communities and making a contribution to them.

You don't have to hold authoritarian, hierarchical views to see the dangers as well as the advantages in this more horizontal modelling of how intellectuals work. Fragmentation, as Edward Said has pointed out, suits oppressive governments down to the ground. For historian Judith Brett the conventional notion of the public actually still has its uses.

Judith Brett

If you believe in such a thing as public opinion (which, I think, does still have some force — we haven't become a collection of mini-publics), you put ideas out as a public intellectual into that arena of public opinion without actually knowing what's going to happen to them, who's going to hear them. There's danger in becoming a whole lot of mini-publics: Tim Costello was talking recently about the dangers that arise when, for example, broadcasting becomes narrow-casting and we all just tune in to our taste groups, and that sense of a broader public debate, being carried out on the ABC, on commercial radio and in the newspapers, fragments. It hasn't happened yet.

The notion of a public has a history, of course. Suzanne Kiernan, who lectures in Italian at Sydney University and has been the most recent editor of the Sydney Review, *spoke about how that notion developed in Western societies.*

Suzanne Kiernan

The public is a very recent invention. You can't talk about a public before the eighteenth century — you simply don't find the word used in any sense we would now give meaning to before then. The public as such invents itself in the eighteenth century as a consequence of and also a function of the burgeoning of the print culture, which became a culture of debate.

And which is still burgeoning and still nourishing a culture of debate in countries with a critical population mass, such as Italy.

Yes, although the Berlusconi empire there is every bit as engulfing and devouring as Murdoch's is here. At the same time, there is, in Italy, a wealth of periodical publications of all kinds, right across the political spectrum, many of them quite long-lived. That's only possible because of the size of Italy's population — that's what allows a press of that diversity and those dimensions, that pluralism of niches, to flourish to the degree it does.

None of this seems to work, however, none of this trafficking in critical ideas, none of this creation of intellectual constituencies, large or small, unless the population is educated, aware of its history and language — or its histories and languages, if you prefer — of its roots in all their hybridity. Yet even to hint at ideas such as these, at least in certain circles, is to risk opprobrium: they smack of much reviled humanism, God's eye views, Grand Narratives and education in official histories.

I'm lucky in the sense that I came to the university at a time when the humanities weren't yet on the run. Now, clearly, they're on the way out, and have been, really, for the best part of a generation. There's great distrust now of higher education because it sounds elitist, so what we have now is a kind of undifferentiated post-secondary education. If you speak of higher education, it sounds as if you're interested in quality, in discriminating, and this is thought to be somehow inimical to popularising — the populist democratic tenor we ought all to subscribe to. In our newer tertiary institutions, in particular, the tendency has been to collapse the humane disciplines into undifferentiated 'communications' or 'cultural studies'.

Now, nobody is saying that the disciplinary boundaries are unchangeable or, even less, that they shquld be unchangeable. After all, the bundle of ideas and methodologies we call the humanities originally emerged, back in that quasi-mythological time we call the Renaissance, as a result of a disregard for the older disciplinary divisions. It was an expression of dissatisfaction with Aristotelian syllogistic method, and produced a cluster of new historical disciplines. And history itself — archaeology, philology, Renaissance humanism — was, of course, a culture of criticism. The form in which we've inherited these disciplines comes out of the Enlightenment with its own intellectual traditions.

Having said that the humanities are on the way out, I acknowledge at the same time that they've been put back on the agenda by the neo-conservatives. This makes it difficult to defend the humanities, because you're immediately thrust into a corner as an old fuddy-duddy. In the 1980s some of the younger fogies in education in the United States became concerned about the lack of focus in the curriculum and about the obsession of university educators with techniques and methodologies, with investigations into the process instead of with causes and effects. They started to talk solemnly about retrieving the humane studies curriculum and even about taking lessons from the Renaissance.

It seems to me, though, that the more you actually know about the Renaissance, the less likely you'll be to talk in those terms. Consider the nature of Renaissance culture: its favourite image for describing itself was the *hortus conclusus,* the enclosed garden, a culture working by exclusion and predicated on the acceptance of inequality. Of what possible use is a model of this kind to us in a mass democratic society where universal literacy is the aim? Indeed, our culture is based on the concept of inclusion. At the present time, when we have mass literacy as the result of compulsory education, and are maximising access to post-secondary education, we're beginning to see a confusion, with quite serious consequences, between the administrative nature of education and the educative nature of administration. It's turning out to be a very vicious circle indeed, letting nothing new in as it closes in upon itself.

In a way, the upsurge of generalised and fairly undifferentiated cultural studies courses is an example of this. Cultural studies doesn't exist as a scholarly discipline. What it is is a kind of packaging for post-secondary education. It derives its content from the disciplines of anthropology, literary criticism, history, ethnology — just about anywhere. This is referred to as 'the new erudition', yet all it is is transgression across old disciplinary boundaries. Of course, it's a very convenient kind of package to deliver. So the graduates of popular culture courses, and their teachers as well, tend to be quite content to know very little about virtually nothing[5].

✧

Peter Beilharz lectures in sociology at La Trobe University in Melbourne, is the author of Imagining the Antipodes: Culture, theory and the visual in the work of Bernard Smith[6] *and has had a long association with a number of 'small magazines', such as* Australian Society, Australian Left Review *and* Thesis Eleven. *He notes other changes in the intellectual culture over the last two decades: on the whole, he thinks, it has become less critical. Yet criticism is a prime function of intellectuals in our kind of society.*

Peter Beilharz

When the Labor Party was in power, it transformed certain intellectual institutions in positive ways. Under Labor, for example, intellectuals began working in the area of cultural policy. But the period of Labor hegemony also had some pernicious effects: it meant that the critical capacities that were previously exercised were eroded, the idea of being critical became more difficult. And, of course, in the universities performance indicators, administrative functions, reviews and so on were introduced, which gave an increased value to certain intellectual activities, but at the expense of criticism. So from the perspective of political criticism, our polity is a lot thinner than it was — richer in various cultural senses because of the democratisation that technologies allow, but thinner in others.

---

5 A critique in similar terms of cultural studies and the curricula of many contemporary English departments in the United States is at the heart of Stanley Fish's *Professional Correctness*. Interesting objections to and qualifications of Fish's argument are raised by Terry Eagleton in his review of *Professional Correctness* in the *Times Literary Supplement*, 24 November 1995, pp 6–7.
6 (Cambridge University Press, 1997).

My point is that, while intellectual activity is now more recognised and valorised than twenty years ago, there are distinct codas about what counts as intellectual activity. We all know the stories about academics getting more points for writing in the *Latvian Journal of Morris Dancing* than the *Age,* but there are other stories about appointment committees for professorial positions considering televisuality to be a major criterion. In other words, intellectuals are subjected to various pressures, one of which includes the sense that outside work is more important than inside work. That's a real risk for the quality of what people like me do in universities: if we're being stretched outwards in so many directions, our capacity to engage in the more traditional areas — teaching, writing for our peers and our students, crticism of society and the economy — are diminished.

So, on the one hand we're supposed to respond to the ongoing controversies — Manning Clark, Hanson, Mabo and so on, having views on everything — while on the other hand we've been stripped of the godlike character we once had and associated with people like Sartre, who actually put his foot in it every second time he spoke. So we're overvalued and undervalued at the same time. We need a new balance.

How easy is it to be independent?

I suspect it's impossible. Independence works better in France and the US where it has been possible since the twenties and thirties to act as an independent because of the enormous potential market. There are a few people who can behave like this in Australia, but we can probably count them on the fingers of one hand — people like Bernard Smith, who retired early and has had twenty years to engage in his own scholarship and with society, when he's thought it appropriate, as a committed intellectual in public life. Engaging with public life on issues such as Demidenko or Manning Clark so often means running with the pack — to lead in one's own modest way, to be innovative, to open up to larger questions in the wider world, are much more difficult. And so many of the controversies I've mentioned are really just running on the spot.

Do you think there are important differences between Antipodean intellectual activity and intellectual activity in the North?

Peripheral intellectuals in general are both the victims and the beneficiaries of the way the world operates. Our situation is one of both frustration and privilege. On the one hand we're less likely to be listened to at the centres, although sometimes they're receptive to our ideas and recycle them. The current emphasis on performance, on being televisual, on beautiful writing, regardless or not of whether you have anything to say, makes it difficult for the Antipodean writer to impress his or her ideas on the centres. However, you're not an intellectual to gain recognition. You're an intellectual because of a commitment to certain things.

On the other hand we can't reasonably exist without knowing a great deal about both their worlds and our own, it's incumbent on us to know more. As a Dutch sociologist once put it, it's like being on the wrong side of a one-way mirror. There are also perspectival advantages: we're both engaged with and detached from the centres, which is something intellectuals need to be. It allows us to articulate positions not so readily available to those working at the centre.

As a teacher, constantly meeting students of a different generation from your own, do you think they have a different attitude to these questions about the public intellectual culture? A less tolerant attitude towards traditional figures of authority, perhaps?

I actually encounter in my students a hunger for ideas of a kind some might define as traditional. Many of them feel deprived, feel they missed out on an exciting period (the sixties) — an unfair denigration of their own experience, I think, and the present possibilities for leading full and interesting lives. There is also a sense of anxiety about having to juggle things we didn't have to juggle — reading, working, surviving, they're very pressed. Many of them think that the university would be a world of riches if only they could get to the library. The generational issue may be significant, but I don't think it's the most useful way to come at a whole range of problems.

In my experience, you need to be about 40 to feel confident about the cultural capital you've imbibed. It takes about twenty years of reading, talking, arguing and writing. However, after twenty years of doing that, many intellectuals shut down, stop reading and try to exist on that cultural capital, which is more or less co-extensive with their PhD training. They start reproducing verbatim whatever they've just been reading. The way that universities and professional training work, and the contemporary need to have a theory, all invite closure. So my students are both open and closed: open to the world, but looking for definitive answers.

✧

To some extent Wendy Bacon belongs to the fraught world of the university (she is Associate Professor at the Centre for Independent Journalism at the University of Technology Sydney), although as a professional journalist she also works in a much more immediately public arena. And not just her words, but her acts of social criticism make her stand out from the more passive role Peter Beilharz feels that intellectuals have lapsed into: ever since the heady days of the Tharunka *obscenity trial and the dangerous fight to save Victoria Street, Kings Cross, from developers, her commitment to free speech has been outstanding[7]. The debilitating separation of thought and action so often mentioned in this series as part of the Australian ethos doesn't seem to affect Wendy Bacon.*

On the question of the arenas available to Australian intellectuals to perform in, Wendy Bacon points out that those that exist can all too easily become just turfs to defend or battlegrounds for supremacy.

Wendy Bacon

Recently I wrote an obituary for one of the people in the Sydney Push, Darcy Waters, and, in thinking about him, I realised that my strongest memories of him were of him reading books and talking in coffee lounges and pubs, meeting him in the street — that sort of

---

7 Wendy Bacon's period of political activism is documented in detail in Anne Coombs' *Sex and Anarchy*.

thing. I think there are few spaces left now for the Darcy Waters of this world, for intellectuals who aren't in a major institution. The marketplace, as well as the cutbacks to public funding, are leaving us with not enough spaces for people to be themselves, to contribute ideas, apart from in their job or profession. Edward Said has interesting things to say about this. I would put it differently because I'm a professional journalist, but he attacks the notion of the professional because for the professional knowledge always has a use[8]. The notion of ideas being discussed and circulated simply for the public good is very much under threat.

Perhaps the sort of thing Darcy Waters did in coffee shops and pubs is now being done in other places — on the Internet, for example.

Yes, I don't want to be too much of an old romantic and go on about the loss of oral spaces, because I'm actually very keen on the Internet and its possibilities, and especially in the new public communities it can create. Here's an example: there's an intellectual in Malaysia who's involved in fighting the construction of a dam in Sarawak. His magazine has been banned in Malaysia, but through e-mail and moving his publication onto the Internet in Australia he's created a community interested in his ideas. And there are, no doubt, other developments out there that I'm just not aware of.

Having said that, I think there's a pressure in all our public spaces, including the Internet, for the market to dominate. If you can't make a profit or at least cover your costs, you can't do it. Even within the universities there's so little 'fat', so little room to move, that community projects (such as the one-day seminar on youth and the media the Australian Centre for Independent Journalism ran recently with a Sydney youth organisation) can't be carried out unless you can get funding — in fact, these days people like you to make a profit.

---

8 Said's ideas about the limitations of professionalism and specialisation are summarised in the chapter 'Professionals and Amateurs' in *Representations of the Intellectual.*

*Despite your optimism about new technologies, someone of my gener-
ation is likely to feel that some sense of community has been lost in
recent decades. If something is discussed in the* Age *or the* Australian *or
on the ABC, there's a real sense that the community as a whole is reading
it or listening to it — perhaps it's largely educated people interested in
ideas, but it's there for everybody. Discussions on the Internet, in small
magazines, or even in some suburban pub, strike me as being for very
discrete publics.*

I know what you're saying, but the *Age* and the *Sydney Morning
Herald* are also geared through their advertising to speak to particular
publics as well. I once gave a course out at Liverpool on the outskirts
of Sydney to a group of women trying to get back into the workforce
after having a family. One of the exercises was to read a whole article
in the *Sydney Morning Herald* and talk about it, but they actually
found that newspaper totally alienating. So I'm not convinced that
the so-called 'quality newspapers' are for 'the community' — your
community is only *your* community. As far as the new technologies
go, the issue arises as to whether or not everybody will have access
to them. At the moment public libraries and schools are connected to
the Internet — at my child's primary school, for example, every child
is able to use the Internet. So partly it's a generation thing, I think —
the audience the new technologies reach will be at least as wide as
that of the *Age* or the *Sydney Morning Herald*.

*Even if we accept that there are many different publics, and that it's an
illusion to think that our public is 'the public', wouldn't it still be true
that those who make the big decisions that impact on us in our society
— who is to own our public transport system, say, or how the education
system is to be run, defence, foreign relations and so on — are reading
the major dailies? They're not listening to what's being said in suburban
pubs or reading groups.*

I agree. One can't underestimate the role of the ABC and the capital
city newspapers in setting the agenda. To some extent they even set
the agenda in the other media. But there's another issue which I think

is even more important: there's been research showing that exploratory stories on social issues — the privatisation of childcare, for example — are appearing less and less frequently in the commercial media. I think this increasing poverty of ideas in our media is worrying. Cultural studies people may say I'm being snobbish, that people read their own meanings into what they find there, that there's resistance, as they'd say, through people's readings, but in the end, if a story isn't there at all (and there are many stories that aren't there at all), how can people participate in discussing it?

Although I spoke about a variety of publics, I still think there's room to talk about a broader public in a democracy. So I'm concerned that we should have media which can circulate ideas in precisely the way our own High Court ruled was an essential part of a democracy.

There are obvious advantages to diversity within a society, but isn't it also important that the many publics you've spoken about find ways to talk to each other in order to create some sort of cohesion? After all, we want to live in a country, not some sort of supermarket of ideas.

The last thing I think we want is a whole series of niche markets. You can see it happening in the magazine market, with every small variation in the demographics around women, and now around men, creating a new magazine. Yet if in the end everyone is isolated inside their own niche market, what happens is that more power goes to those who make decisions and there's less scrutiny of them. When there are big issues to do with the reshaping of society — handing over public services to the private sector, for example — people can't then participate in the decision-making, or even hold developed views on it.

So, although I might be a supporter of the Internet, I actually think that what's interesting about the Internet is whether or not it's going to be dominated by the advertising and selling of products. Or will its real value lie in creating links between communities and across borders?

As a journalist teaching Media Studies, to what extent do you think our journalists write as citizens rather than as mere employees of this or that media empire? I'd have thought that the notion of citizenship, of speaking as a citizen to other citizens, was important in finding the right kind of voice.

I think you've touched on something important. If journalism isn't about giving a voice to citizens to talk to other citizens — to a public and for a public — then I don't think that journalism is anything more than just writing for an employer. And I think that many of our journalists do see themselves as citizens in this sense.

Working as a journalist is a constant negotiation over finding the space to do the work you really want to do. Most people, I think, see their journalistic careers as a series of ups and downs — the times when you're able to do what you want to do, the times you're not. Journalists work in large, hierarchical organisations, agendas are set, you're sometimes told what to do — that's true. But if we lose that sense of speaking out for the public, then we've lost the essence of the profession. Calling ourselves professionals and intellectuals, with some sort of ethical practice underlying what we do, is absolutely tied to the notion of citizenship and the public.

Recently the Media Alliance has been reviewing its Code of Ethics. In the revised code there are lots of mentions of the public, but what has gone — and this concerns me — is the clear link in the old code between journalism and the public right to know. The point is the rights of the public, not journalists' rights. In the face of a media culture militating against that idea, I feel very strongly that it's time for some sort of professional renewal amongst journalists. The job of people such as myself in the universities is, while criticising the media, to give support to fellow journalists trying to speak as citizens to other citizens.

Education is also tied to some notion of the public. At the moment in every sphere of our education — indeed, of our existence — there's a move towards the niche market, developing and selling new products, competition between universities — education for consumers. There's a kernel of something good there — students will have more right to ask for what they want — but young people need to be able not only to survive in the world, but to find some meaning in what they do.

✧

'Speaking the truth to power' is how Edward Said sums up his view of what a public intellectual does. This series of discussions has been about some of the Australians who do this, with eloquence, wisdom and spirit.